I0793428

IMAGES
of America

Carolina Tractor & Equipment Company

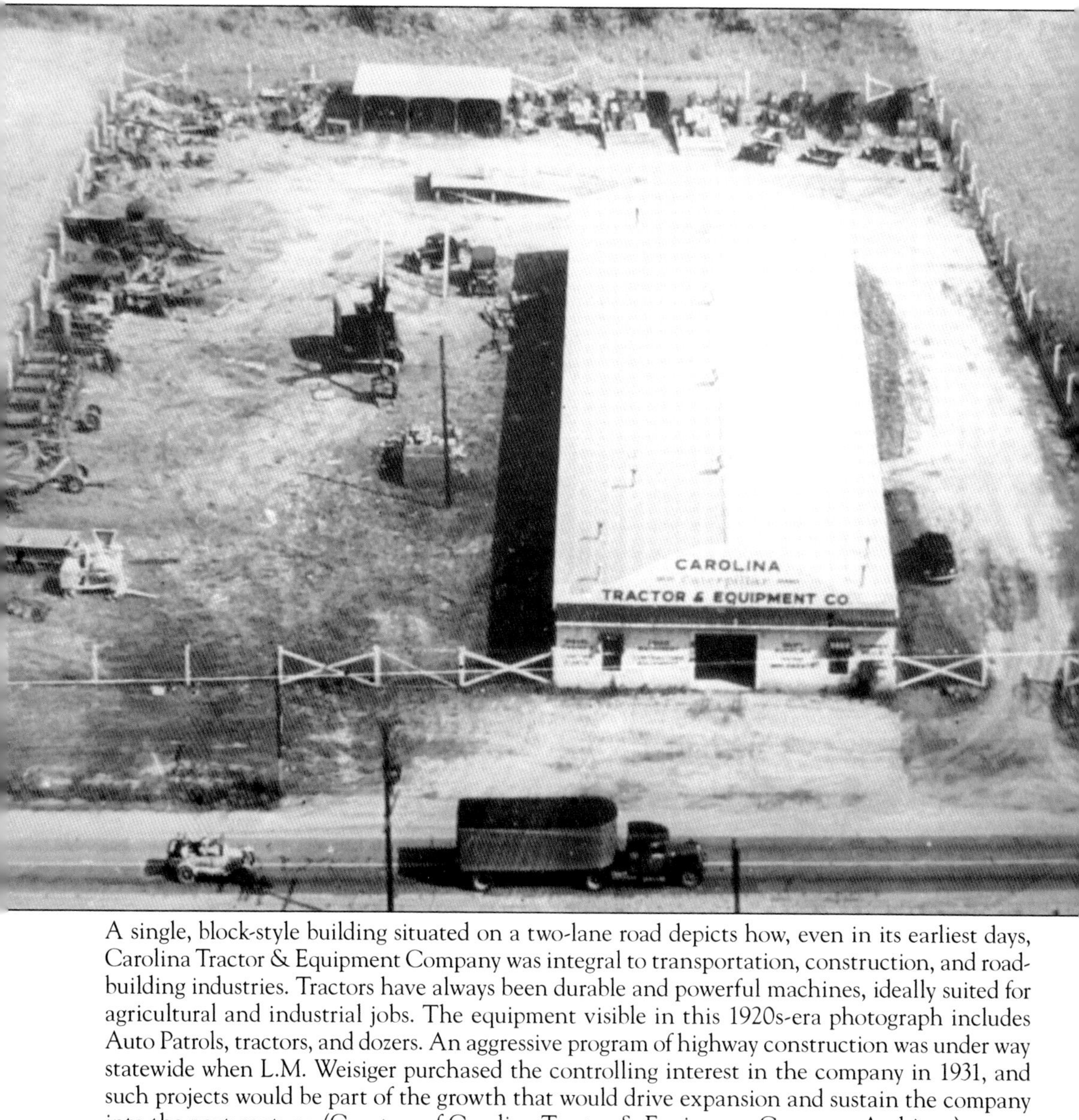

A single, block-style building situated on a two-lane road depicts how, even in its earliest days, Carolina Tractor & Equipment Company was integral to transportation, construction, and road-building industries. Tractors have always been durable and powerful machines, ideally suited for agricultural and industrial jobs. The equipment visible in this 1920s-era photograph includes Auto Patrols, tractors, and dozers. An aggressive program of highway construction was under way statewide when L.M. Weisiger purchased the controlling interest in the company in 1931, and such projects would be part of the growth that would drive expansion and sustain the company into the next century. (Courtesy of Carolina Tractor & Equipment Company Archives.)

On the Cover: A continuous-track bulldozer with a compactor attached, like the one in this 1930s-era picture, is typical of the thousands of machines Carolina Tractor & Equipment Company has sold, serviced, repaired, leased, and brokered since its founding in 1926. From the construction of agricultural irrigation ponds to interstate highways to massive public works, including the Blue Ridge Parkway, the company has long been an industry leader. Now in its third generation of family ownership, Carolina Tractor & Equipment Company is meeting the challenges of the 21st century with the acumen, innovation, and vision that continue to be the hallmarks of its success. (Courtesy of Carolina Tractor & Equipment Company Archives.)

IMAGES
of America

CAROLINA TRACTOR & EQUIPMENT COMPANY

Amy Rogers

ARCADIA
PUBLISHING

ISBN 978-1-4671-2069-2

Published by Arcadia Publishing
Charleston, South Carolina

Printed in the United States of America

Library of Congress Control Number: 2013941301

For all general information, please contact Arcadia Publishing:
Telephone 843-853-2070
Fax 843-853-0044
E-mail sales@arcadiapublishing.com
For customer service and orders:
Toll-Free 1-888-313-2665

Visit us on the Internet at www.arcadiapublishing.com

Contents

Acknowledgments

Since Carolina Tractor & Equipment Company was founded in 1926, many people have contributed to the success of the company. We would like to thank all of our employees and customers who have been part of this story and the members of the Weisiger family for their contributions to the success of this book. It is not possible to thank everyone individually, but this book highlights some of our milestones and the people who made them possible.

Throughout the years, our employees have helped to preserve the images that are included in these pages. Because of their help we had over 1,000 images from which to choose for inclusion in the book. For that, we extended special thanks.

We would like to express gratitude to our author, Amy Rogers, for her time learning about and capturing the long history of Carolina Tractor & Equipment Company. We want to recognize our company's marketing administrator, Christy Baker, as the book's project manager. We would also like to recognize Elizabeth Bryant, marketing manager, for her efforts in editing the book.

Finally, we would like to thank Ed Weisiger Sr. for sharing his extensive knowledge for every single picture in this book but most of all for the many hours he spent being interviewed. There would be no book without him, and we are proud to honor the legacy of the story he has brought to these pages.

INTRODUCTION

There is no way to fit into a single book the entire history of Carolina Tractor & Equipment Company since its founding on December 17, 1926. There are too many stories to tell and too many people to recognize but too few pages.

It all began when paving contractor Leslie M. "Mr. Les" Weisiger became the majority owner of the company in 1930, and the history of Carolina Tractor and the Weisiger family became forever intertwined.

During the Depression years of the 1930s, when many businesses failed, Carolina Tractor & Equipment Company helped maintain its solvency by selling dairy supplies to farmers.

As the Caterpillar Tractor brand grew as the market leader, so too did this family-owned dealership. Carolina Tractor brought the machinery to the individuals and contractors who undertook construction projects of every size and scope, from small farm ponds to massive interstate highways to military installations.

And so Carolina Tractor continued to make its mark not only upon the economic health of North Carolina, but by contributing to the state's built environment of roadways, bridges, hospitals, dams, communication networks, and many other public works by selling and servicing the equipment that brought such ambitious and essential projects from the drawing board to reality.

To be close to its customers, the company expanded beyond its original Salisbury location to open facilities in Charlotte, Greensboro, Asheville, and Raleigh, North Carolina over the next 30 years.

Solid management skills are essential to a company's survival, but diversification and adaptability are also crucial. Not only did the company add to its product line offerings, it established rental and used equipment divisions to service customers unable to absorb the expense of purchasing new equipment.

Heavy equipment was not the only type of machinery to make Carolina Tractor & Equipment Company an industry leader. It became one of the first companies to implement computers for ordering, invoicing, inventory tracking, and other office functions. The computers and printers shown in photographs from the 1980s appear antiquated by 21st-century standards, but at the time the machines were in use, they were state of the art. Employees with the ability to operate the innovative technology became highly sought after. The company kept pace with its customers' needs by implementing computerized systems for tracking inventory and parts.

Even more critically, Carolina Tractor sent crews of technicians to work on job sites to minimize downtime and lost production for large projects. These crews often braved challenging and dangerous working conditions complicated by mountainous terrain, extreme heat or cold, and exposure to the elements to assure the customer's equipment was running properly.

Even a fire that gutted the Asheville location one weekend in November 1955 did not affect the company's ability to serve its customers. By the following Monday, it was operating out of a temporary location nearby.

The Highway Aid Act of 1956 and the funding it provided drove demand for heavy equipment, as did sewer, water treatment, mining, and other large-scale engineering projects. Carolina Tractor expanded its service and warehouse operations to keep pace with its customers' needs during this time.

Ed Weisiger Sr. became president of the company in 1965 when his father, Mr. Les, stepped aside to take on the role of chairman of the board. Ed Sr.'s son Ed Weisiger Jr. became president of the company in 1991, and by doing so, he represented the third generation of family leadership.

As the 20 century drew to a close, the company continued to assert its role as a market leader and met head on the unavoidable periods of economic uncertainty, both in the United States and internationally. With the opening of a new facility in Greensboro, promotional literature accurately proclaimed, "No recession in the Greater Triad area."

From the years spanning the Great Depression, World War II, and into the computer age that heralded the arrival of the 21st century, Carolina Tractor remained an industry leader and trusted partner to its customer base. Its machinery and customers played pivotal roles in the construction of iconic landmarks and attractions, such as the Charlotte Motor Speedway, the Linn Cove Viaduct, Grandfather Mountain, and additional sections of the Blue Ridge Parkway in Western North Carolina.

In 1992, a new state-of-the-art facility opened in Asheville. By 1995, Carolina Tractor & Equipment Company became the seventh fastest-growing business in North Carolina and the 33rd largest in the state.

Over the years, many employees who came to work for Carolina Tractor found not just a job, but a career. To the customers who deal with them face-to-face, employees *are* Carolina Tractor and the Caterpillar brand. In every aspect of the business, from sales to service and every other task imaginable, these men and women have loyally represented the company.

It has been a privilege for three generations of the Weisiger family to have been involved with this enterprise. There is nothing quite like being a part of a Caterpillar dealership network. Perhaps it is most rewarding because the work that its customers do benefits so many people across the state, region, nation, and world. From a small company founded in 1926 to a major corporation operating in a new millennium, Carolina Tractor & Equipment Company remains committed to the growth and prosperity of North Carolina.

The photographs in this book have been selected from company archives to highlight some of the people and events that have shaped Carolina Tractor & Equipment Company over the years. Professional photographers documented the projects and equipment that modernized the region's infrastructure, along with images of the workers who performed the often dangerous jobs. Pictures capture the meetings and award ceremonies that marked milestones, everything from facility openings to employee retirement celebrations. Completing this collection are archival newspaper clippings, along with never before seen images from the Weisiger family's personal album.

The vignettes that accompany the photographs help tell the story of Carolina Tractor & Equipment Company, its history, and the people whose dedication continues to make the company a success today.

One

The 1920s–1940s

Since its founding in 1926, Carolina Tractor & Equipment Company has established itself as an industry leader by supplying equipment to the construction, road-building, utility, forestry, agriculture, waste, paving, and mining industries. It is one of the oldest Caterpillar dealerships established in the United States. North Carolina governor Cameron Morrison was a strong supporter of road-building projects during this era. At the same time, a young engineer named L.M. Weisiger from Hickory benefited from the new initiative to go on to become a successful contractor with partners J. Roy Pennell and J.M. Gregory. By 1930, L.M. Weisiger was the Caterpillar equipment distributor for the Asheville region. He became an investor in Carolina Tractor, eventually becoming the sole owner of the company that would be headed by two future generations of the Weisiger family.

During the Great Depression years of the 1930s, many successful businesses folded. When contracts for large-scale projects dried up, Carolina Tractor adapted to its customer base, whose needs and resources had changed dramatically, by selling everything from dairy processing materials to cleaning supplies.

L.M. Weisiger, known to all as "Mr. Les," saw the company through the lean years of the Depression. As the US involvement in World War II grew, so did the need for heavy equipment. Carolina Tractor opened facilities to support North Carolina training bases in New Bern and at Camp LeJeune. Rather than retooling to build combat machinery, the company was directed to provide construction equipment that would build roads and airstrips at home and abroad.

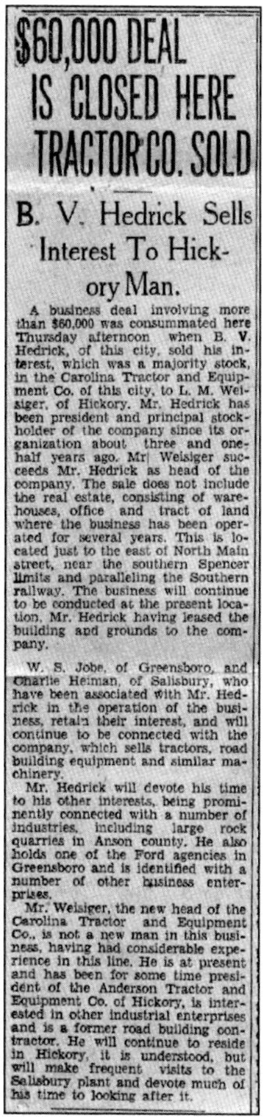

$60,000 DEAL IS CLOSED HERE TRACTOR CO. SOLD

B. V. Hedrick Sells Interest To Hickory Man.

A business deal involving more than $60,000 was consummated here Thursday afternoon when B. V. Hedrick, of this city, sold his interest, which was a majority stock, in the Carolina Tractor and Equipment Co. of this city, to L. M. Weisiger, of Hickory. Mr. Hedrick has been president and principal stockholder of the company since its organization about three and one-half years ago. Mr| Weisiger succeeds Mr. Hedrick as head of the company. The sale does not include the real estate, consisting of warehouses, office and tract of land where the business has been operated for several years. This is located just to the east of North Main street, near the southern Spencer limits and paralleling the Southern railway. The business will continue to be conducted at the present location, Mr. Hedrick having leased the building and grounds to the company.

W. S. Jobe, of Greensboro, and Charlie Heiman, of Salisbury, who have been associated with Mr. Hedrick in the operation of the business, retain their interest, and will continue to be connected with the company, which sells tractors, road building equipment and similar machinery.

Mr. Hedrick will devote his time to his other interests, being prominently connected with a number of industries, including large rock quarries in Anson county. He also holds one of the Ford agencies in Greensboro and is identified with a number of other business enterprises.

Mr. Weisiger, the new head of the Carolina Tractor and Equipment Co., is not a new man in this business, having had considerable experience in this line. He is at present and has been for some time president of the Anderson Tractor and Equipment Co. of Hickory, is interested in other industrial enterprises and is a former road building contractor. He will continue to reside in Hickory, it is understood, but will make frequent visits to the Salisbury plant and devote much of his time to looking after it.

L.M. Weisiger was well known and well respected by his colleagues who knew his work as a paving contractor. In 1930, Mr. Les had the opportunity to purchase the majority interest of Carolina Tractor & Equipment Company from B.V. Hedrick. When the $60,000 transaction was complete, not only did Mr. Les have controlling interest in the company, but he was also able to merge Anderson Tractor and Carolina Tractor & Equipment Company's territories. With the merger, Carolina Tractor & Equipment Company was the sole Caterpillar dealer for the western half of the state.

The earliest versions of the company's sign, which included the Caterpillar logo, date back to the period between 1926 and the 1930s, when Leslie "Mr. Les" Weisiger formed a paving and grading company, Pennell & Weisiger Contractors, with partners J. Roy Pennell and J.M. Gregory. Eventually, that company would grow and evolve into the successful enterprise that has lasted more than 80 years under family ownership.

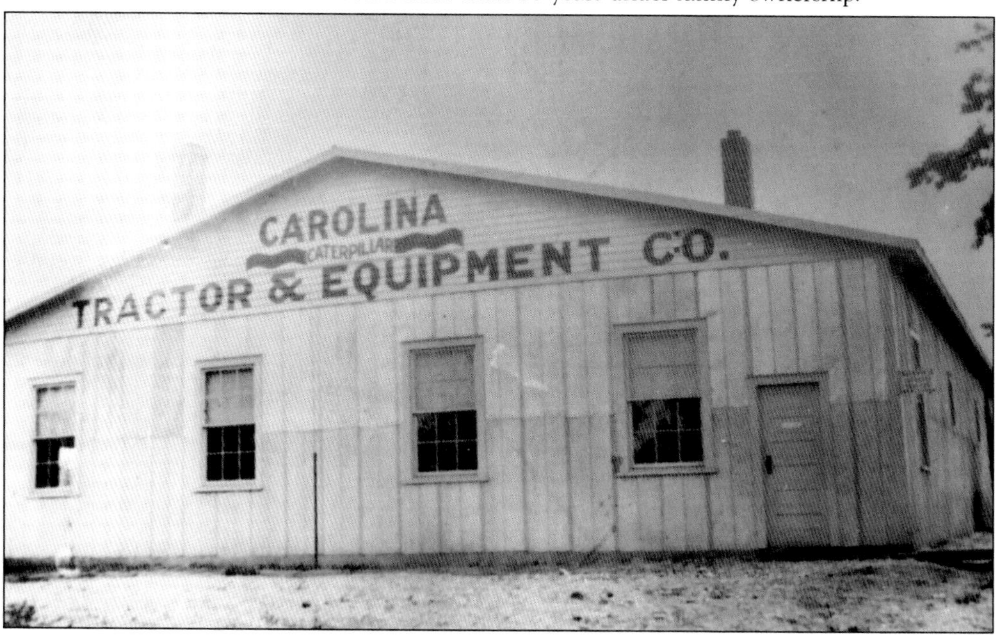

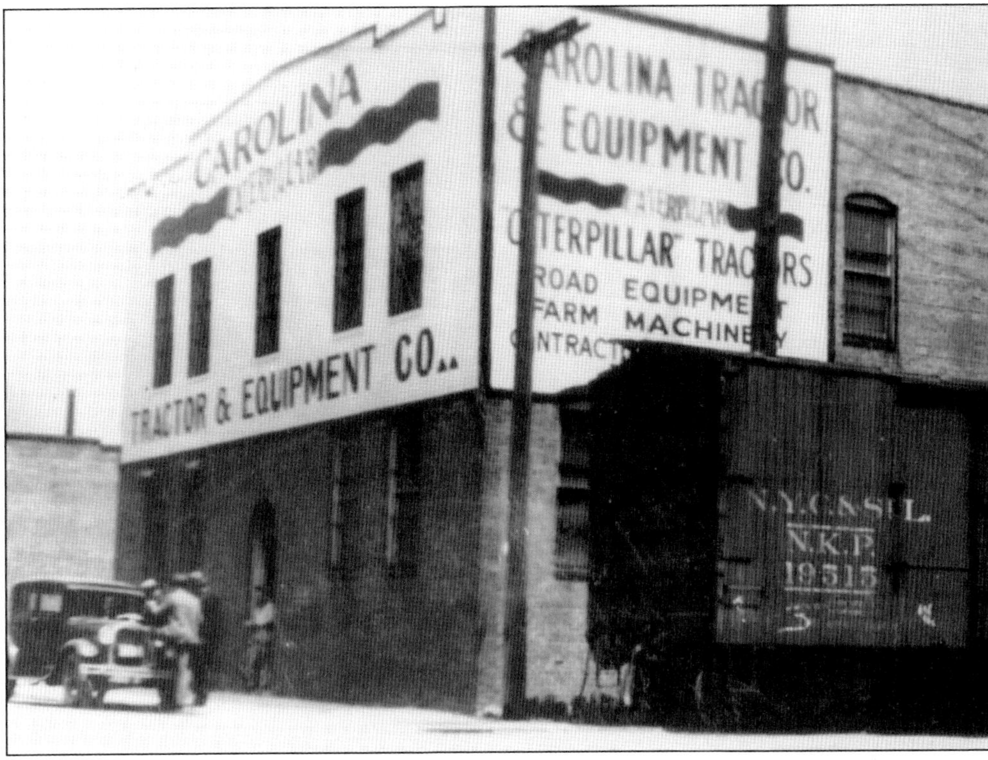

On September 5, 1934, Carolina Tractor & Equipment Company purchased Raleigh Tractor & Equipment Company, which lead to Carolina Tractor being the sole Caterpillar dealership for the entire state of North Carolina. Pictured is the Fayetteville facility that was now owned by Carolina Tractor. It was situated right next to a railroad line, which provided easy access to manufacturing plants. Most machines and parts were delivered by railroads in the 1930s.

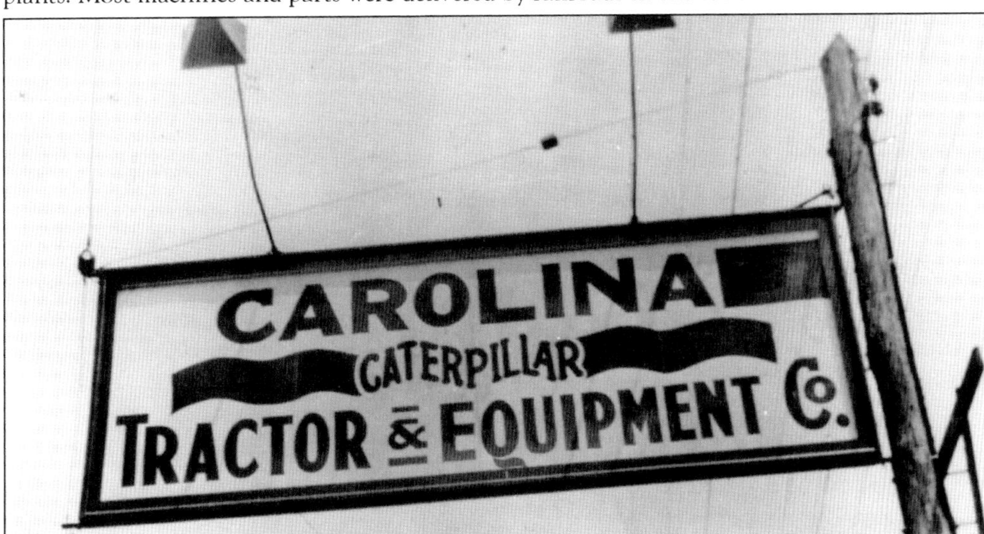

Carolina Tractor & Equipment Company has long been affiliated with the Caterpillar name, although it has also offered other branded machinery to its customers. In the company's earliest days, it also sold Lorain shovels and Athey wagons that were used in mining and construction projects.

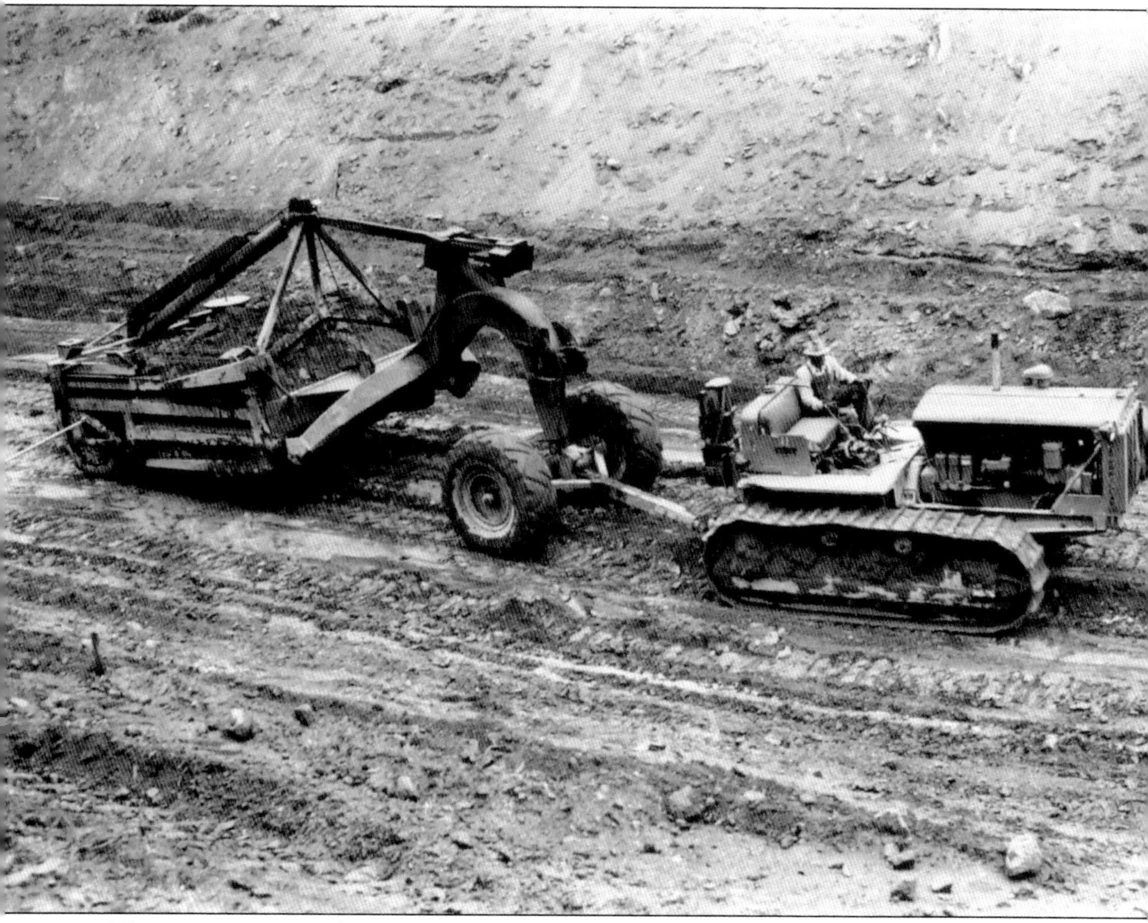

The campaign to implement an extensive road development program across the state was the vision of Gov. Cameron Morrison, North Carolina's "Good Roads Governor," as far back as the 1920s. Highway expansion continued during the subsequent decades with projects such as this one near Asheville, identifiable by the mountainous terrain.

The Blythe Brothers Company was founded in 1921 and, like Carolina Tractor & Equipment Company, it played a significant role in the road building, heavy construction, and industrialization of the region. Both companies were family owned and passed down their legacies and leadership through successive generations. They worked closely together on the expansive program of interstate construction projects. This portrait depicts F.J. Blythe Sr., who joined the company in 1938 following his graduation from the University of North Carolina and later rose to become the company's chief executive officer.

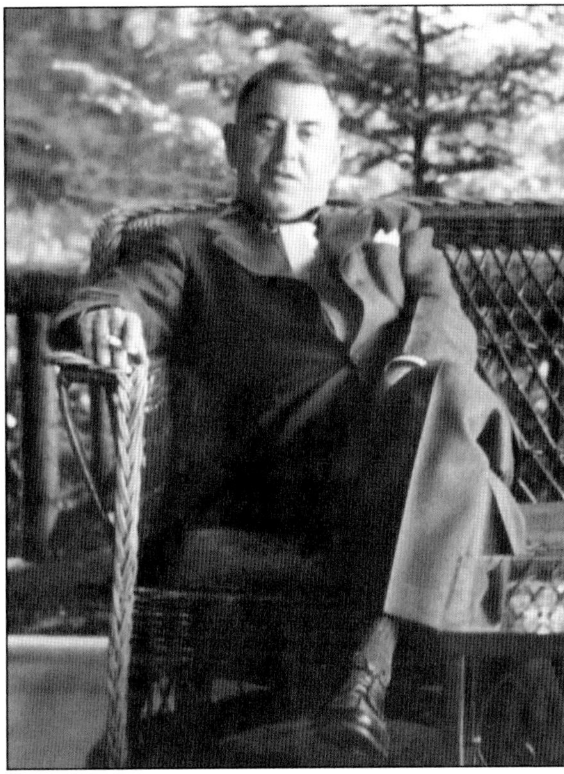

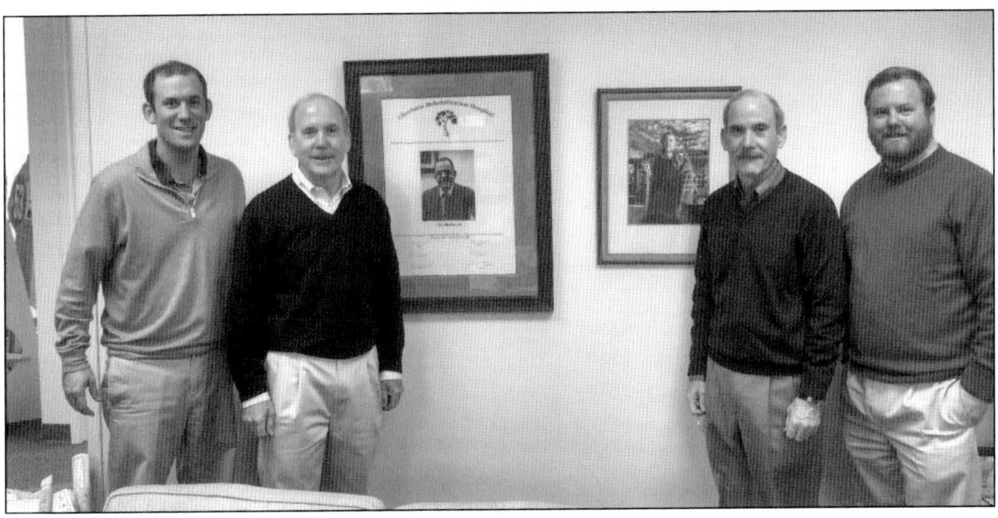

As in generations past, the Weisiger and Blythe families continue to partner on construction projects that are essential to the growth of North Carolina and South Carolina and the surrounding region. Franklin Jackson Blythe Sr. founded his company in the 1920s and was succeeded by his son Franklin Jackson Blythe Jr. in the 1950s. The third generation of management is led by twin brothers Jack and Frank Blythe, who came to work for the company in the 1960s. Under their leadership, the present-day Blythe Development and Blythe Brothers Asphalt companies were established, and they remain committed to providing their customers the highest quality construction services. Pictured here are, from left to right, Luke Blythe, Frank Blythe, Jack Blythe, and Alec Blythe.

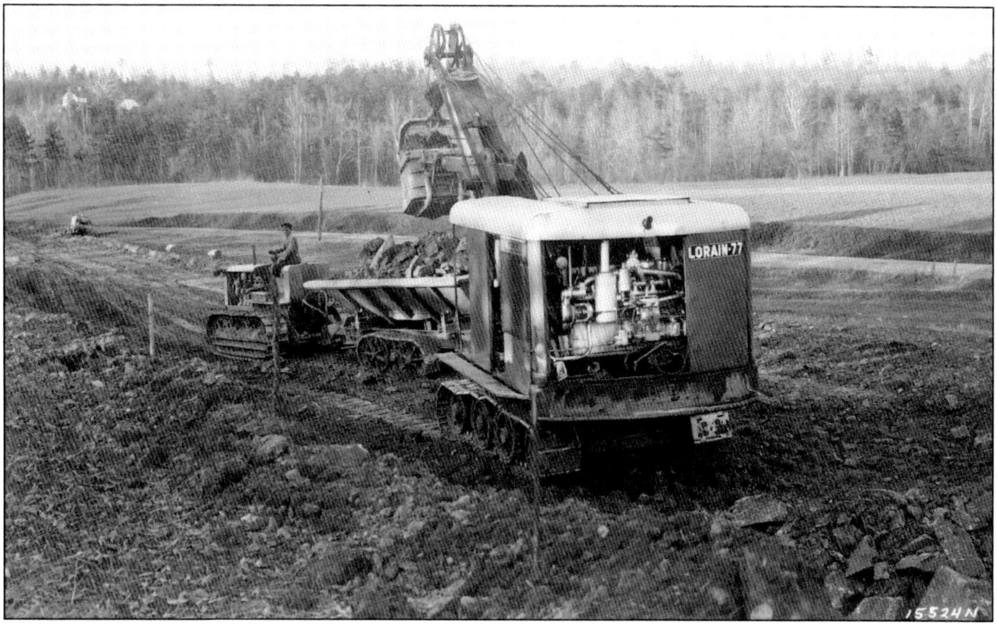

This March 1937 image from Mocksville, North Carolina, is one in a series produced by professional photographers who documented the equipment at work on various job sites. This state highway project utilized a Caterpillar D11000 diesel engine in a Lorain 77 shovel. "Tractors hauling and bulldozing move 125 yards per hour. The shovel consumes 3 gals. 8-cent fuel per hour. The tractors 2-1/2 gals. each unit," the notes detail.

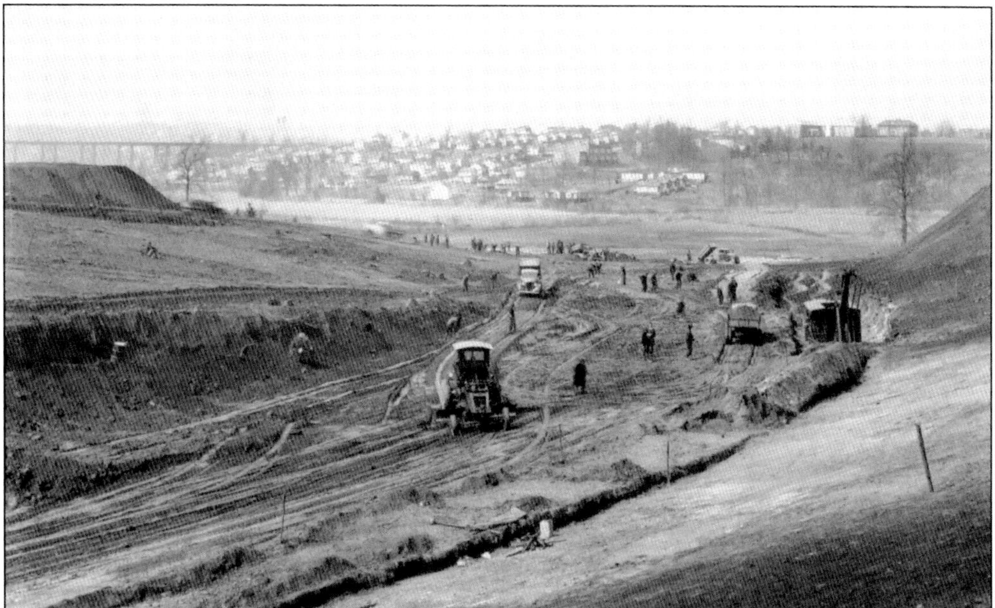

Pictured is the building of the Bowman Gray Stadium in Winston-Salem, North Carolina, in March 1937. The stadium took five years to build and was completed in 1949. The stadium is home to NASCAR's sanctioned quarter-mile asphalt flat oval short track and football games. The machine pictured in this photograph was the Caterpillar No. 11 Auto Patrol, which consumed three gallons of fuel per hour. This machine was widely used for grading and street maintenance.

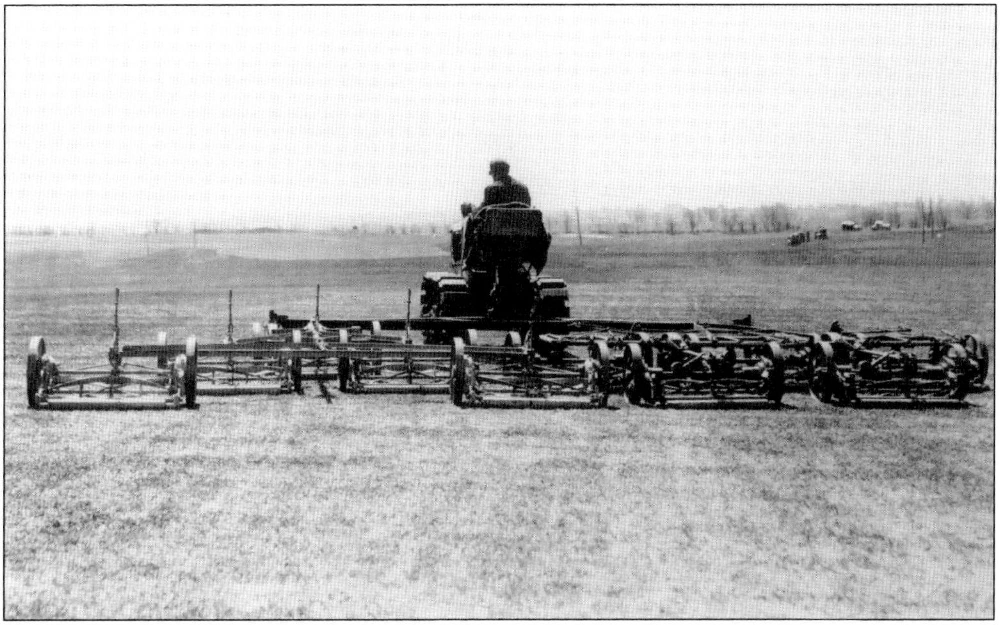

Not every Carolina Tractor & Equipment Company customer project involved heavy machinery and industrial work. This worker is mowing grass on a golf course in the late 1930s. Rubber pads on the equipment protect the grass from the weight of the machinery.

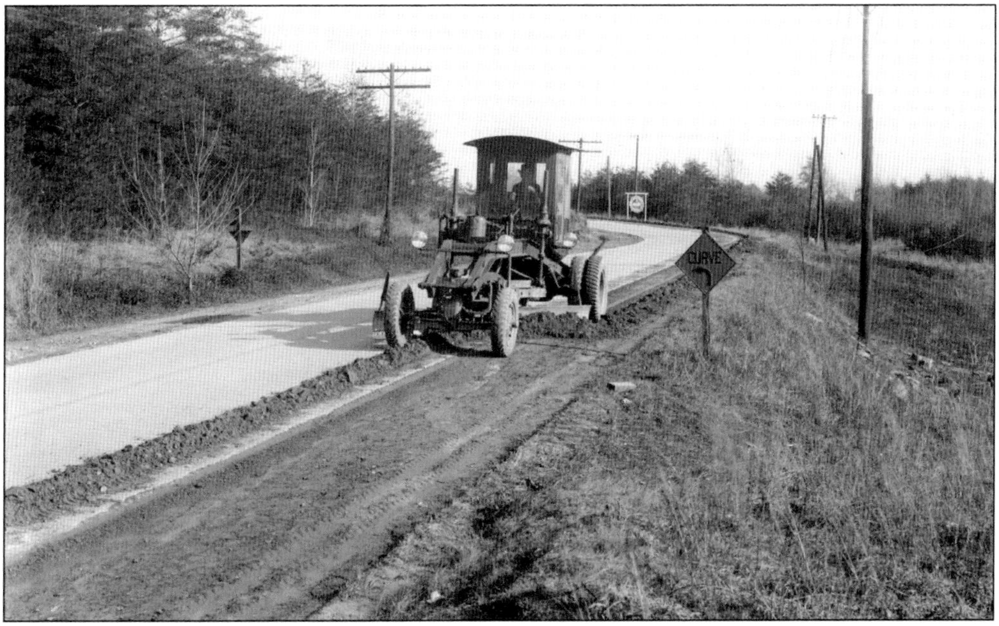

This Auto Patrol machine, now called a motor grader, worked on the shoulders of paved highways. Horse-drawn graders originally did highway grading until the introduction of the self-propelled grader in the late 1920s. This job site was near Reidsville, North Carolina, and the photograph is dated March 1937. The customer who operated the equipment was A.B. Odell, and he was reported to say, "I've been with the state 23 years and have operated all kinds of road equipment, but this Auto Patrol is the best ever." Auto Patrols were a milestone in the road maintenance industry during the 1930s.

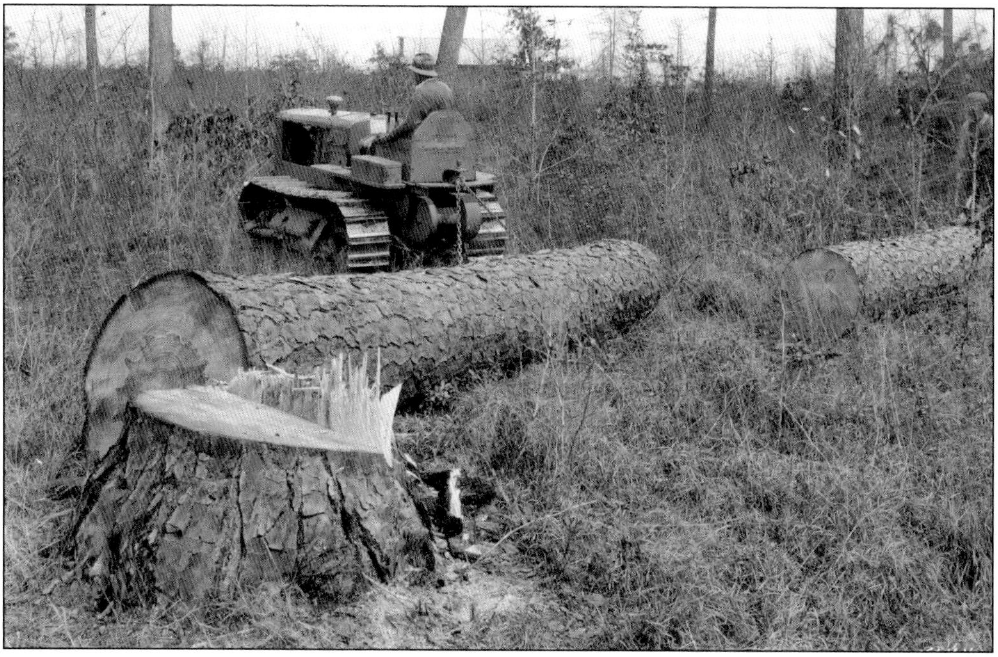

Brought to market in the 1930s, this 22 Model tractor is shown on a logging job near Laurinburg, North Carolina, in the late 1930s. Notes on this company photograph indicate that the tractor consumed 9.25 cents' worth of fuel per hour during a 10-hour day. "This owner is saving $10.50 to $13.50 per day over mules for this work," the comments on the back of the image further explain.

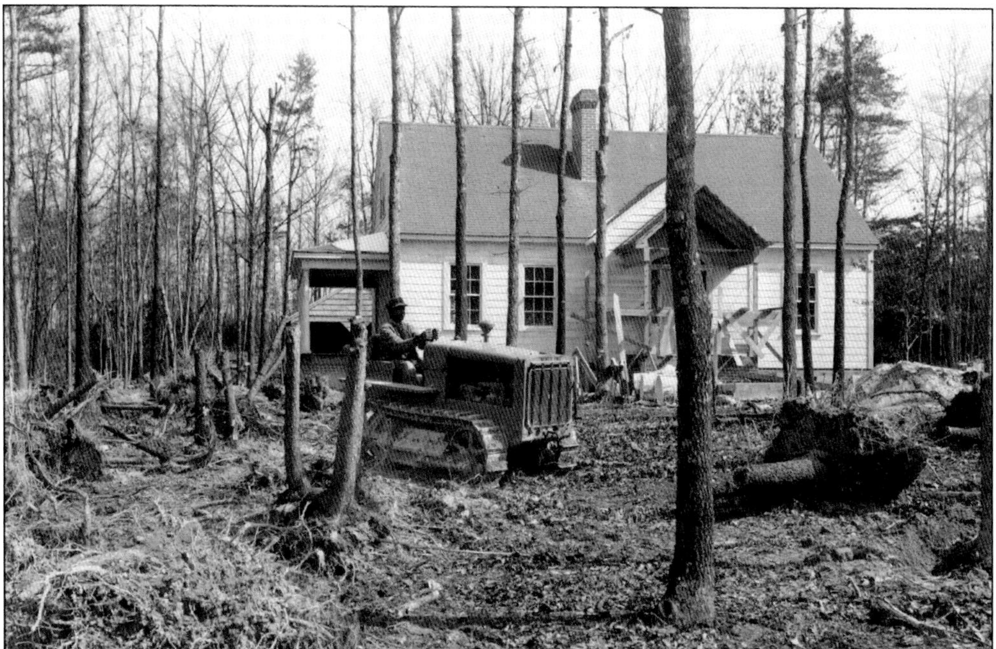

In March 1937, a photographer from Caterpillar took this picture of work being done by C.L. Stanfield to clear a homesite in Brown Summit, North Carolina. The homeowner said, "That man Stanfield pulled more stumps in two hours than two men could dig in two weeks."

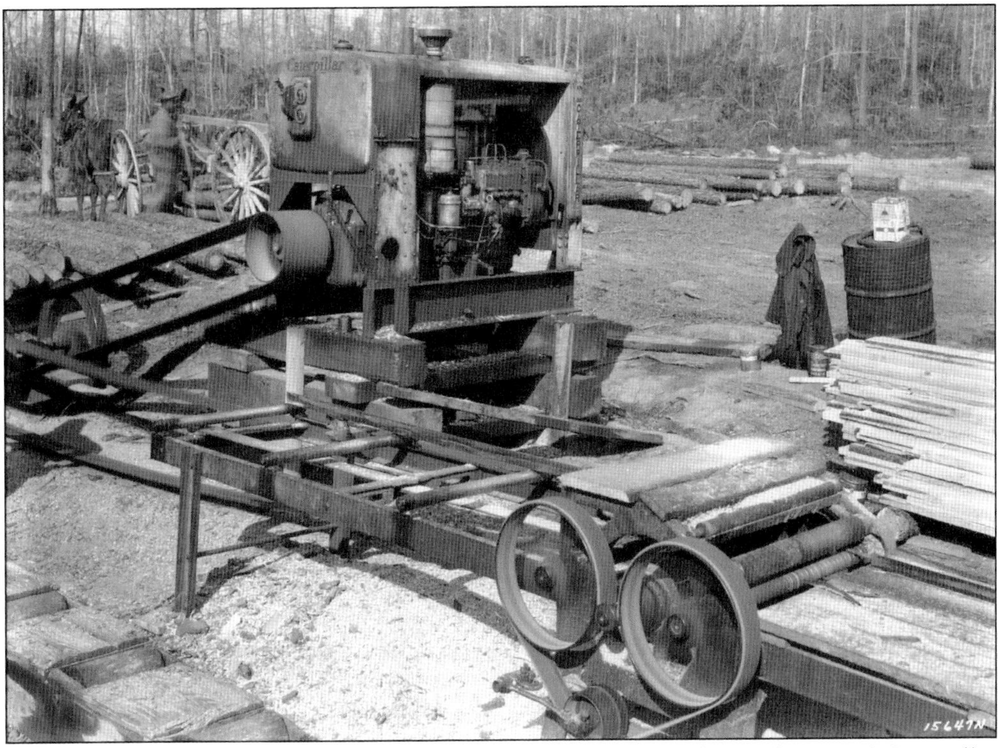

In March 1937, M.A. Lewis and H.A. McKinnon of Biscoe, North Carolina, used Caterpillar equipment to operate their sawmill. They commented: "Runs 10 hours a day on 15 to 17 gals. 8 cents fuel, cutting 10,000' feet a day. Fuel, lub., and maintenance cost 19.7 cents per hour for total of 4475 hours. In fuel alone it saves 41 cents per 1000 feet, over another mill gasoline driven. Total productions to date 3-1/2 million feet."

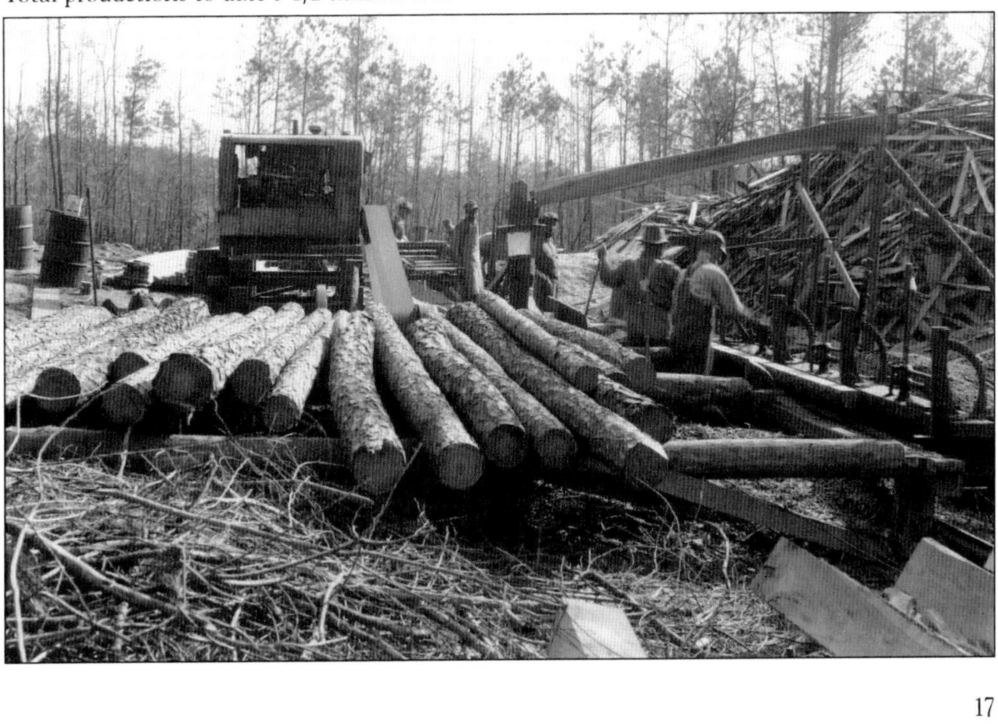

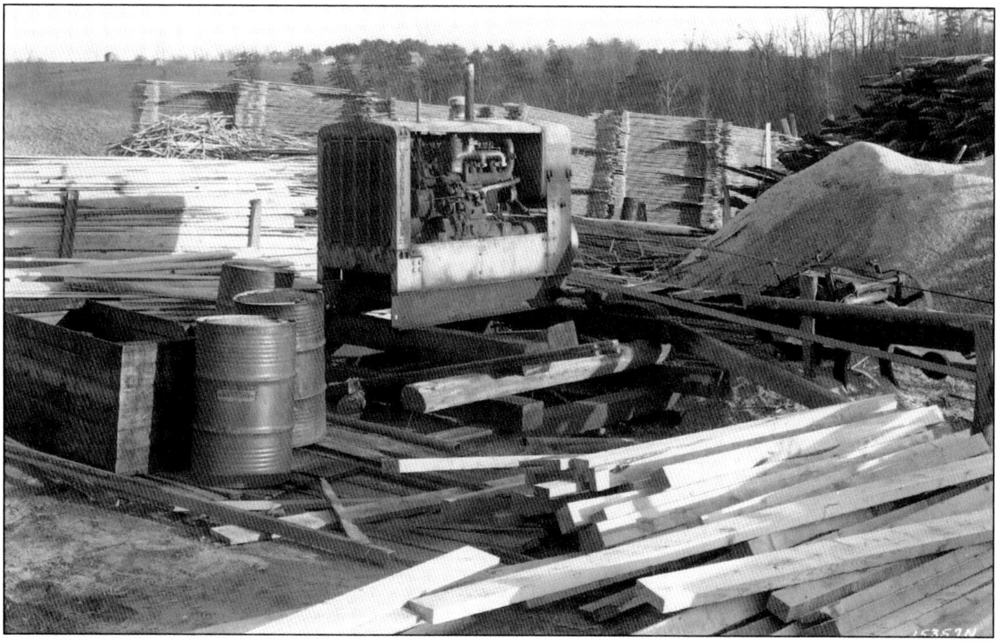

In the 1930s, transporting downed trees to remote sawmills was not always feasible, so loggers set up temporary sawmills in the fields. This photograph from March 1937 shows a Caterpillar D8800 diesel engine being used to power one such operation at Belew Creek, North Carolina. It had been installed in December 1935 and operated an average of 190 hours per month, with an output of 14,000 feet of lumber per 10-hour day. "Consumes 1.7 gallons of 8-cent fuel per hour. Engine operating cost 21 cents an hour for fuel and lube oil," the notes explain. "No repairs."

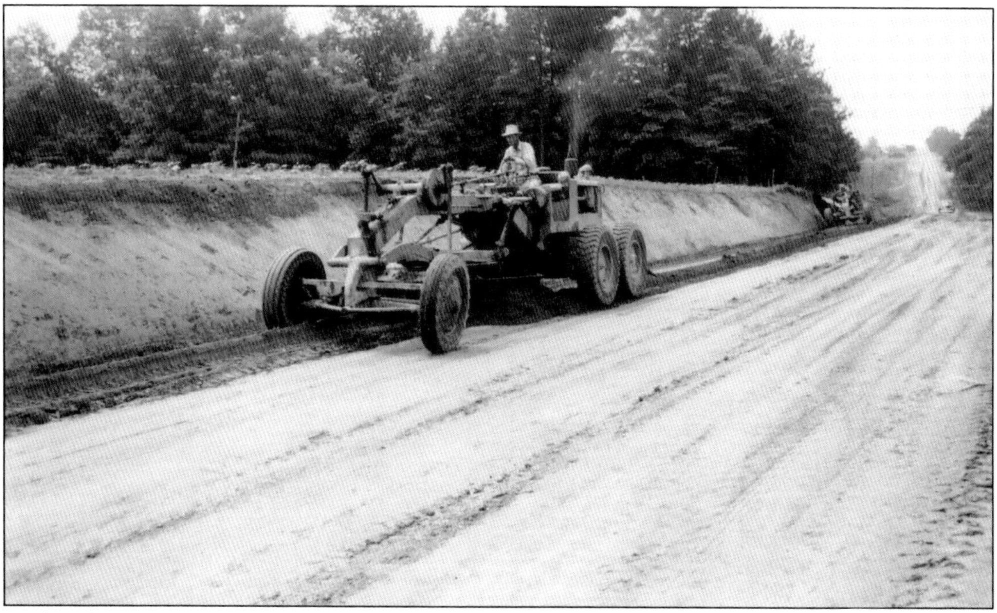

In this photograph from August 1947, Caterpillar diesel motor graders are used to improve a road near Middlesex, North Carolina. This Auto Patrol would grade the roadbeds and slope the banks before the road was paved. They were equipped with wide front axles and leaning front wheels to allow for better stability and control when working in ditches.

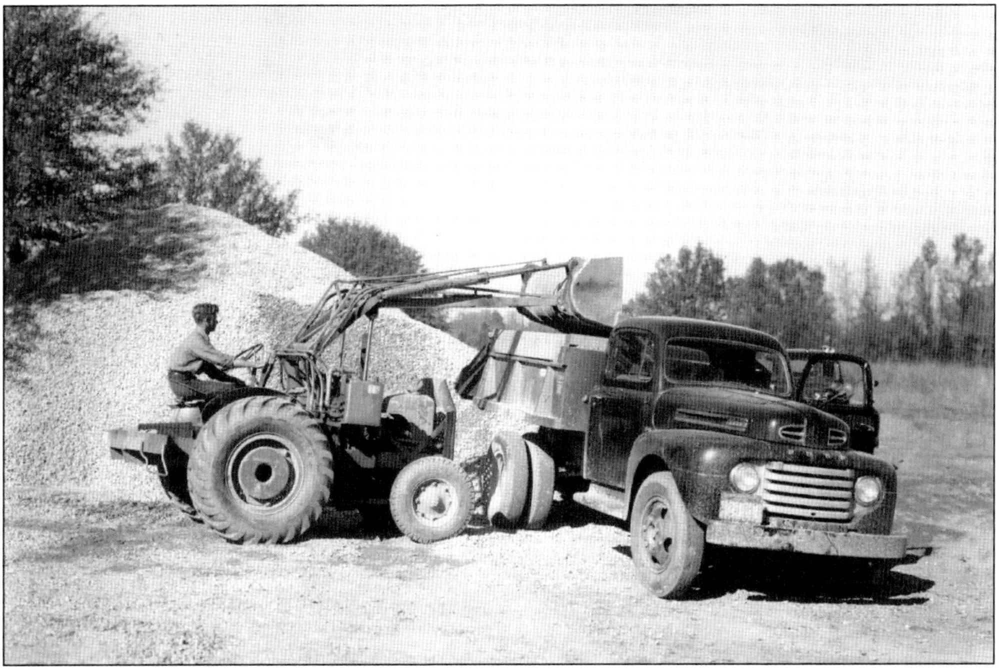

In addition to Caterpillar, Case was another manufacturer of construction and farm machinery whose products Carolina Tractor & Equipment Company sold in the 1940s. The equipment was used primarily to load and move stone for residential construction work. Case represented only a small portion of the company's business, and it eventually became a competitor, after which time Carolina Tractor was no longer a dealer.

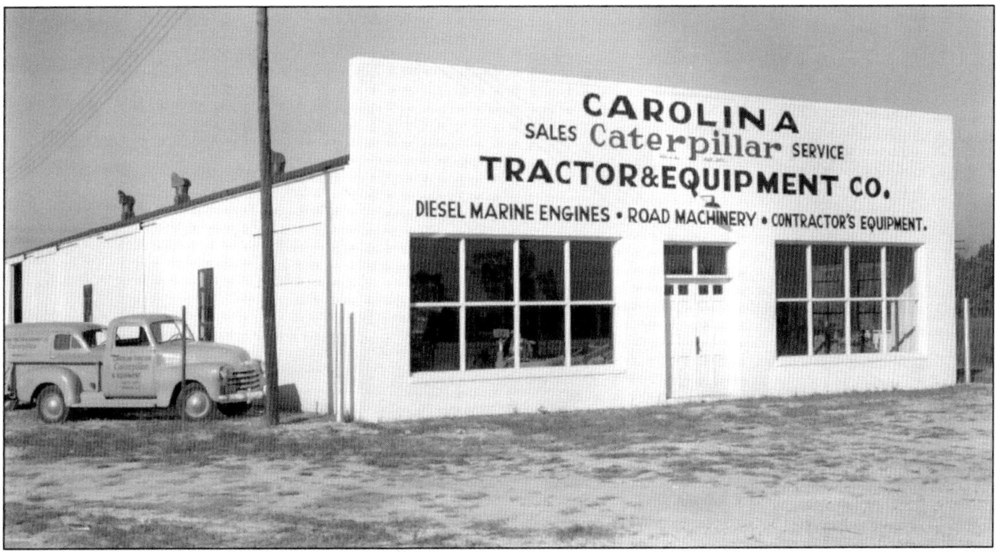

World War II provided a big boom for Carolina Tractor & Equipment Company in the 1940s. Pictured is the New Bern store, which opened in 1940. The facility was built to support the construction of Cherry Point Marine Corps Air Station at Havelock and Camp LeJeune at Jacksonville. By the end of the war, a demand for new equipment began to impact the market. Carolina Tractor & Equipment Company responded to this need by expanding the business even more.

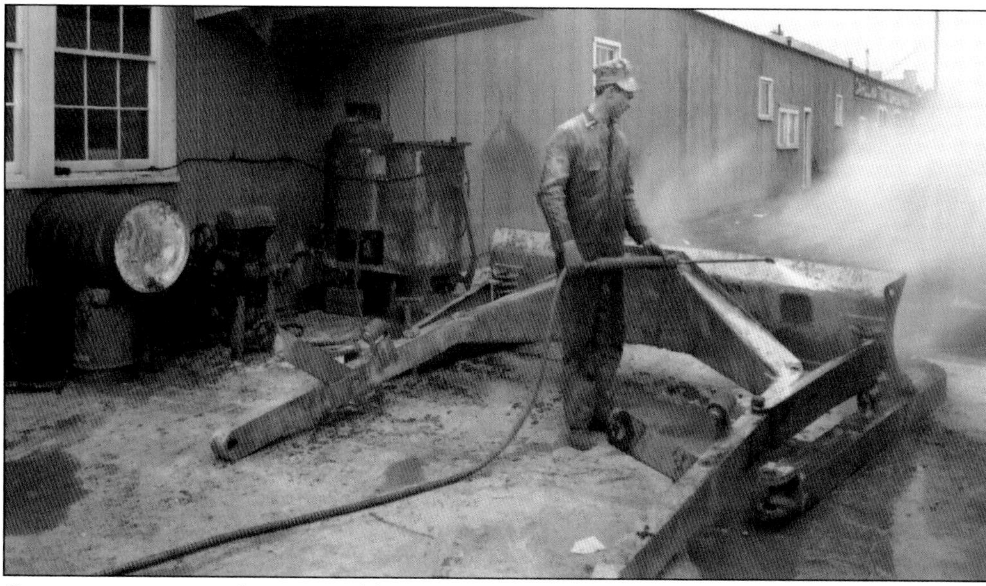

Construction, mining, logging, and farmwork were hard on machinery. Before a mechanic could service the equipment, it had to be cleaned. In this photograph that dates back to the late 1940s, a worker is steam-cleaning soot and other debris from machinery before he begins to perform the necessary work.

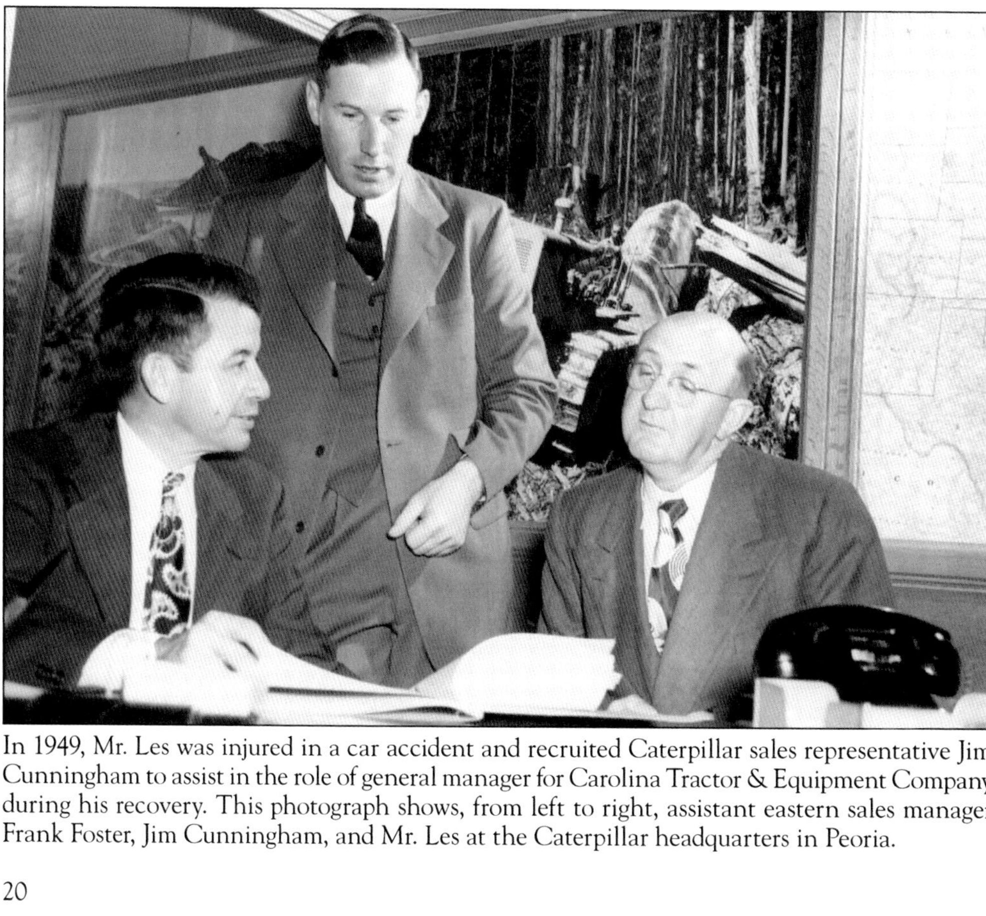

In 1949, Mr. Les was injured in a car accident and recruited Caterpillar sales representative Jim Cunningham to assist in the role of general manager for Carolina Tractor & Equipment Company during his recovery. This photograph shows, from left to right, assistant eastern sales manager Frank Foster, Jim Cunningham, and Mr. Les at the Caterpillar headquarters in Peoria.

Two

The 1950s–1960s

After the war years, the US economy grew at a healthy pace, but there were still unexpected hurdles for Carolina Tractor & Equipment Company. In 1951, Caterpillar's management team decided to split North Carolina's sales territory in half and give the eastern section to Gregory Poole Equipment Company. The income from the profitable Raleigh and New Bern locations was lost. Then in the fall of 1955, fire broke out late one Saturday evening and gutted the successful Asheville store. Still, Carolina Tractor was able to open for business the following Monday by borrowing a facility nearby. Management considered it an inconvenience but not an interruption. Still, it would take more than a year to reclaim and clean what could be salvaged at the Asheville store.

Like his father, Mr. Les's son Ed Weisiger Sr. was also an engineer. He had served in the US Army as a heavy equipment supervisor and, upon his return home, joined Carolina Tractor in 1956 at the age of 25. Before long, he would be promoted to manager of the Salisbury location.

At the same time, the federal Interstate Highway System was established to provide tremendous funding for highway expansion projects and to connect the cities across North Carolina. Construction of the Blue Ridge Parkway, which had begun in the 1930s, moved toward completion. Carolina Tractor established a Charlotte facility location on Graham Street to support its customers working on these and other projects in the western region.

With the support of the Charlotte store in 1959, construction began on the Charlotte Motor Speedway in Concord, just a few miles away. Crews still had to race toward completion for the slated 1960 opening.

In 1965, Ed Weisiger Sr. was named president and general manager, while Mr. Les took on the role of chairman of the board. In 1966, Carolina Tractor & Equipment Company opened their fourth location in Greensboro to serve the Triad region, where most of the state's manufacturing companies were based. As the state's transportation budget grew, so did the scope of the projects for Carolina Tractor.

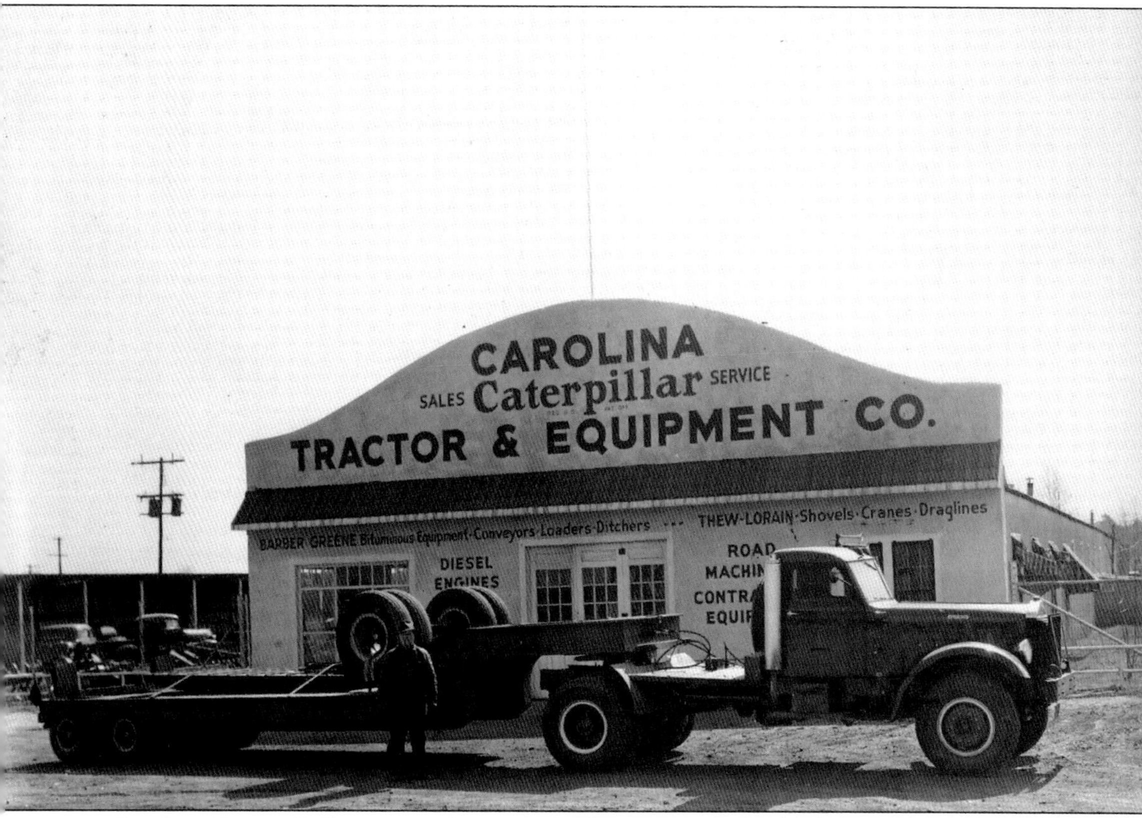

Carolina Tractor & Equipment Company had a presence in Raleigh since the 1930s. In 1950, Raleigh and New Bern accounted for more than 42 percent of the company's $6.9 million in sales. On April 1, 1951, Caterpillar announced the reassigning of the eastern half of North Carolina to Gregory Poole Equipment Company. Carolina Tractor suffered a $1.4 million loss in revenue in 1951, and it would not be until 1962 before the company surpassed the 1950 mark.

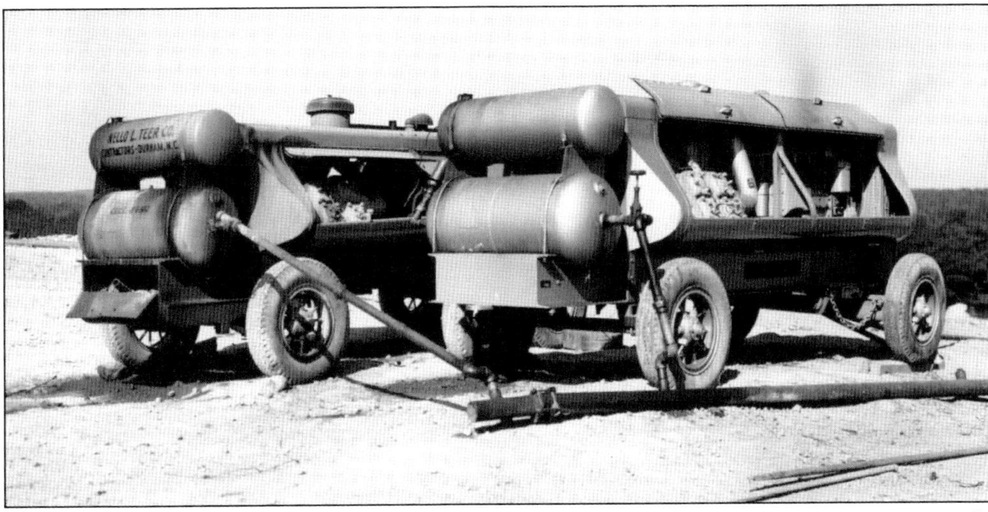

Giant air compressors with Caterpillar engines were used on large construction projects. In this photograph from 1950, the Nello L. Teer Company uses this diesel-powered machinery to generate air pressure to operate rock drills at a stone quarry and crushing plant near Durham, North Carolina. The crushed stone would then be transported to one of the many highway projects under way in the region.

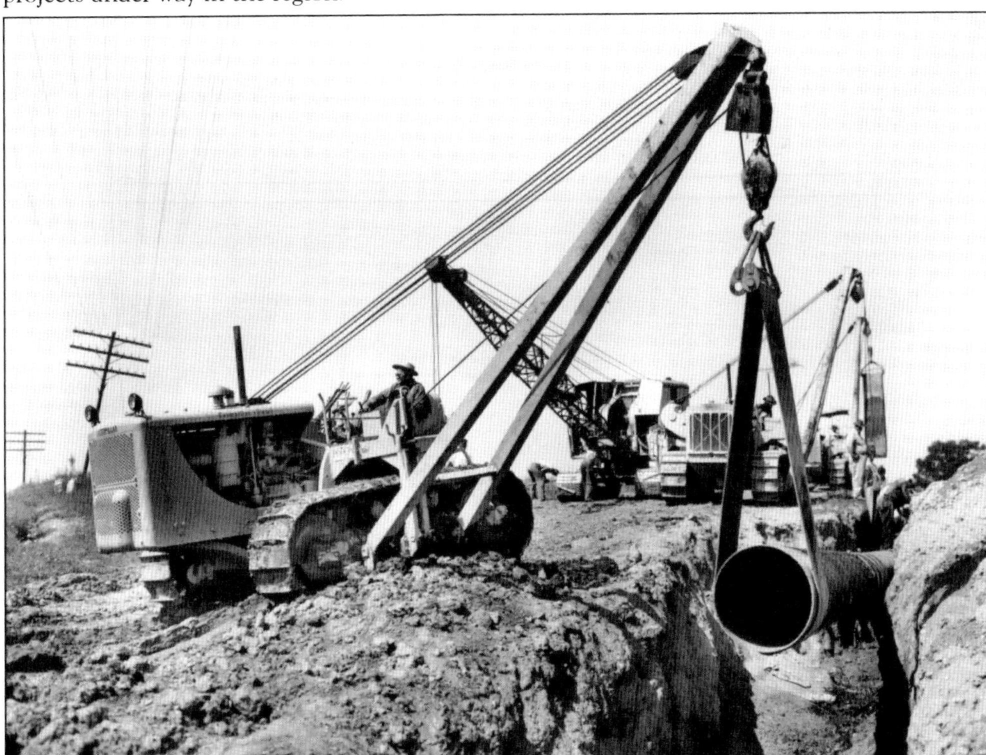

Multiple machines sold by Carolina Tractor & Equipment Company are seen on this pipeline construction job site near Draper, North Carolina. The 1950 photograph depicts a Caterpillar diesel D8 tractor with Trackson side boom in the foreground. The men were most likely laying piping for a residential neighborhood.

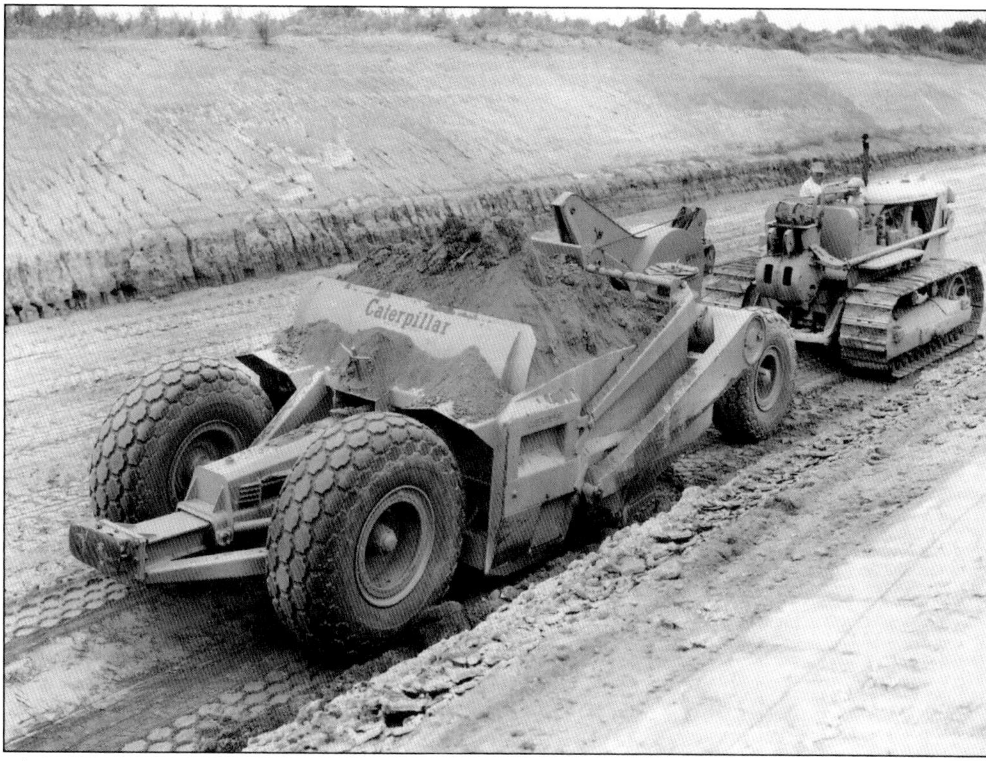

This project was an extension of North Carolina State Highway 421. The highway today stretches 328 miles across North Carolina—from Fort Fisher to the Tennessee state line. The Caterpillar diesel D7 tractor with a scraper worked on the job that was situated near Greensboro. These photographs date back to July 1950.

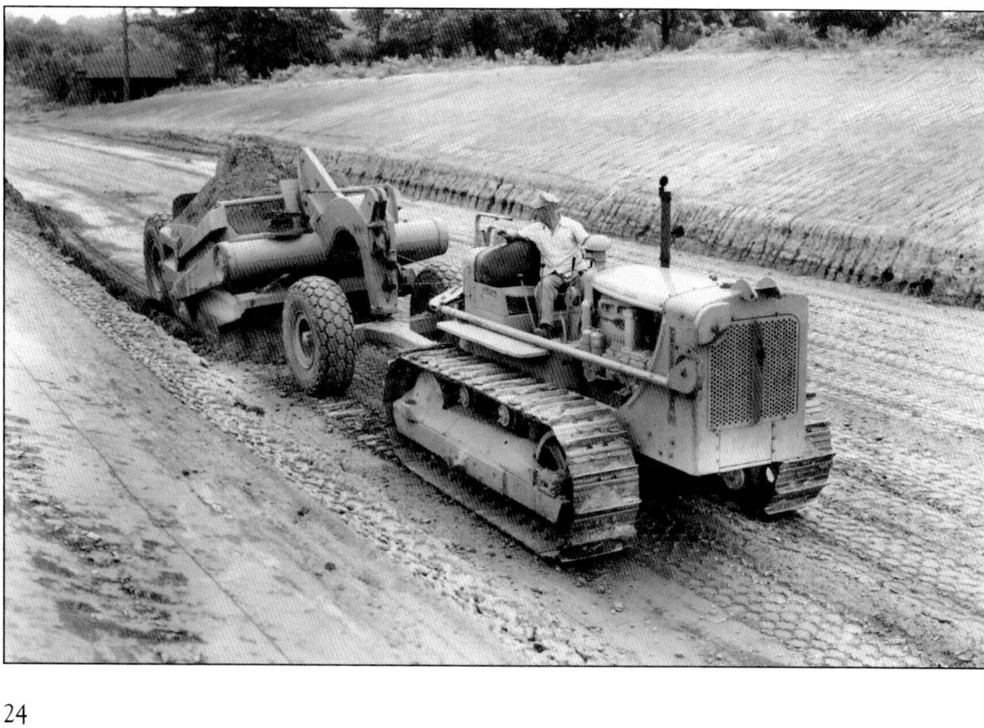

In these July 1950 photographs, a Caterpillar diesel D4 tractor equipped with a Trackson HT4 Traxcavator and sold by Carolina Tractor & Equipment Company is shown on the job in Greensboro. This equipment was owned by Lambeth Construction Company and was used on this job site to clear land and fill it in preparation for a filling station that was to be built at the location.

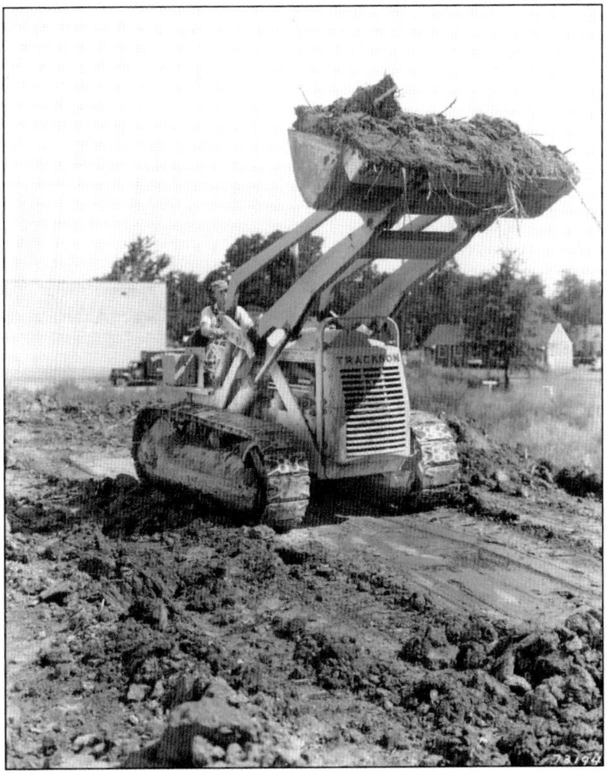

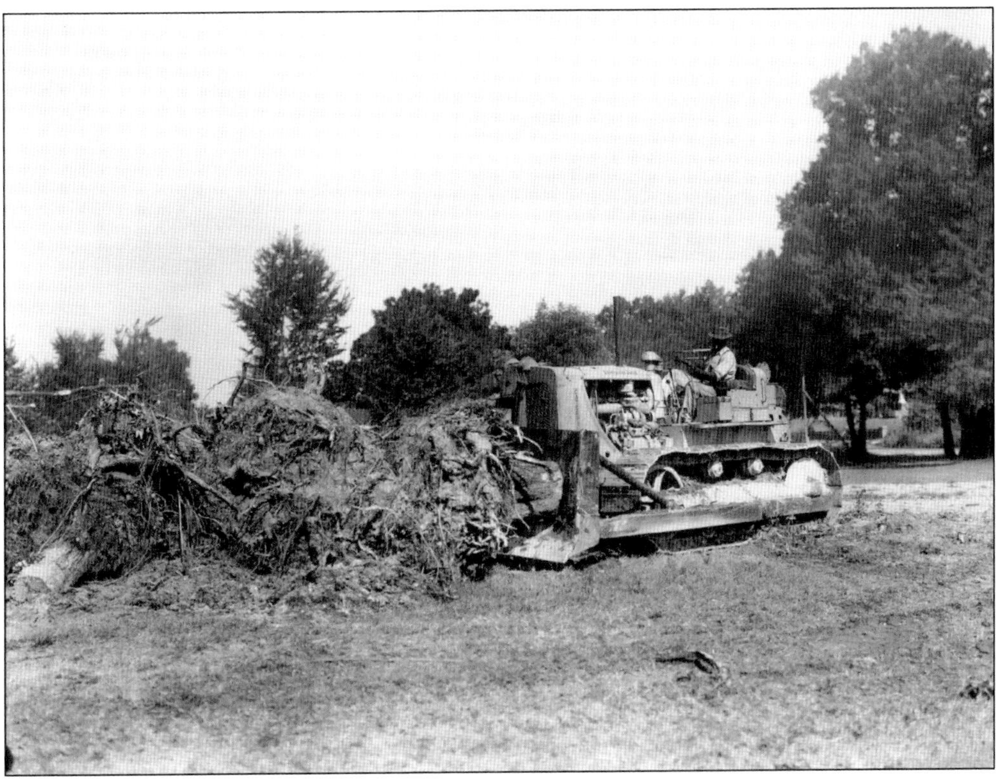

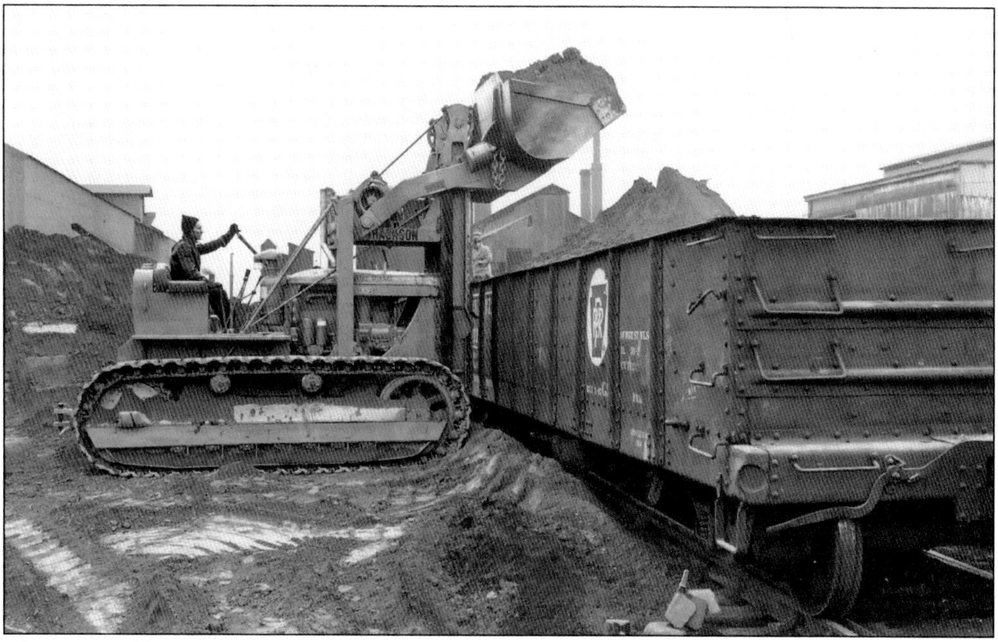

This Caterpillar D7 tractor equipped with a Traxcavator was versatile and found in many types of industrial settings. From the 1940s through the 1950s, the machines were often used in brick manufacturing. The photographer who took this undated image noted on the back that the equipment could be seen "loading 60-ton gondola cars with zinc ore in 12 minutes."

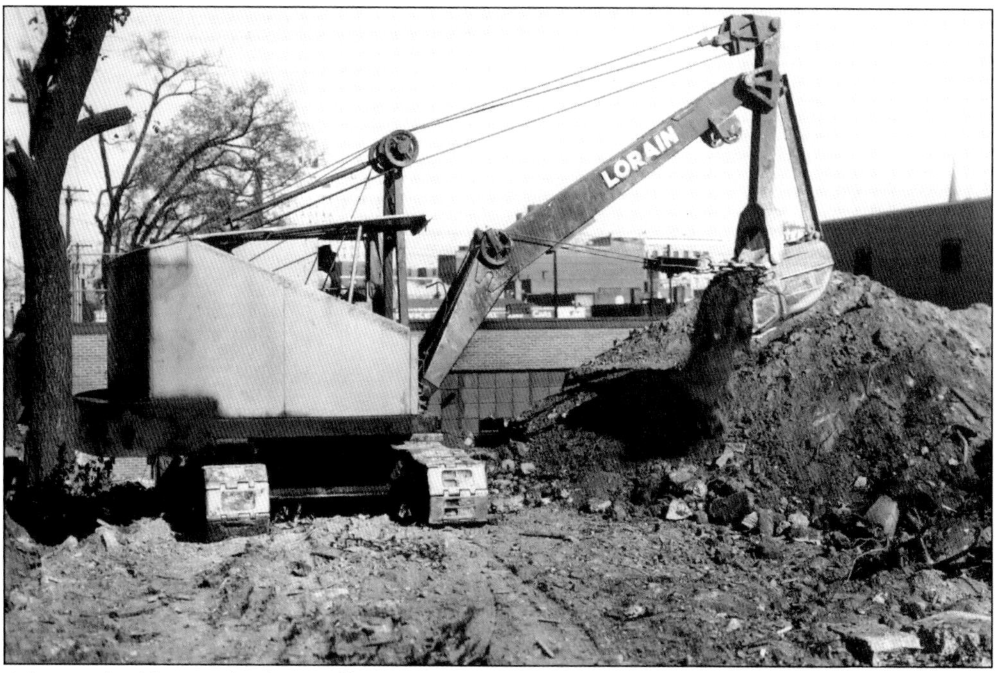

A Lorain backhoe and a Caterpillar D5 tractor work on preparing a building site for a job being done by A.V. Blankenship's construction and excavation business that was located in Charlotte. This photograph dates back to 1950, before the tremendous expansion of road projects that would be implemented to establish an interstate highway system across the United States.

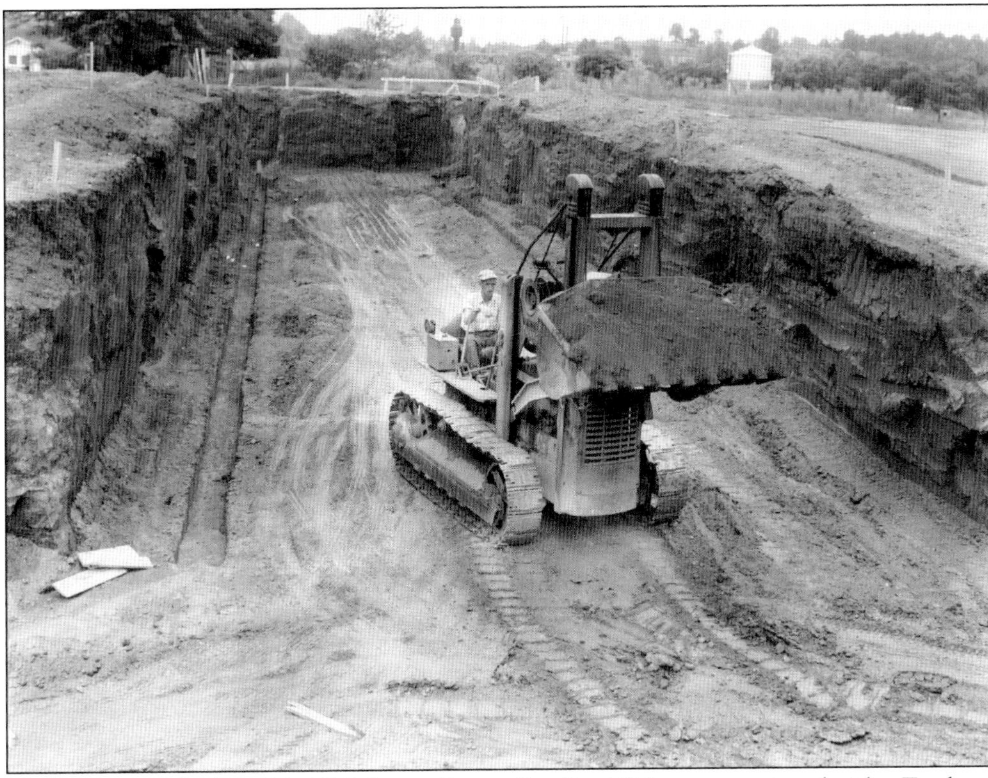

These photographs from July 1950 show a Caterpillar diesel D4 tractor equipped with a Trackson Traxcavator digging basements for new homes in a residential development on Watson Avenue in Winston-Salem. The owner of the equipment was L.A. Reynolds. In December 1951, Caterpillar purchased the Trackson Company, which produced the Trackson attachment for machines.

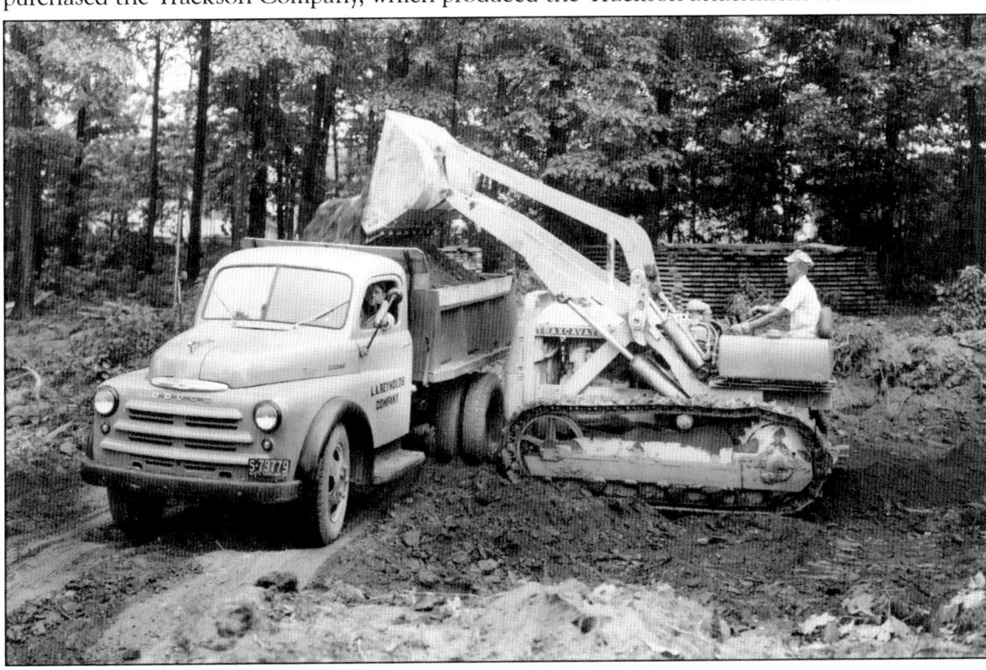

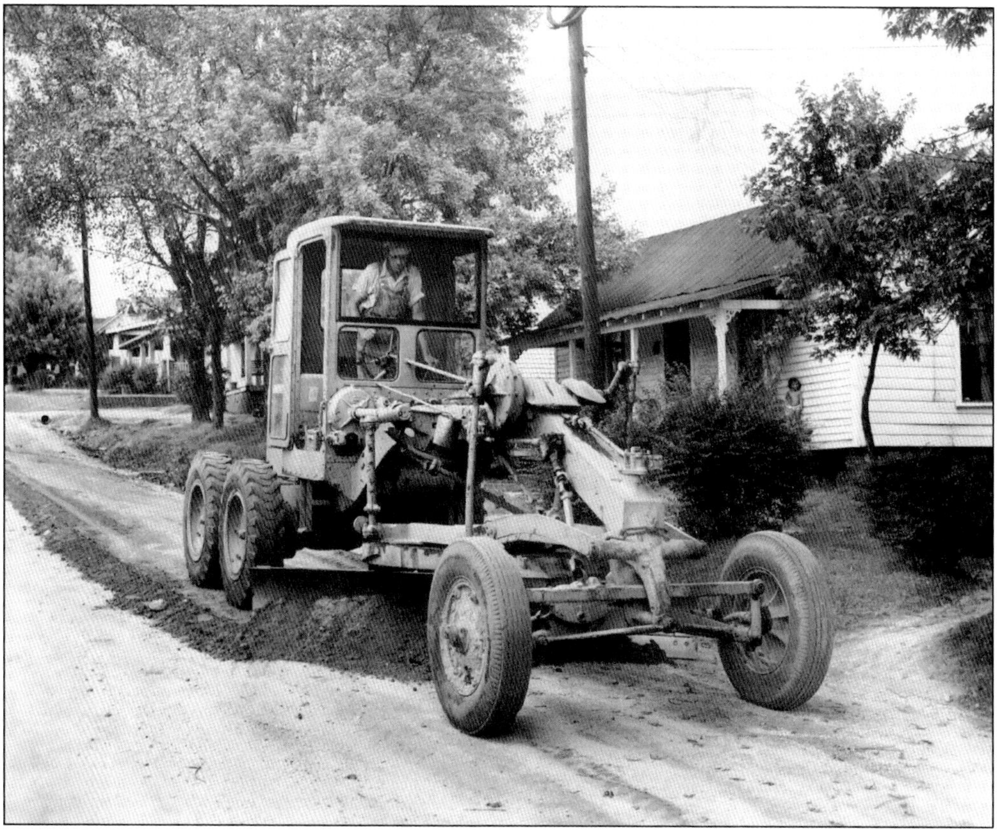

The work shown in this photograph from August 1953 is being done by the City of High Point. A motor grader operated by Stanley Thomas prepares the ground for streets that would be constructed in a residential neighborhood.

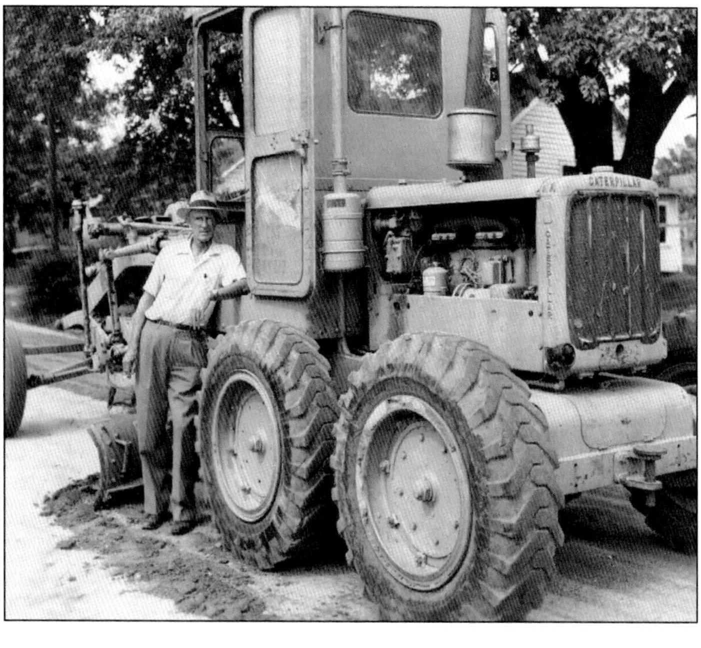

In this photograph from August 1953, E.J. Sharpe is shown on a job where a Caterpillar 212 motor grader is being used to do street work. Sharpe was the street superintendent for the City of High Point. Such public works projects provided economic growth for the state and helped modernize its transportation infrastructure. This type of equipment would continue to be used widely, especially when the Federal-Aid Highway Act of 1956 was enacted.

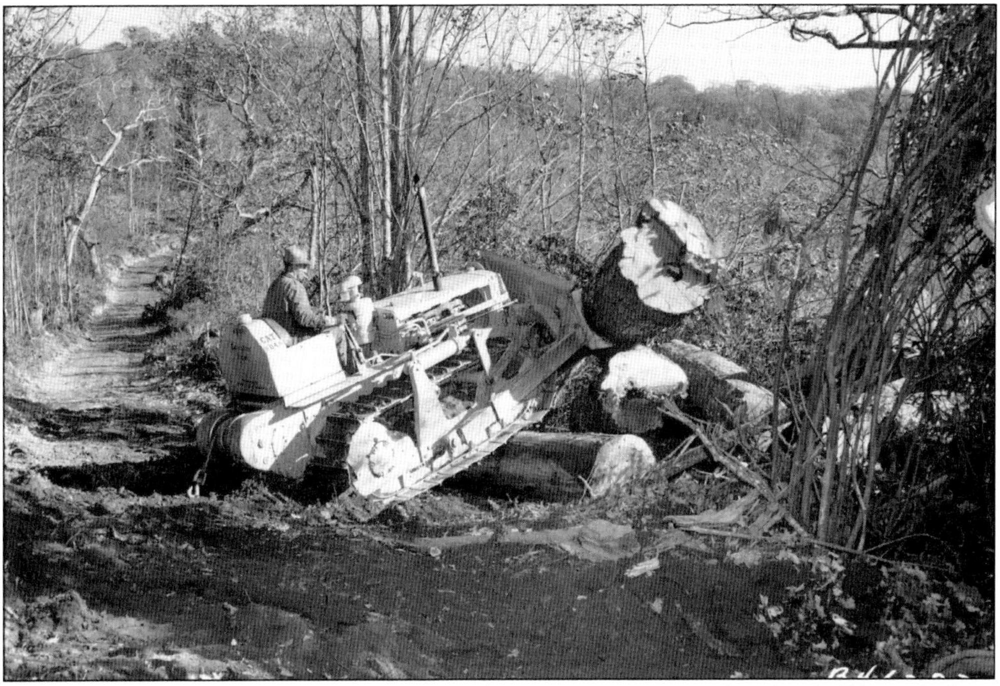

This photograph from 1955 depicts a Caterpillar D4 tractor equipped with a bulldozer decking logs that will be taken to the sawmill. Operations such as this one were commonplace around the Waynesville area of Western North Carolina.

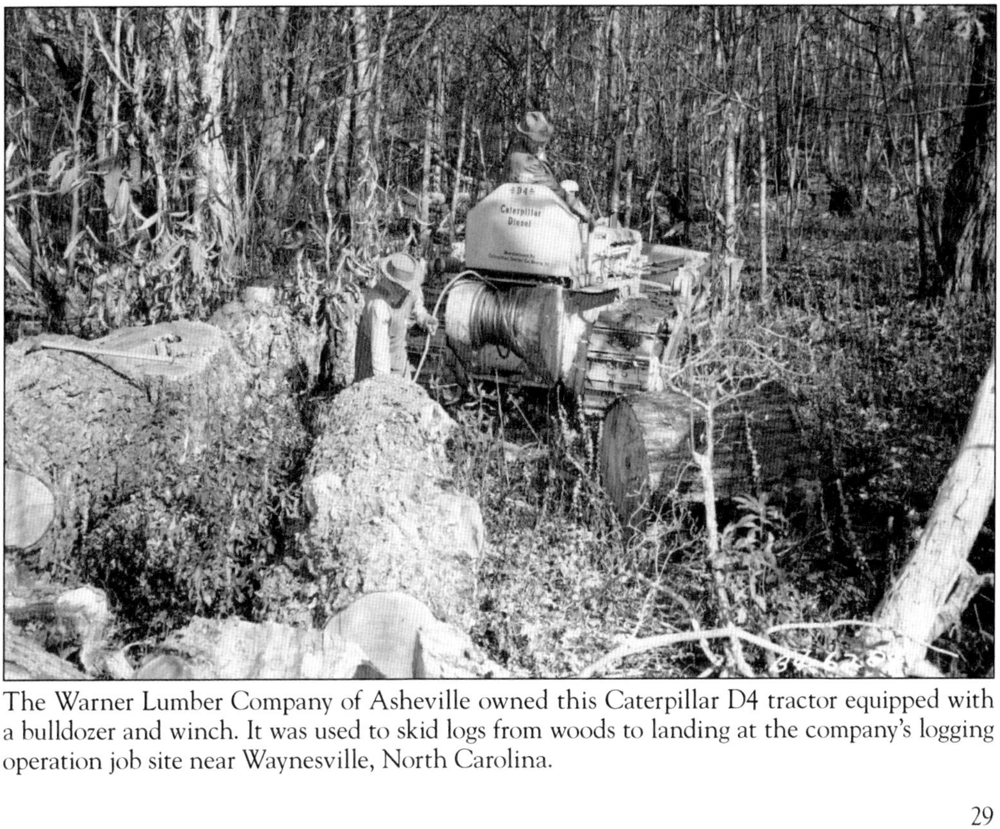

The Warner Lumber Company of Asheville owned this Caterpillar D4 tractor equipped with a bulldozer and winch. It was used to skid logs from woods to landing at the company's logging operation job site near Waynesville, North Carolina.

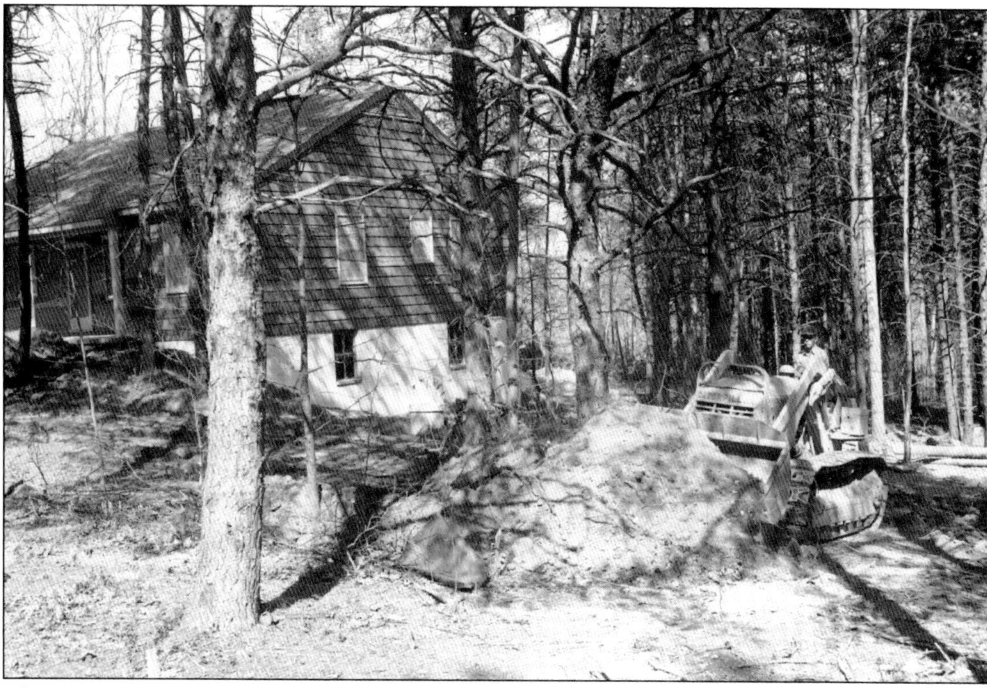

This, too, is a residential construction job being undertaken by the L.A. Reynolds Company of Winston-Salem. The Caterpillar diesel Traxcavator, purchased from Carolina Tractor & Equipment Company, is working to backfill earth around a newly constructed dwelling.

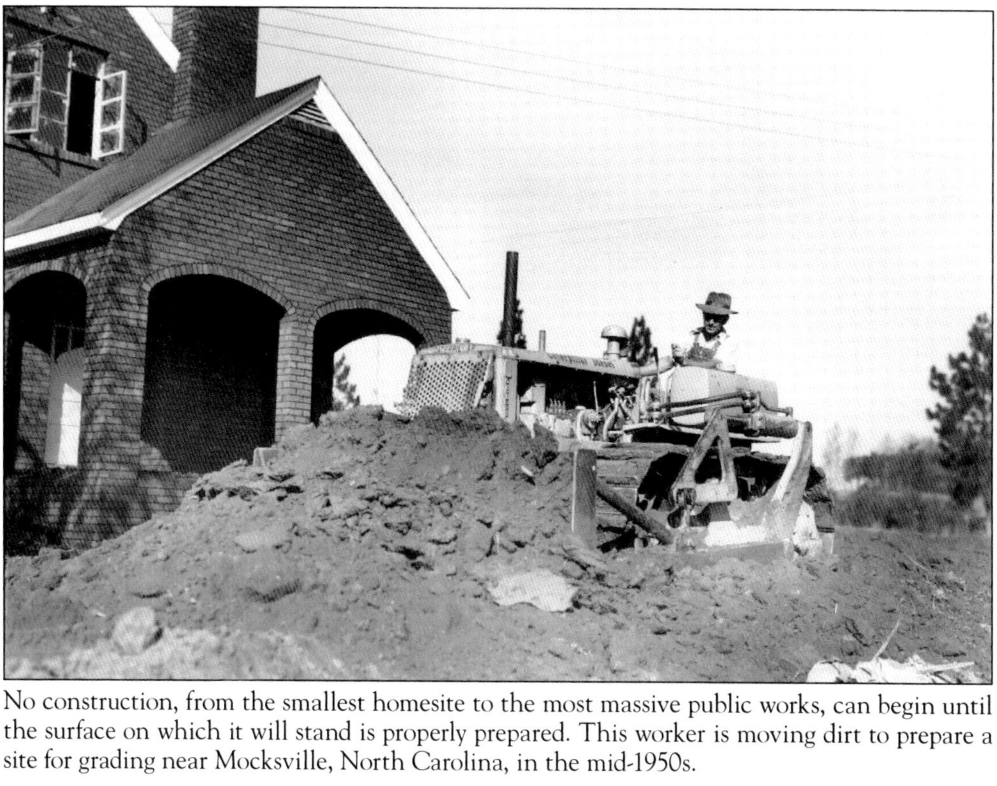

No construction, from the smallest homesite to the most massive public works, can begin until the surface on which it will stand is properly prepared. This worker is moving dirt to prepare a site for grading near Mocksville, North Carolina, in the mid-1950s.

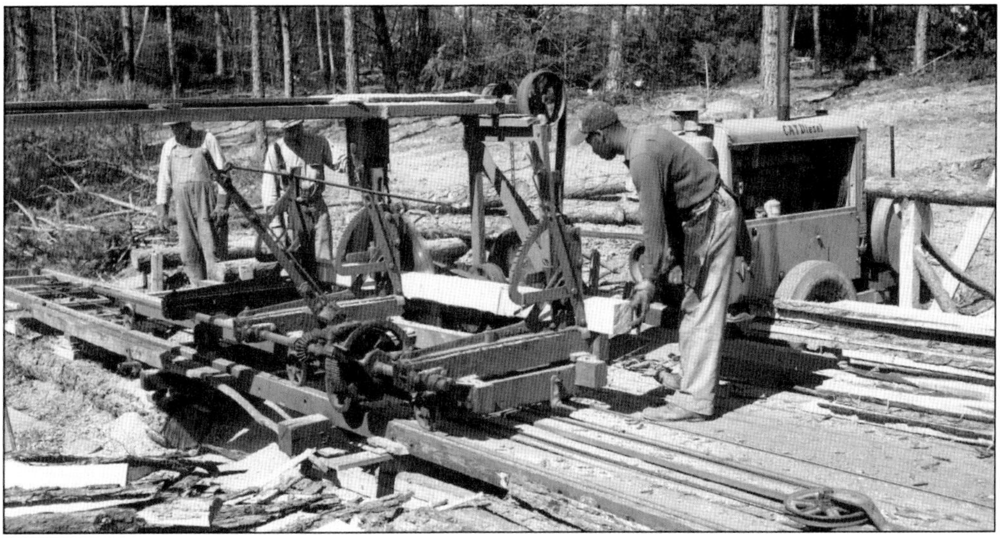

This is the W.W. Owens lumber and logging job site in Mocksville in April 1955. A Caterpillar D315 diesel engine provided the power for this temporary sawmill these workers set up in the field. In this way, they could mill the logs on-site without the extra labor, time, or costs that would result from having to transport the felled trees to a sawmill that could be many miles away from where the logging was being done.

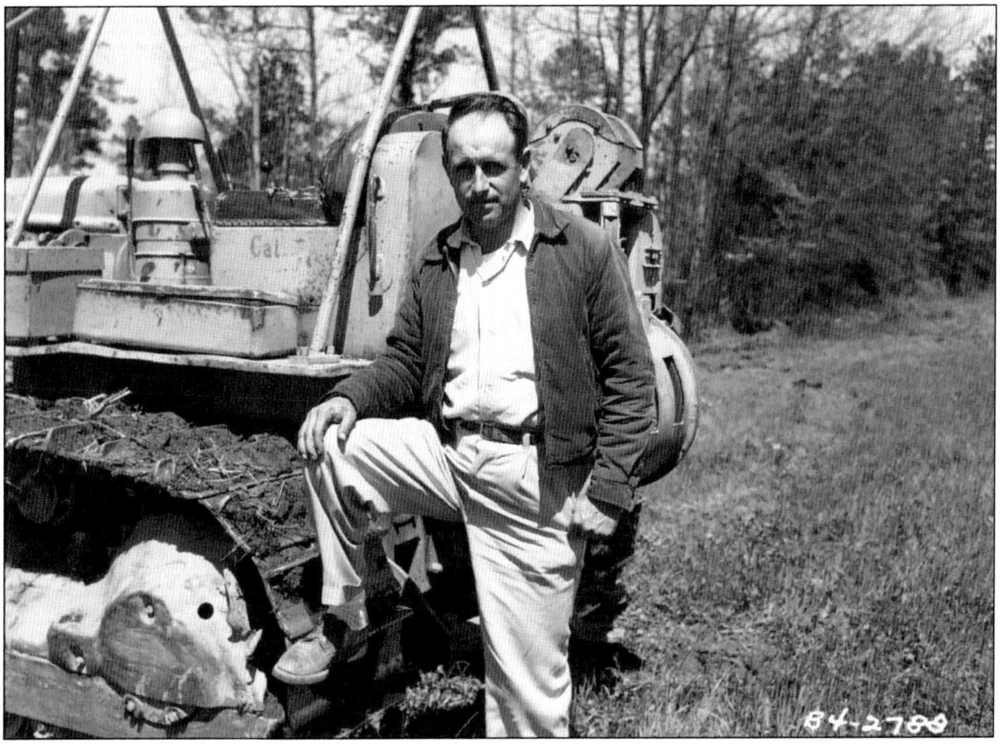

T.W. Brown of Mocksville owned several pieces of Caterpillar equipment he utilized in his land clearing and earthmoving operations. The photographer who took this casual portrait in April 1955 noted that Brown gave a "testimonial [that] concerns ease of operation and long life" of the machinery he purchased from Carolina Tractor & Equipment Company.

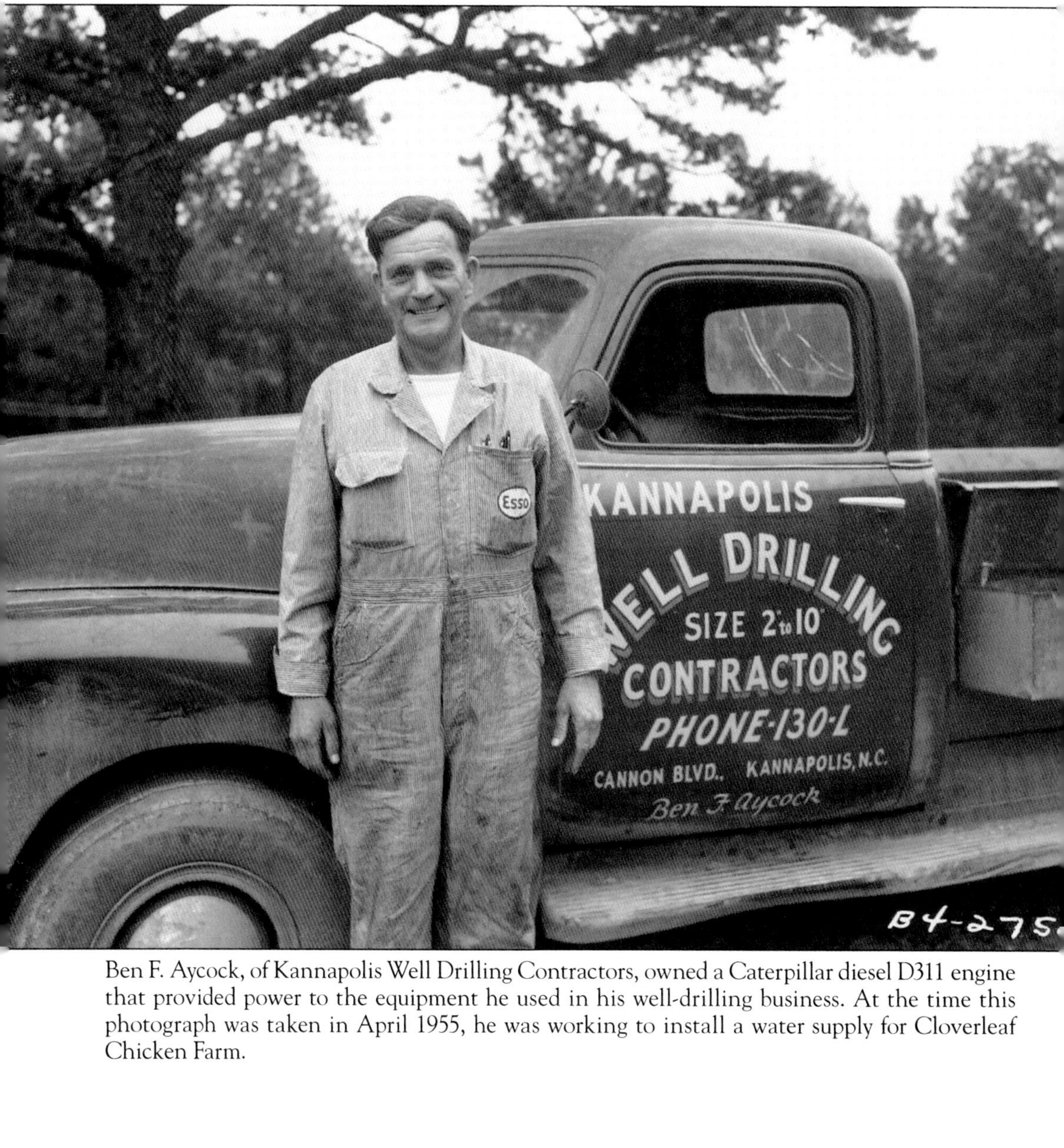

Ben F. Aycock, of Kannapolis Well Drilling Contractors, owned a Caterpillar diesel D311 engine that provided power to the equipment he used in his well-drilling business. At the time this photograph was taken in April 1955, he was working to install a water supply for Cloverleaf Chicken Farm.

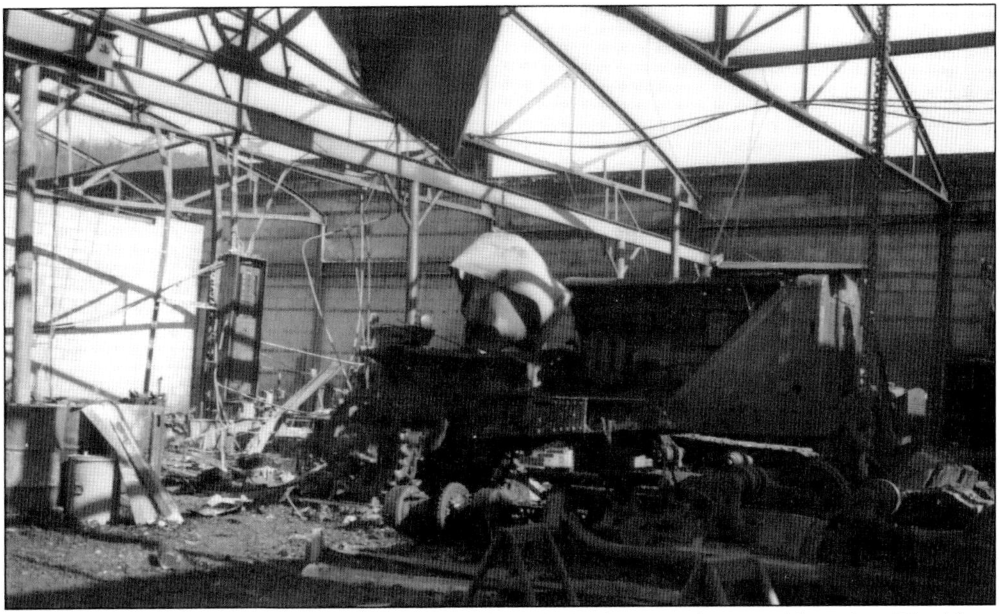

On November 26, 1955, Carolina Tractor's Asheville facility was destroyed by a fire. The blaze broke out right before midnight and burned unchecked for 45 minutes before two companies of Asheville's fire department arrived at the scene. Carolina Tractor estimated a loss of more than $200,000. Equipment lost in the fire included three new tractors, two trade-ins, and a D6 belonging to a customer.

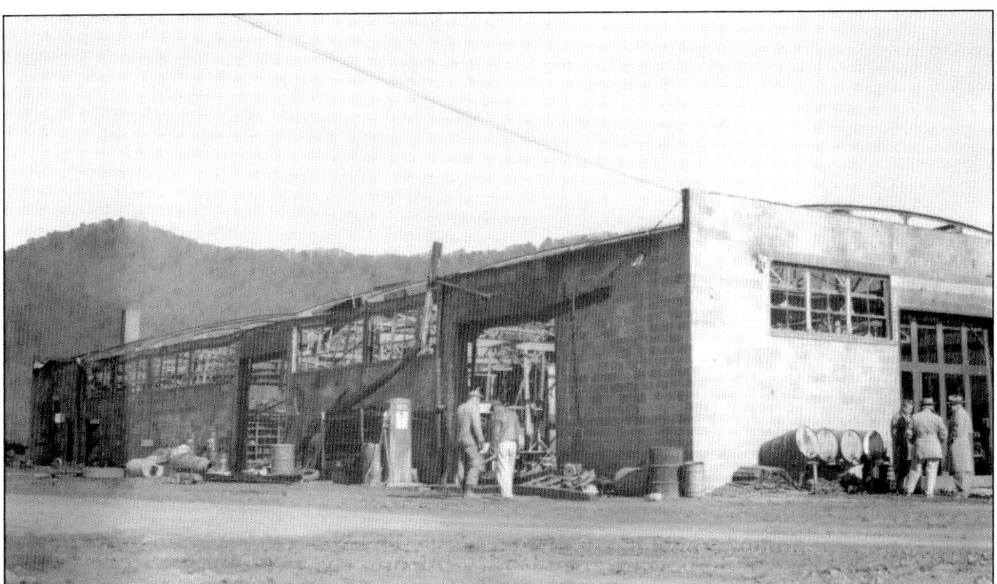

Carolina Tractor employees survey the shell of the Asheville store, which was destroyed by the fire. By the next Monday morning, the company was up and running in a temporary facility. Despite their rapid responses to the loss, it would take employees more than a year to clean up and repackage all the salvageable parts left by the fire.

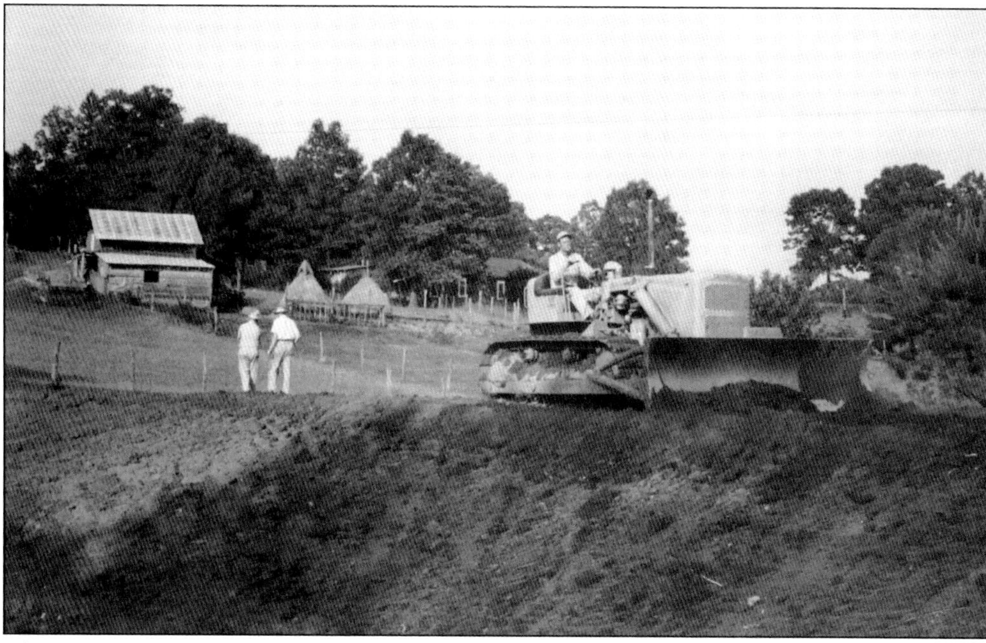

This image from the mid-1950s depicts work under way constructing a farm pond. It was one of the many such jobs initiated during a time when the federal government funded irrigation projects.

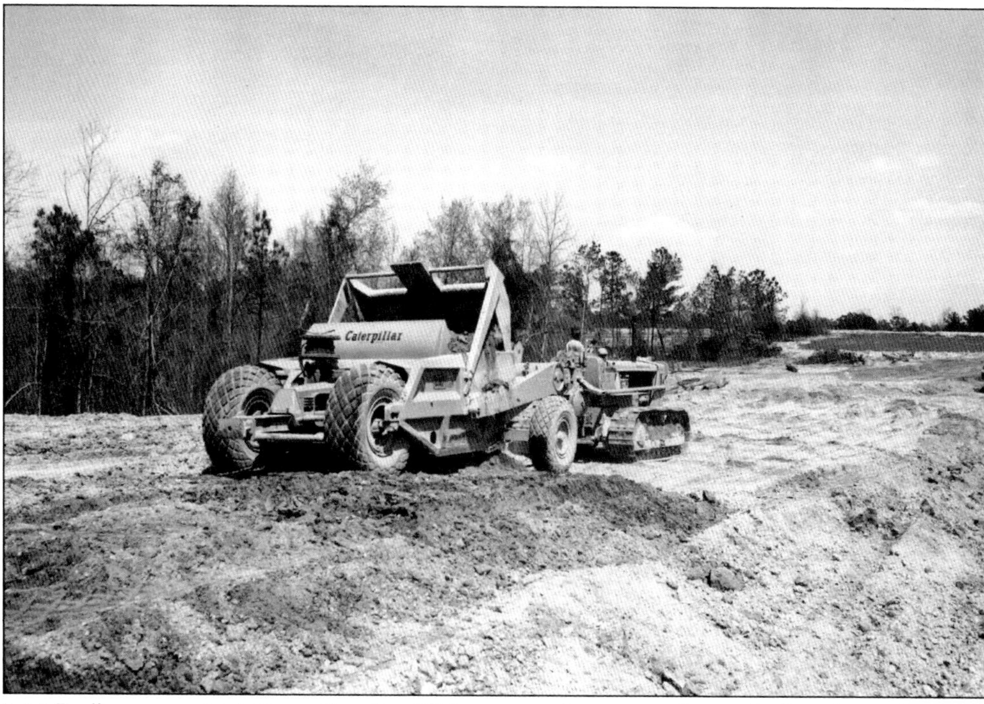

L.M. Faulkner owned this Caterpillar diesel D6 tractor with a scraper that worked on the earthmoving phase of the job to build an irrigation pond in 1955. Like many others, he obtained the equipment with which he earned his livelihood from Carolina Tractor & Equipment Company. Often, the government would provide funding for such projects. This one was located in the Montgomery County town of Candor, North Carolina.

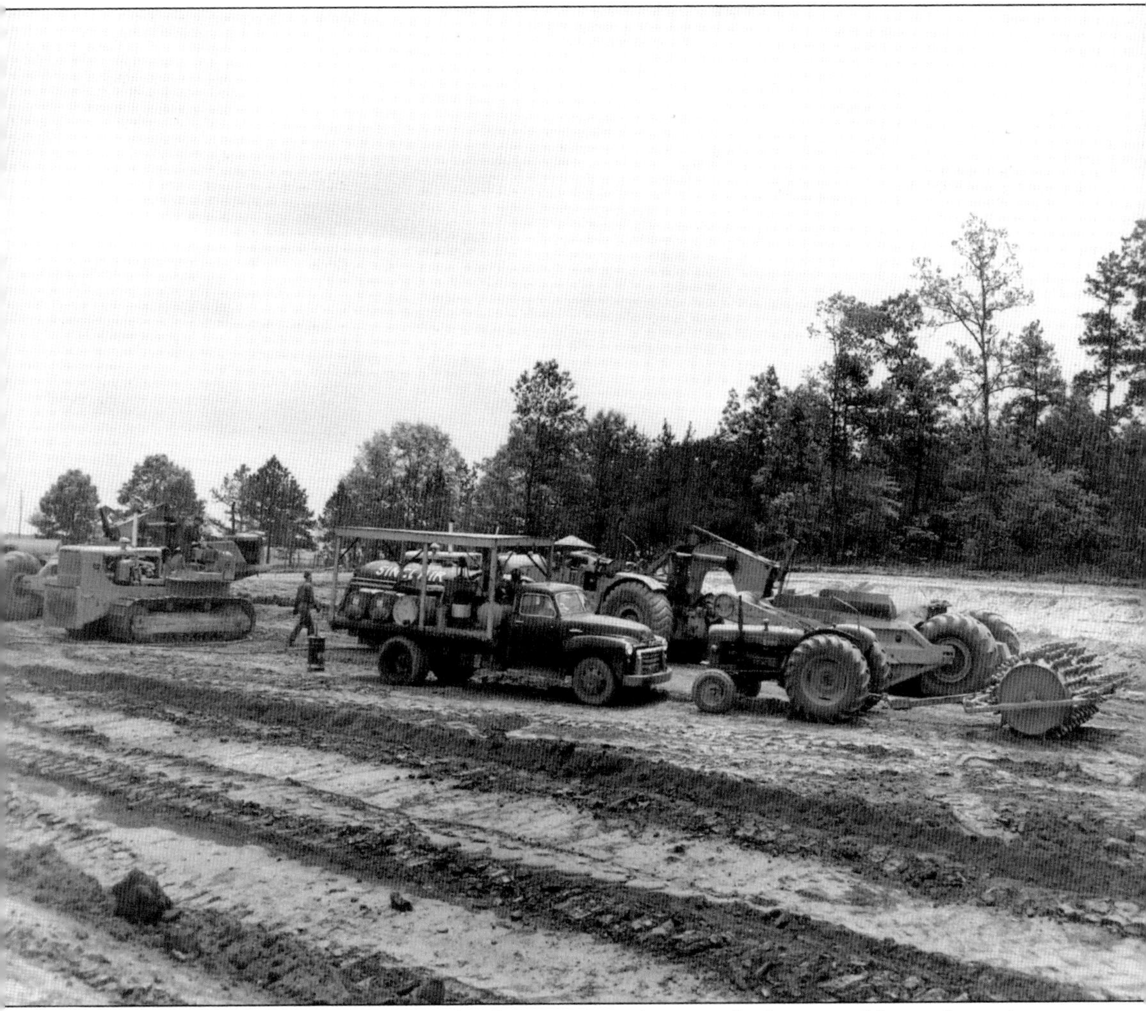

When the Federal-Aid Highway Act of 1956 was enacted, it was the largest public works project in the United States to date. It promised to fund the construction of more than 40,000 miles of interstate highways. Carolina Tractor & Equipment Company sold and serviced the machinery contractors purchased to build the growing network of roads. The equipment in this photograph is typical of the kind that worked on these projects.

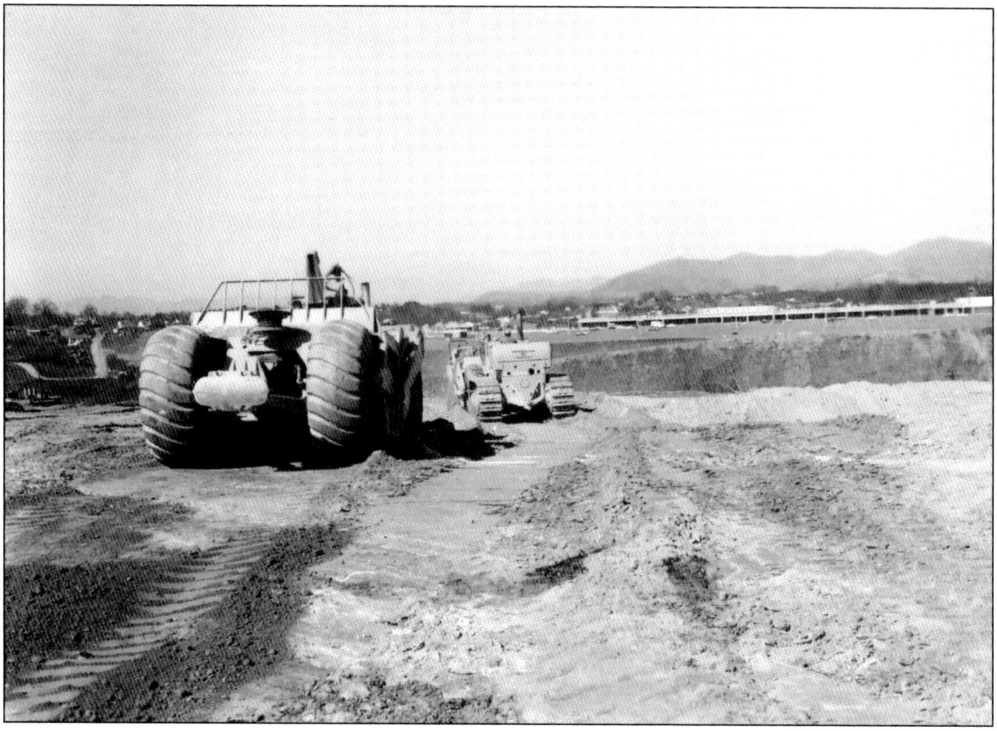

When a highway contractor won a bid to work on an interstate construction project, he could be assured that the labor would keep his crews busy. This was because the federal government, under the direction of Pres. Dwight Eisenhower, funded the extensive program to plan, develop, and build the system of highways that would employ thousands of workers across the country and bring revenues to the industries that built, sold, and serviced the machinery used on the projects. Carolina Tractor & Equipment Company was one of the companies whose products and services were part of this effort.

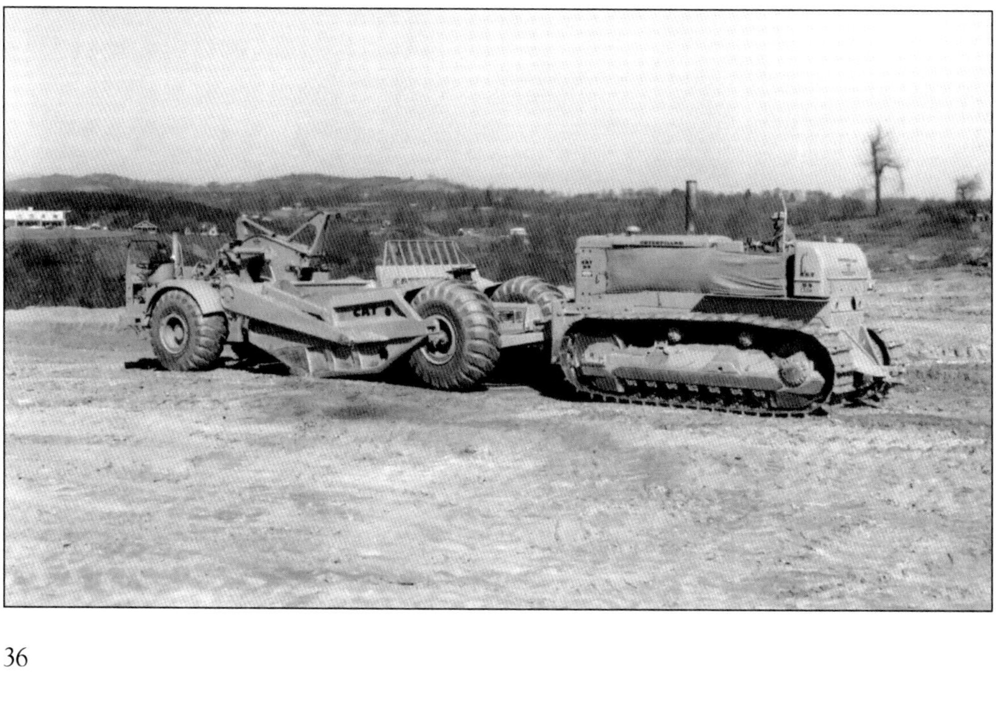

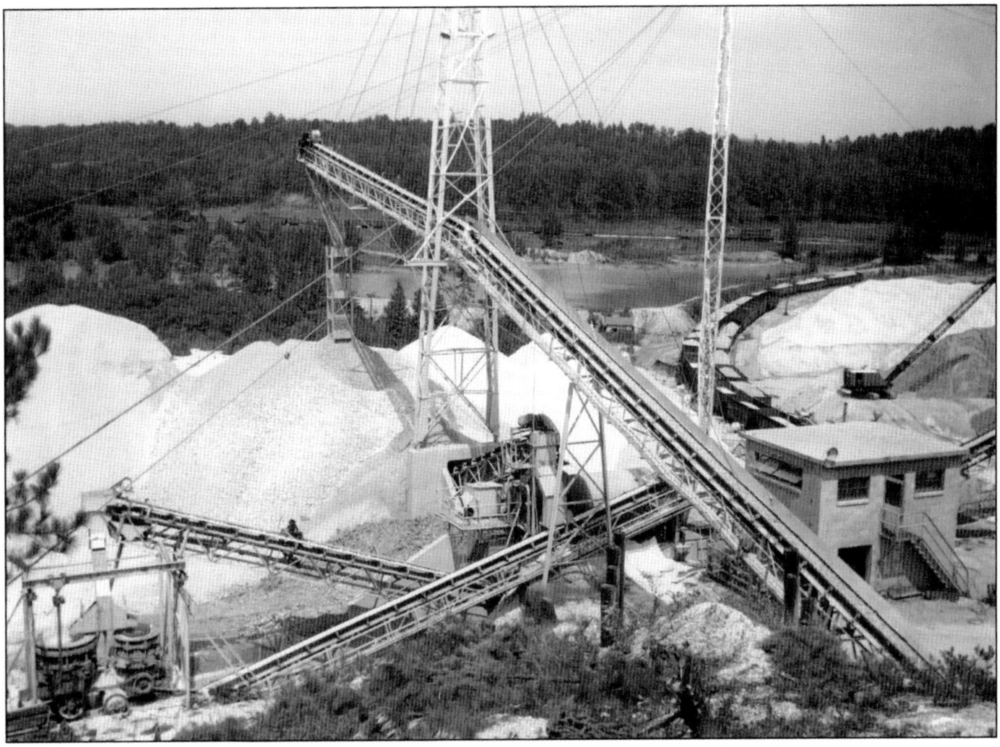

This sand plant near Lilesville, North Carolina, processed and loaded sand onto train cars using shovels and cranes sold by Carolina Tractor & Equipment Company. The need for such material remained strong throughout the 1950s, in large part due to the Federal-Aid Highway Act of 1956, also known as the National Interstate and Defense Highways Act, which was enacted to build a modern transportation network that would stretch across the country.

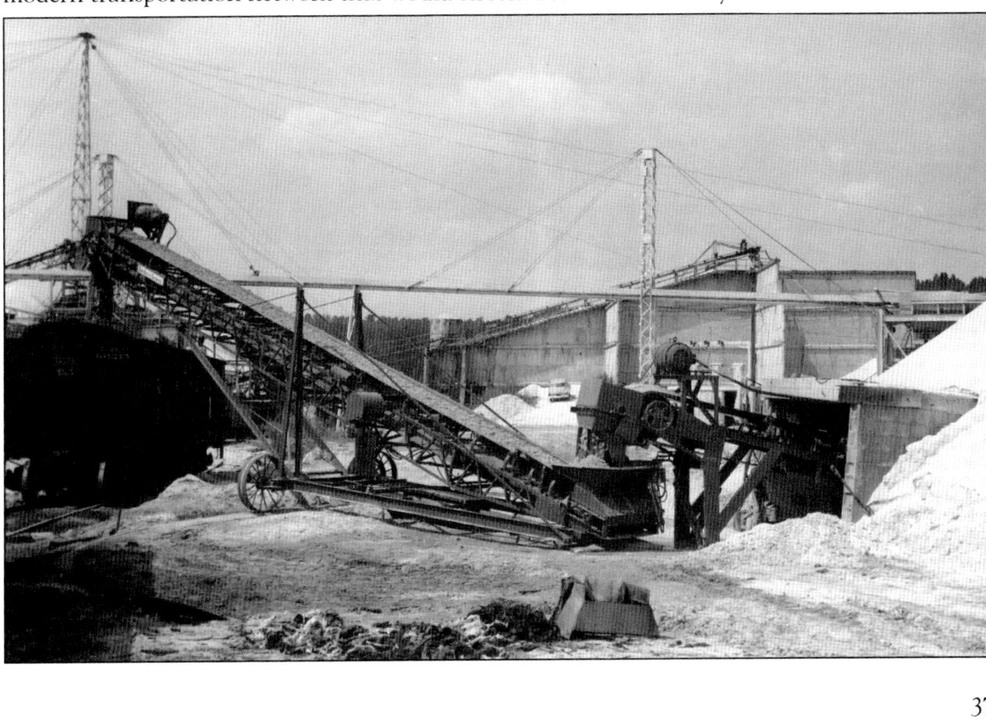

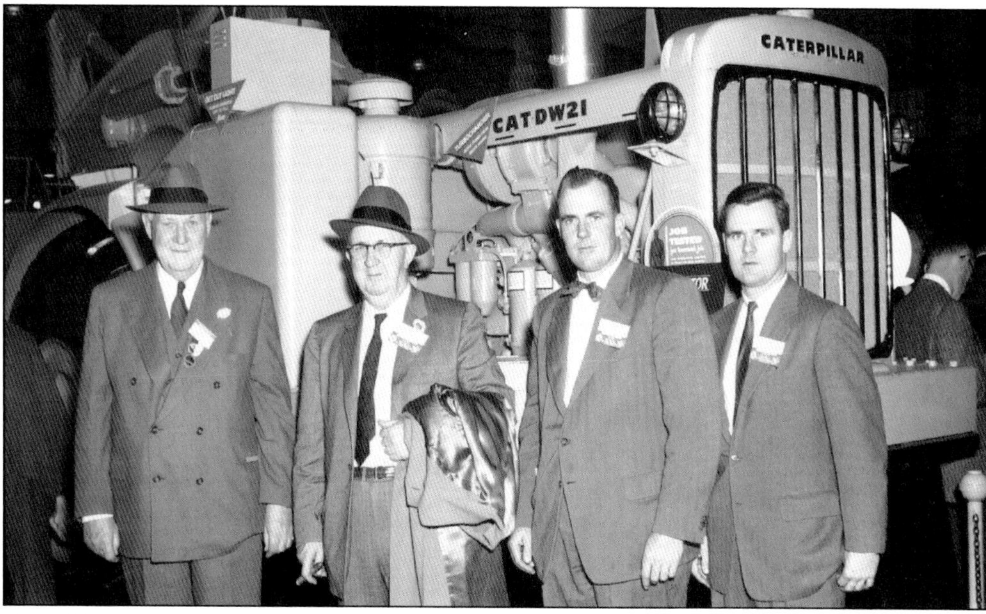

The 1957 American Road Builders' Association Road Show in Chicago, Illinois, was attended by an estimated 200,000 people. Held once each decade, it showcased the newest equipment being brought to market. Since the Federal-Aid Highway Act of 1956 had been implemented, the show attracted large numbers of contractors and highway officials. The Caterpillar display boasted "more than a million dollars' worth of the newest earthmoving equipment." Attending are, from left to right, P. Ransome, L.M. Weisiger, Percy A. Ransome Jr., and Ernest L. Ransome.

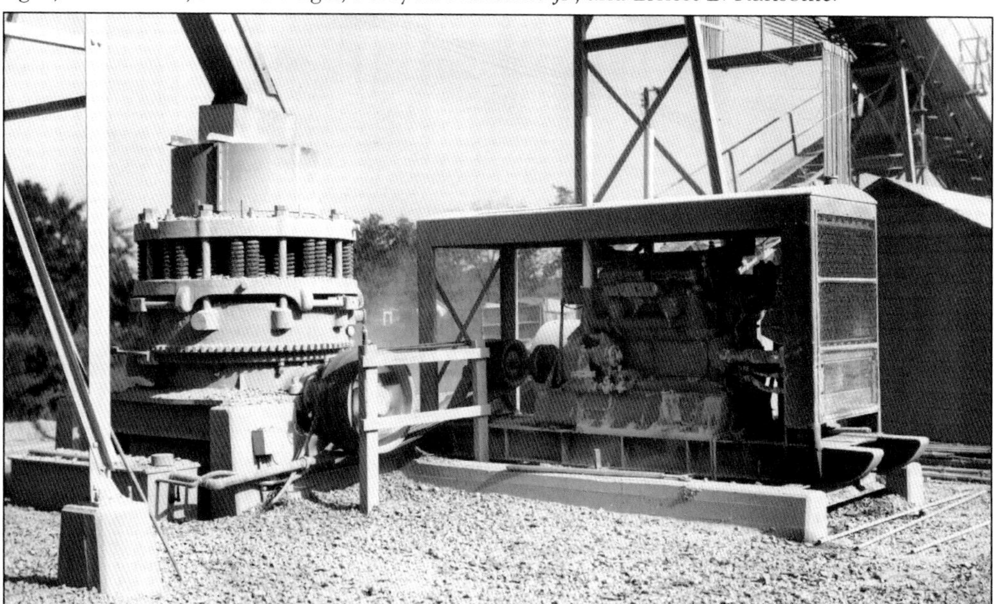
This rock crushing plant was in operation near Durham, North Carolina, during the late 1950s. Like others of its time, it made gravel that was used in highway projects. These public works were part of the post–World War II boom during which the nation's interstate system was established. Carolina Tractor & Equipment Company sold the machinery that provided both diesel and electric power for this Nello L. Teer Company job.

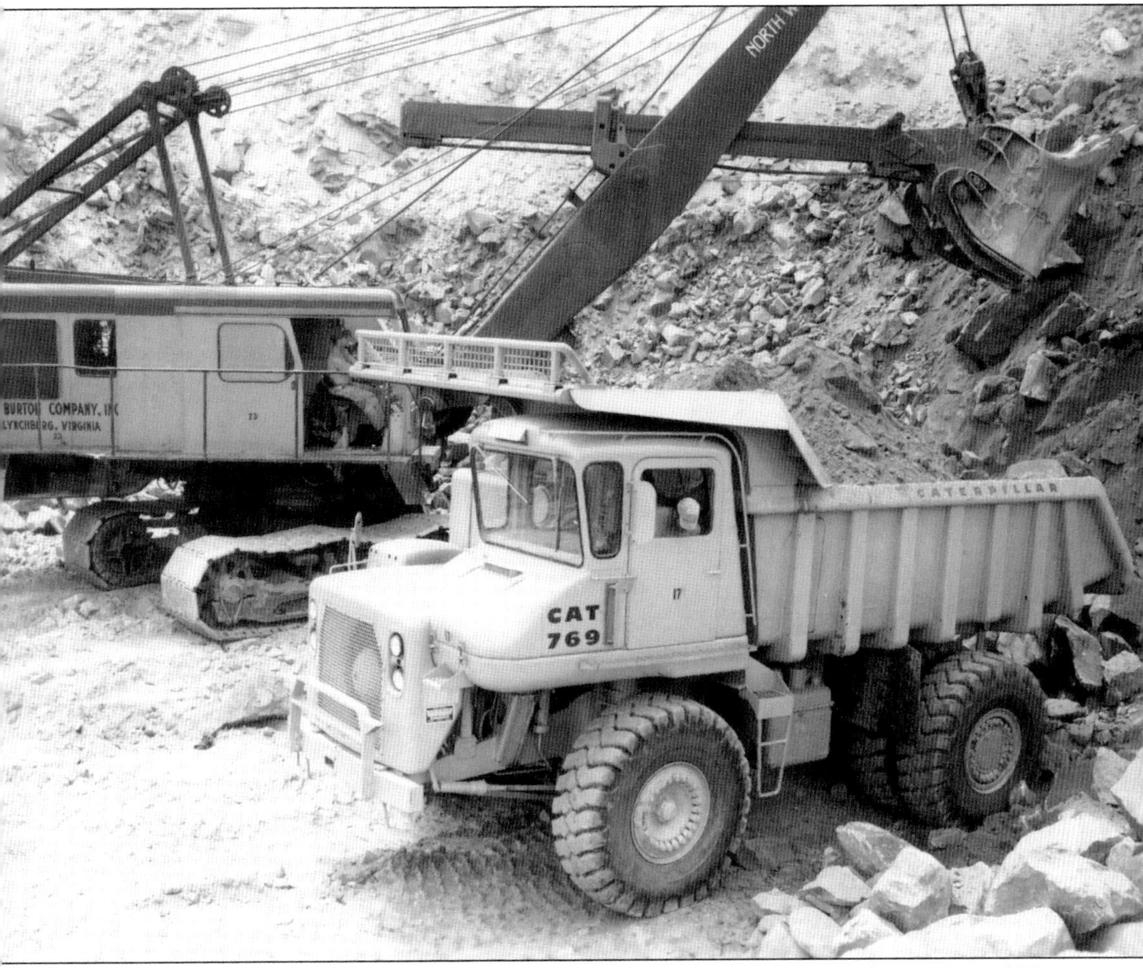

This Caterpillar 769 truck and crane are working on a job site in the late 1950s for customer A.V. Burton in Asheville. The mountainous region of Western North Carolina presented daunting challenges to the companies working to bring roads, utilities, services, and other development to the area. High winds would threaten worker safety; heavy rains could cause mud and rock slides as well as flooding.

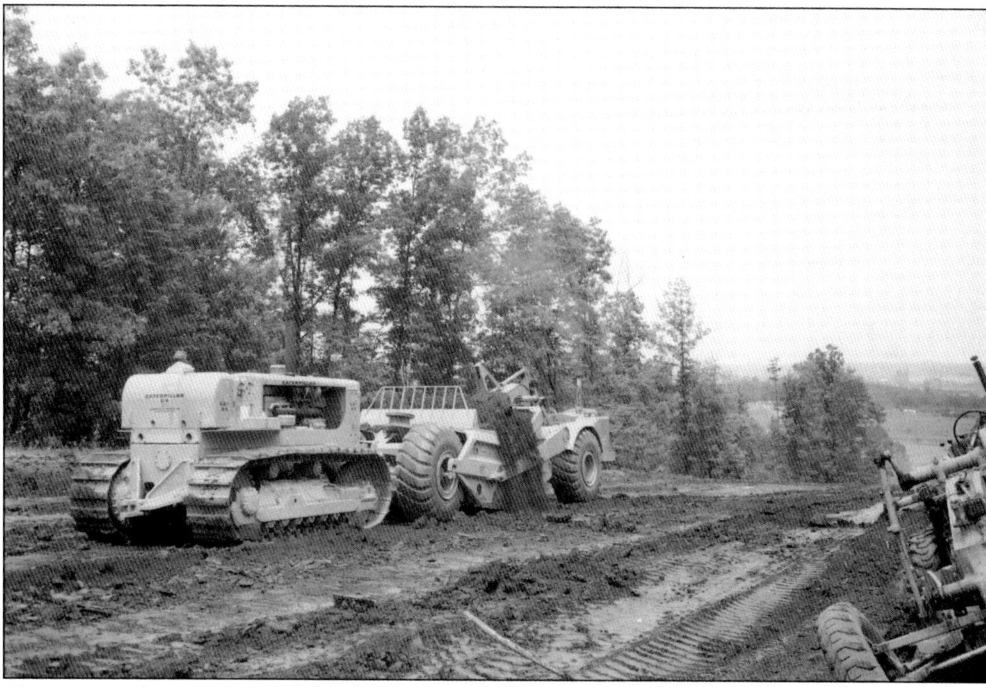

The impact of constructing the new east-west Interstate 40 through North Carolina could not be overstated. Contractors hired for even preliminary work, such as preparation of the roadbeds shown in these photographs from the late 1950s, could be assured of steady work until the completion of the job. Interstate 40 would grow to traverse 420 miles across the state. Although originally conceptualized as part of a cross-country defense network, the interstate system would grow to function so well that commercial carriers, commuters, travelers, recreation seekers, and essentially everyone else would utilize it across the nation.

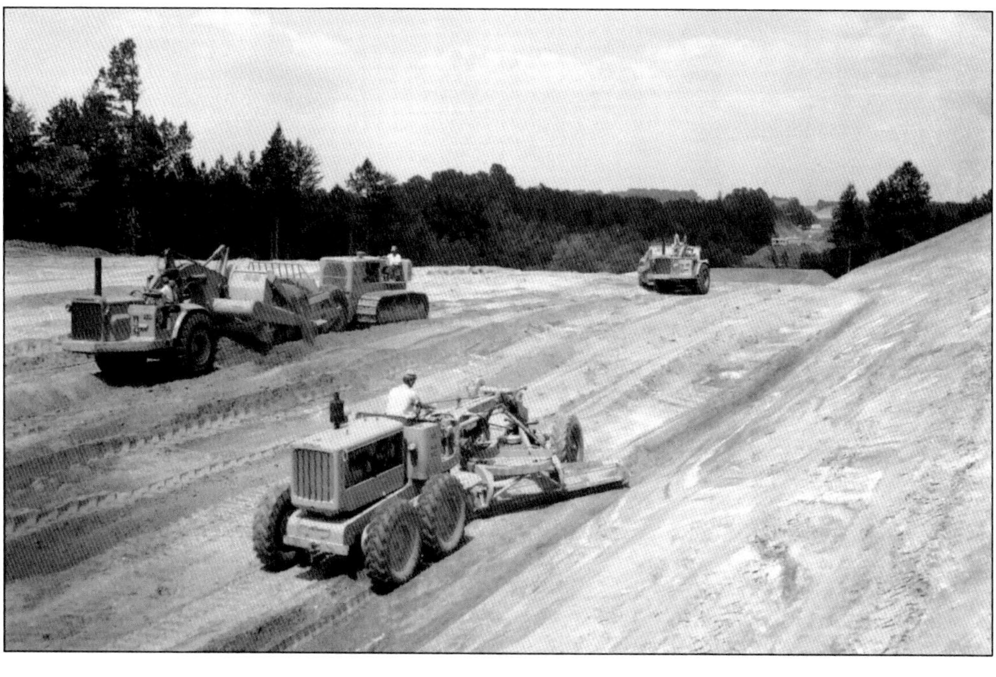

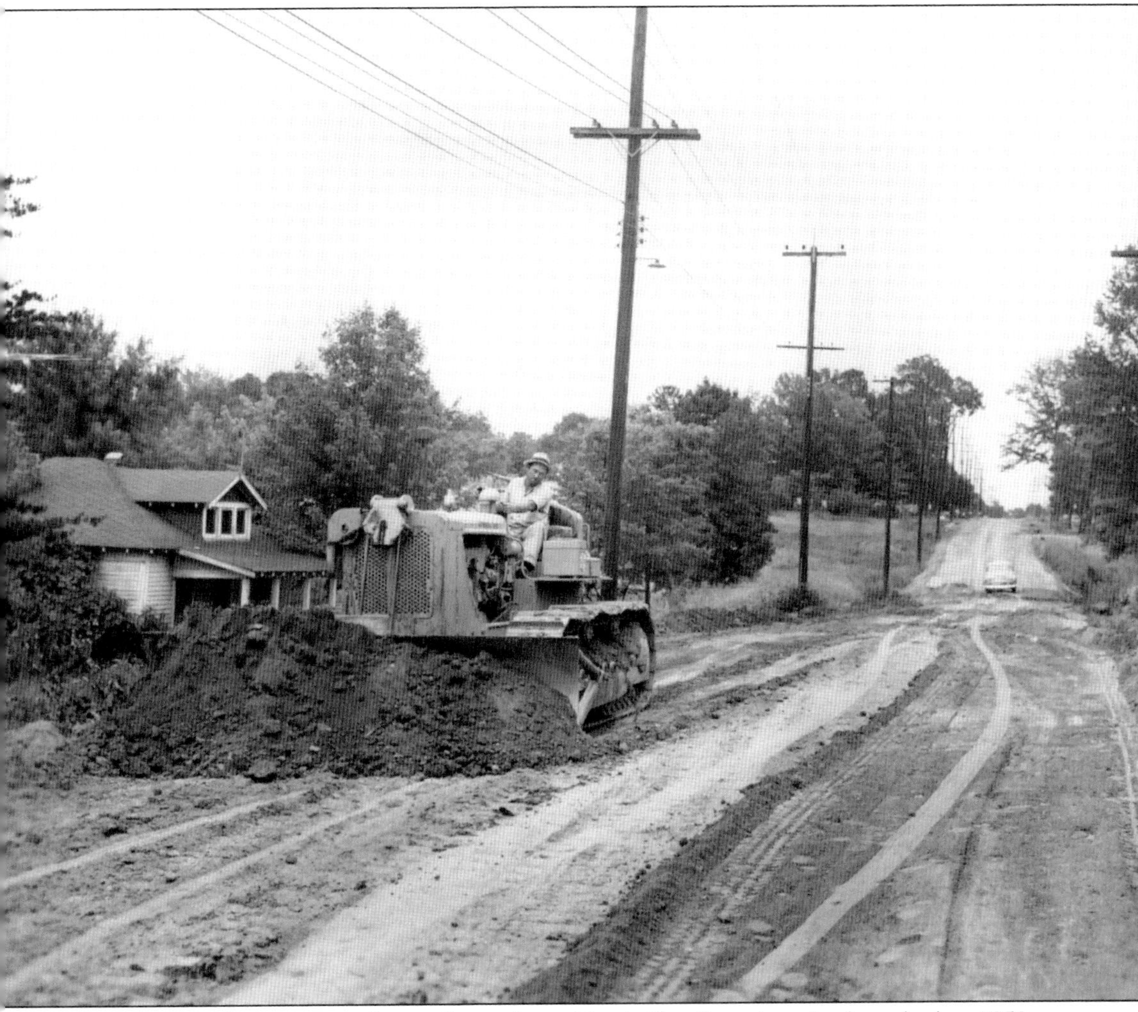

This widening of a county road near Greensboro, North Carolina, dates back to the late 1950s. A Caterpillar D7 tractor is doing the work and is well suited to the task since its size allows it to maneuver around objects in its path, such as power poles or dwellings that have already been built in proximity to the road.

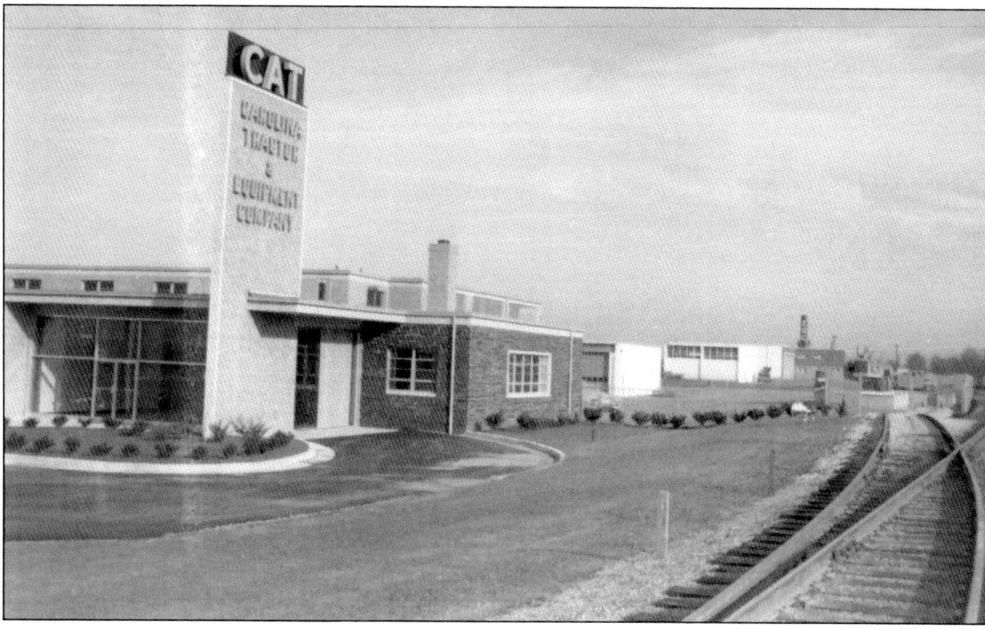

Carolina Tractor opened its first branch in Charlotte on Graham Street in 1956 in a building leased from Blythe Construction. Placing a branch in Charlotte put the company in better position to support projects such as the construction of Lake Norman, I-85, and Charlotte Motor Speedway. The Graham Street store would serve the Charlotte area until Carolina Tractor consolidated its Salisbury and Charlotte operations into a new headquarters on Statesville Road in Charlotte in 1971.

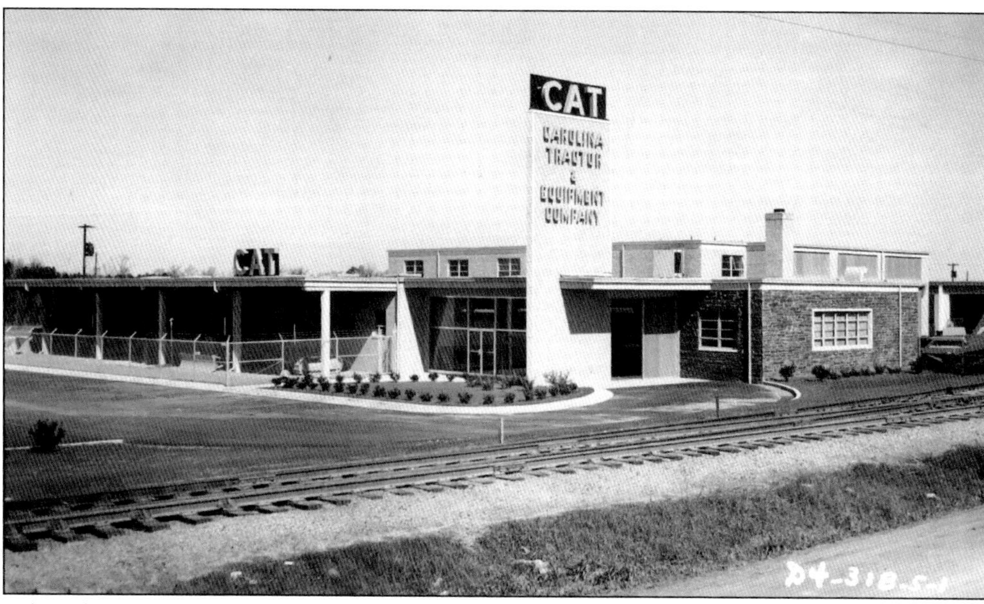

When the Charlotte branch of Carolina Tractor & Equipment Company relocated from Graham Street to Statesville Road, the owners chose a site for the new plant that would provide easy access to rail transportation, since much of the heavy equipment traveled by rail. Also in 1956, Mr. Les's son Ed Weisiger came to work for the company, which at that time had a total of three locations.

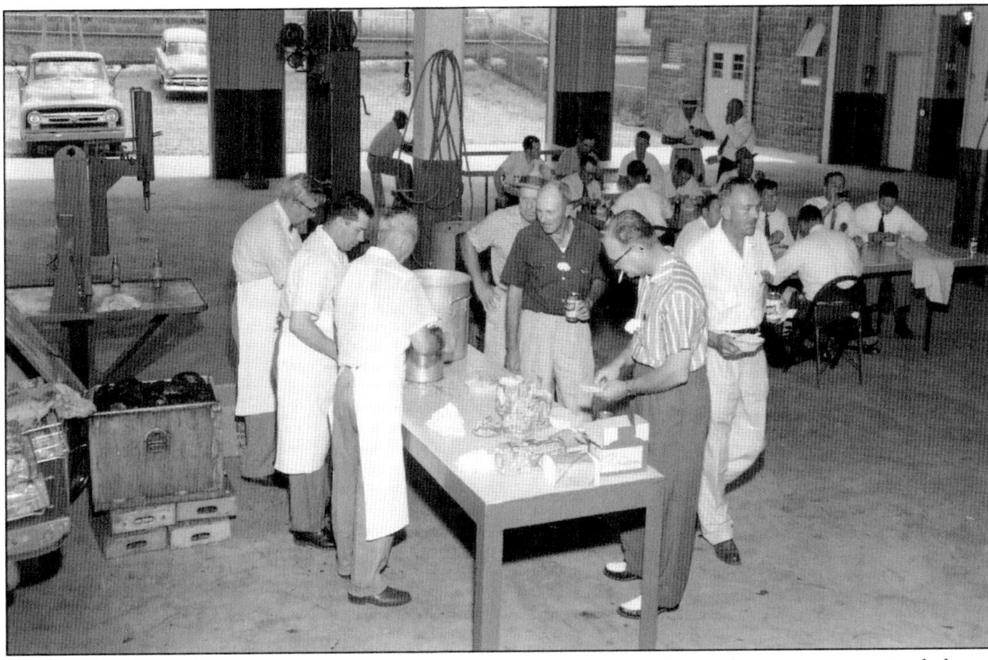

When the new branch opened in 1957 on Graham Street in Charlotte, the company invited clients and their families to visit for an open house celebration. Attendees could tour the modernized shops where equipment was serviced and rebuilt, view the expansive parts warehouse, and partake of some of North Carolina's finest barbecue.

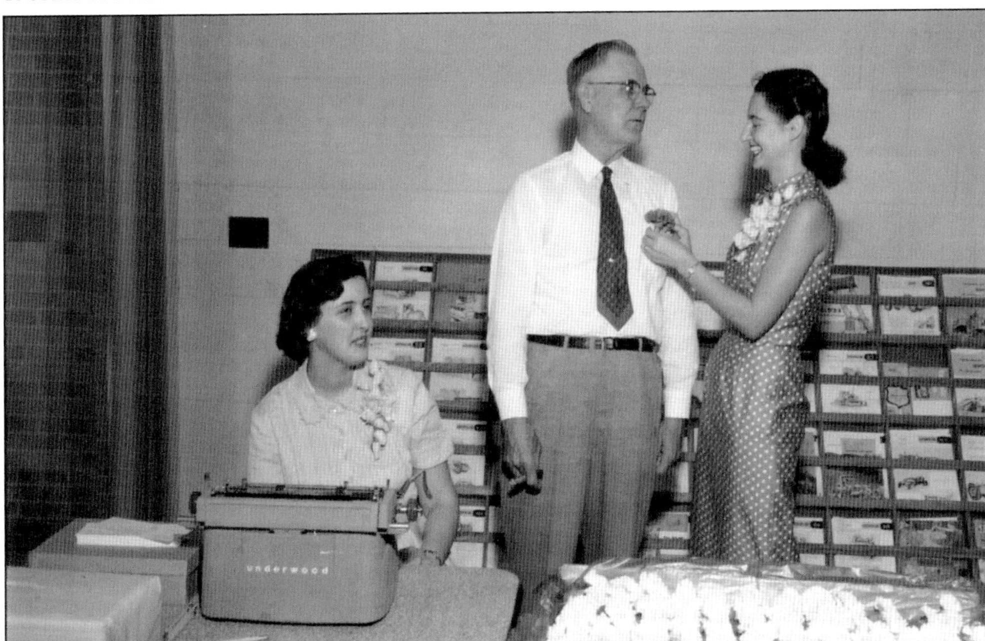

Ladies who worked in the office wore corsages for the open house event at the Charlotte branch in 1957. In addition to the Charlotte staff, key employees from the other Carolina Tractor & Equipment Company locations were recruited to help host the celebration. Here, two secretaries from Salisbury are seen welcoming Lamar Pittman, a visiting Caterpillar dealer.

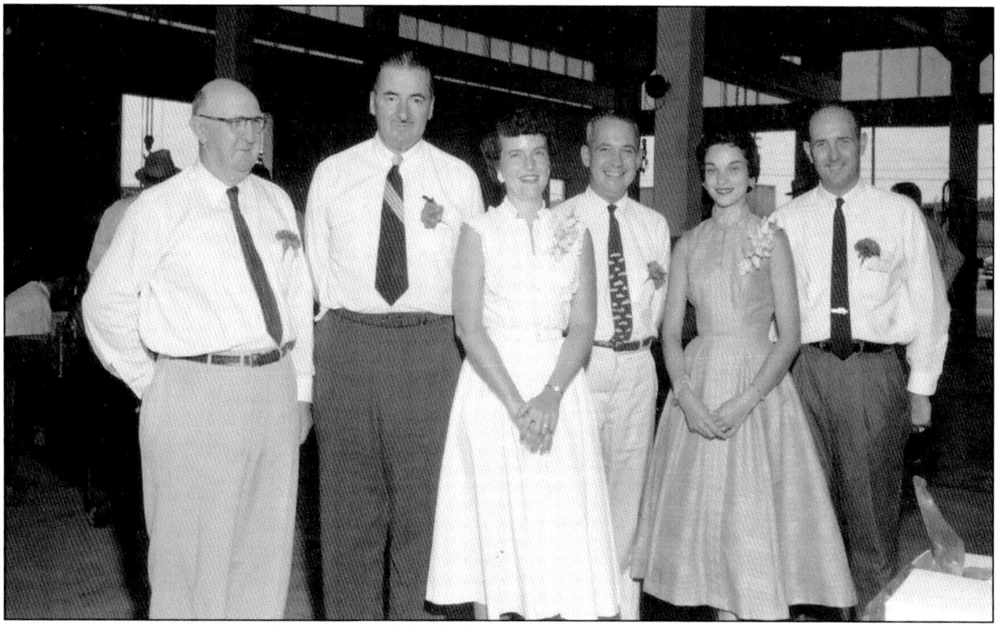

Posing for the event photographer during the 1957 open house celebration for the Charlotte location are, from left to right, Mr. Les, Bill Zeigler, Jewel Wolfe Ziprik, Chappy Chapman, unidentified, and Ed Weisiger Sr. Employees addressed between 400 and 500 invitations to the event that welcomed the customers, dealers, suppliers, and their families to tour the new Carolina Tractor & Equipment Company facility.

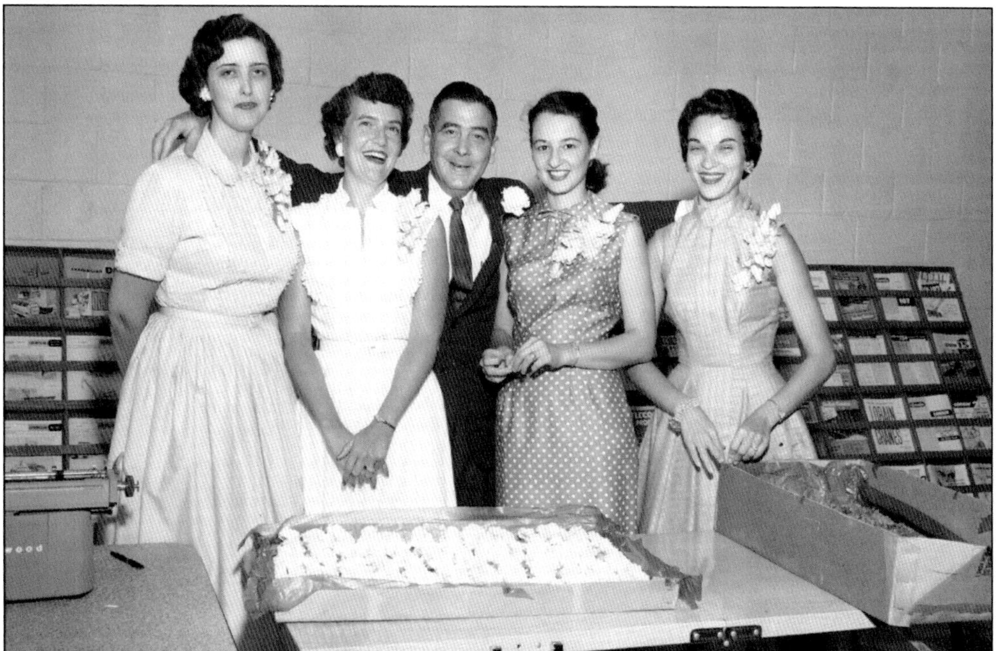

Here, ladies from the office staff show off their corsages along with a gentleman sporting a boutonniere at the 1957 open house celebrating the new Charlotte location of Carolina Tractor & Equipment Company.

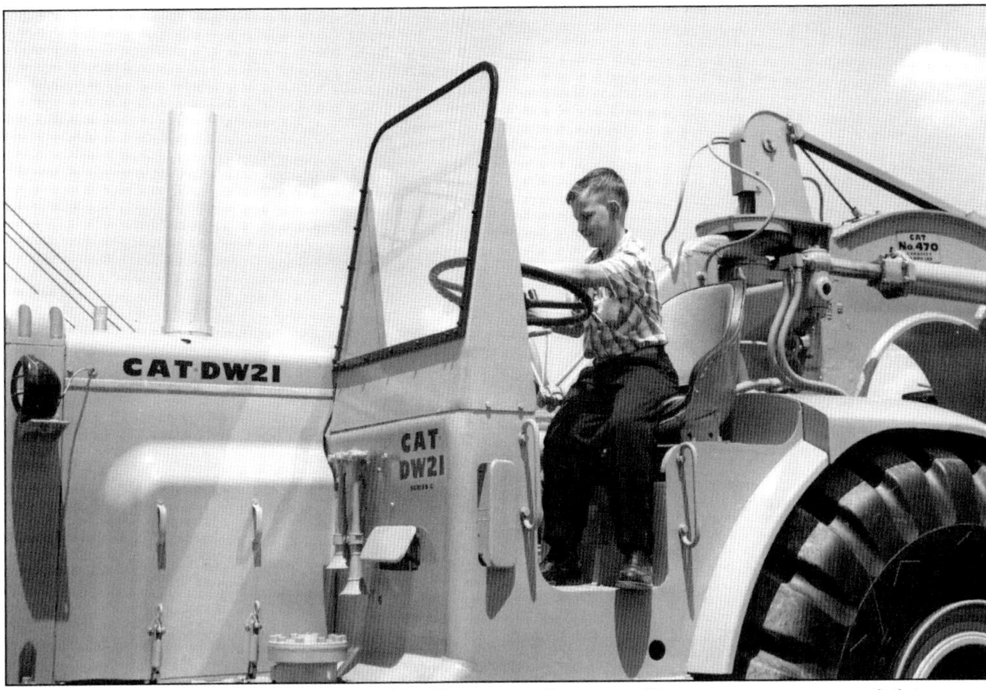

Children have always been fascinated by the size and power of heavy equipment, and this young son of a Carolina Tractor & Equipment Company customer is no different as he enjoys pretending to pilot this DW21 scraper in the late 1950s during a customer appreciation event.

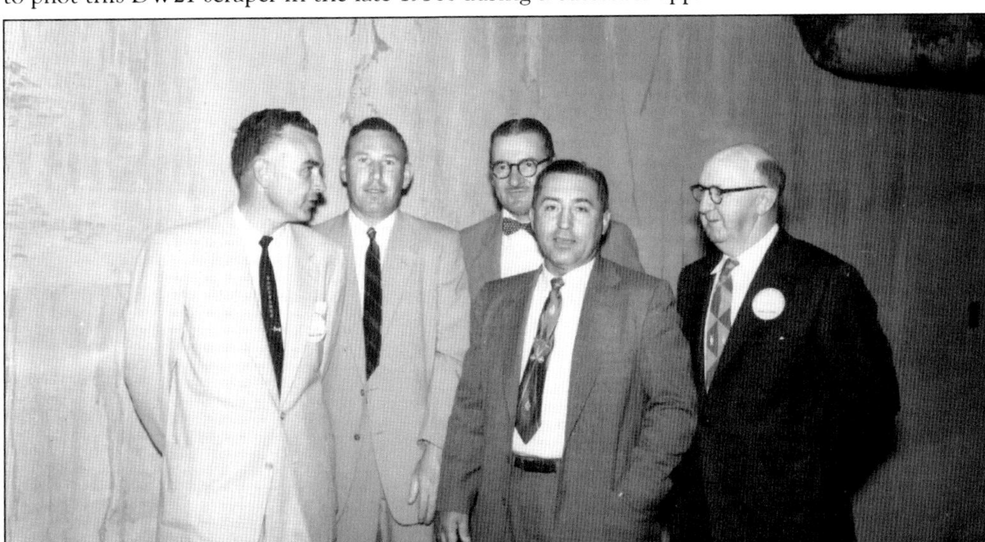

Sales managers, seen touring a facility during an open house, were crucial members of the teams that not only provided sales and service to equipment purchasers, but also helped to build long-term customer relationships and loyalty. Since dealers each had a dedicated territory, they were not in direct competition with each other but were more collegial. Mr. Les is pictured on the far right in this photograph of executives.

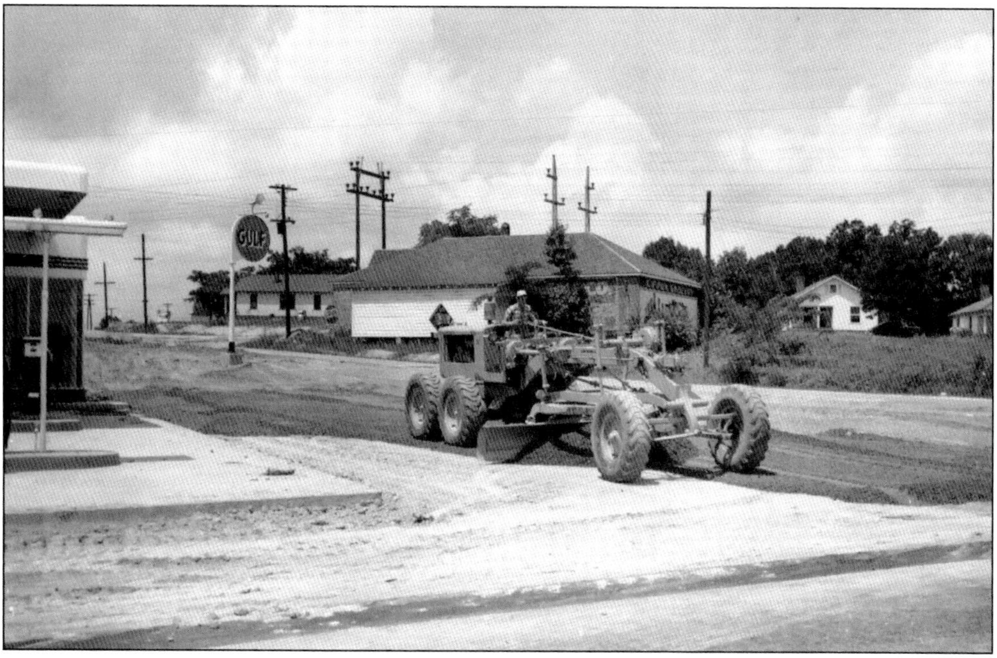

A Caterpillar motor grader works to level the rock base around a new gas station being built in Kannapolis, North Carolina, in this June 1957 photograph. The purchaser of the equipment was E.L. Powlas of Salisbury, who was the owner of the local construction business performing the work with machinery purchased from Carolina Tractor & Equipment Company.

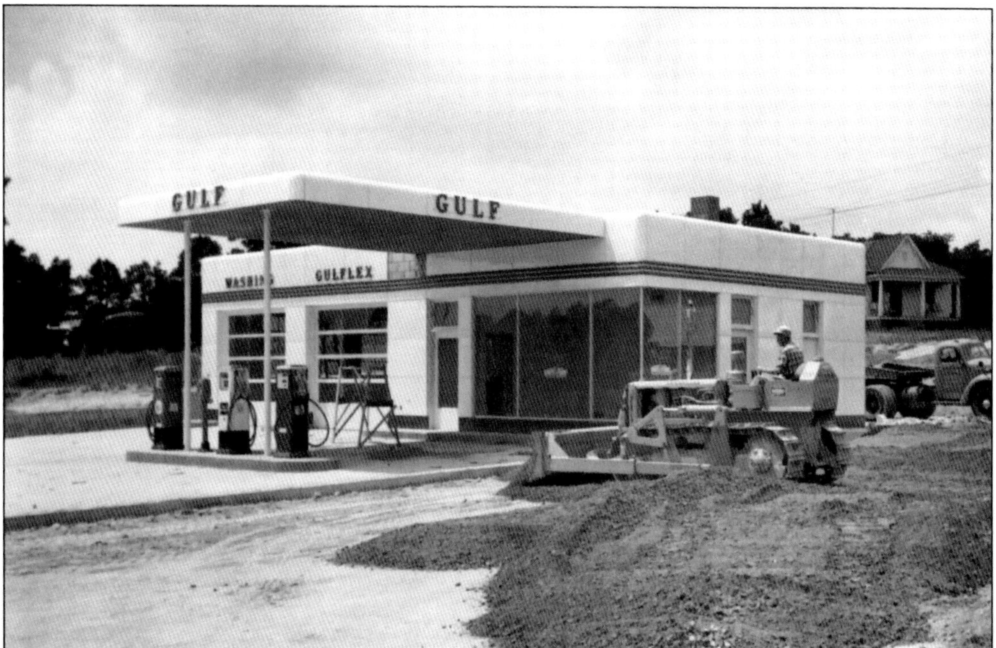

Pictured is a D4 working on the same Gulf gas station in 1957. The D4 was equipped with a No. 4a bulldozer, which was used for leveling the rock base around the new station. The D4 tractor was also widely used for farming and grading during the 1950s.

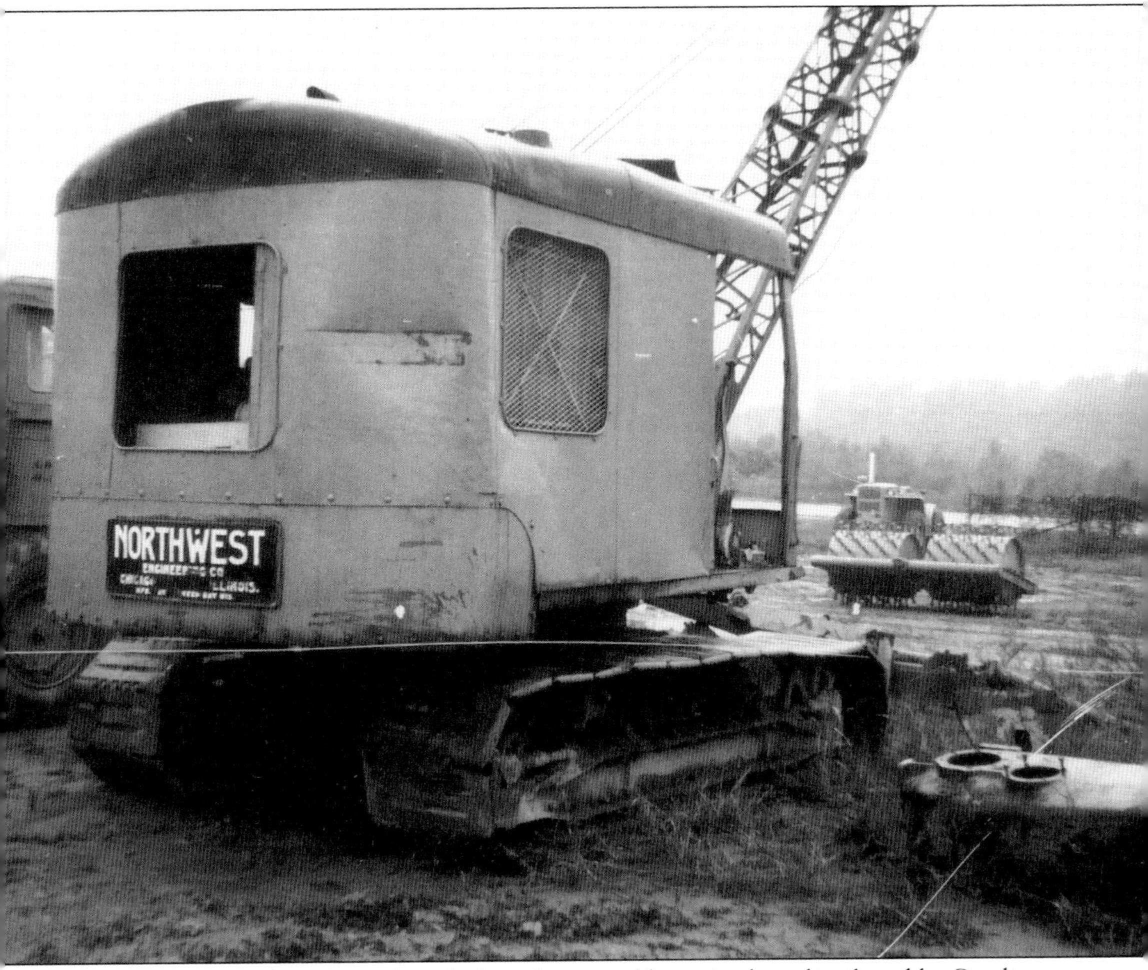

Northwest was not the primary brand of machinery sold, serviced, or distributed by Carolina Tractor & Equipment Company, but it was one of several supplemental lines. The company branched out into offering used equipment for customers unable purchase new machinery. This used Northwest crane is shown on a customer's job site in the late 1950s.

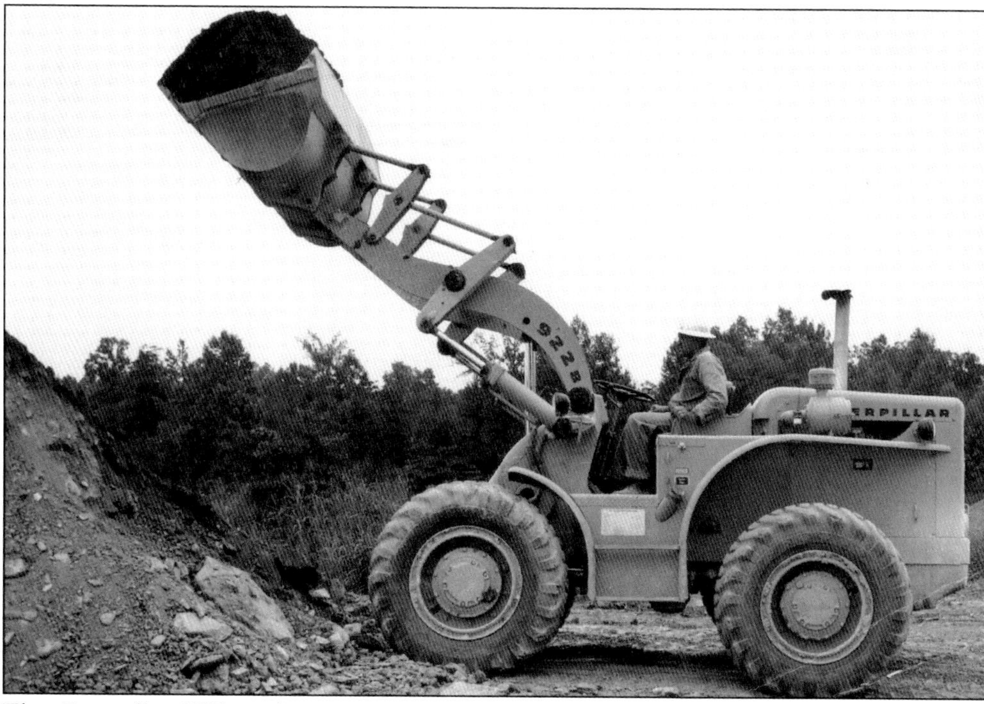

This Caterpillar 922B was known as a Traxcavator and was in use widely through the 1960s to load dirt. The name was changed from Traxcavator to Wheel Loader in 1959 due to customer confusion with newer models. All Traxcavators were steered with their rear wheels until articulated steering design was introduced, which allowed for increased speed and maneuverability. Shown here on a North Carolina customer's job, the machine was built in Winston-Salem. Within a few decades, the 922B would be utilized on jobs not just across the United States, but internationally as well.

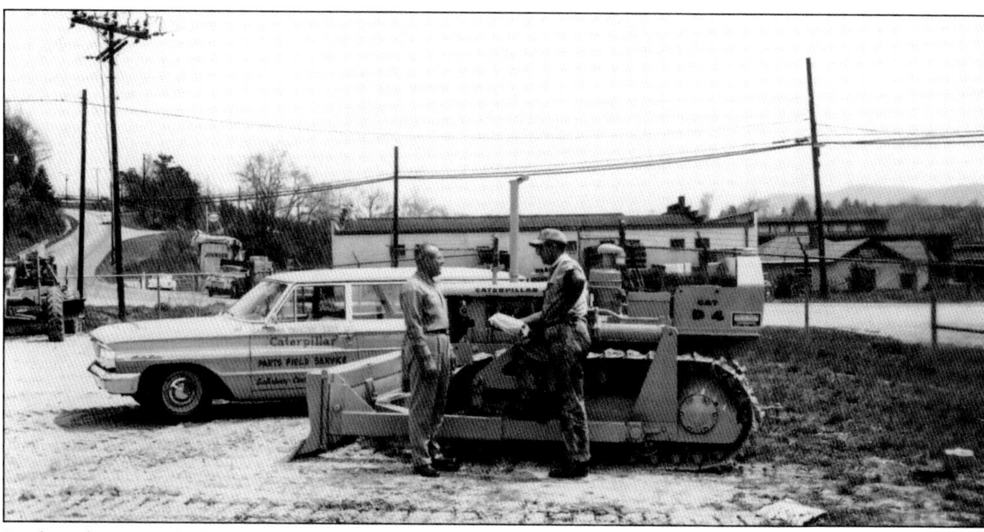

In this photograph from the 1950s, Carolina Tractor & Equipment Company employee Walt Bailey is seen discussing a job with a customer who is using a Caterpillar D4 tractor. Compared to other, more massive machinery, the D4 is much smaller, but its strength lay in its maneuverability. It could operate in smaller spaces, such as grading around houses.

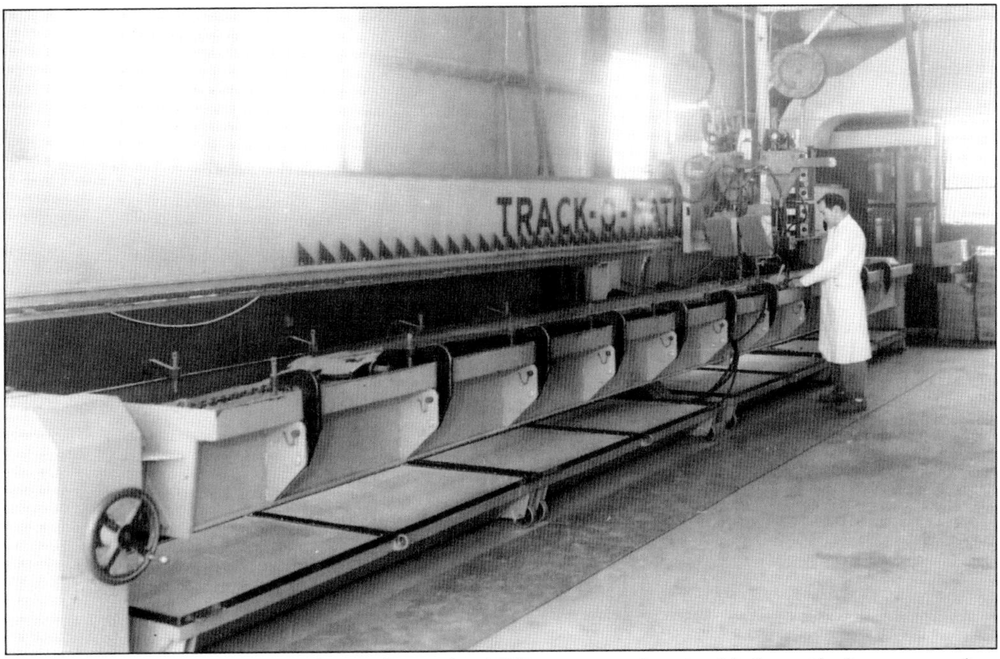

This Track-O-Matic system, shown from the 1950s, was used to build the rails for tractors but could also rebuild rails that were used and worn, to make them serviceable again. The machines were operated by welders who learned on the job and were trained to develop the skills that would allow them to work on new models of equipment as they were introduced. The Track-O-Matic system was located at the Salisbury plant and remained in use constantly.

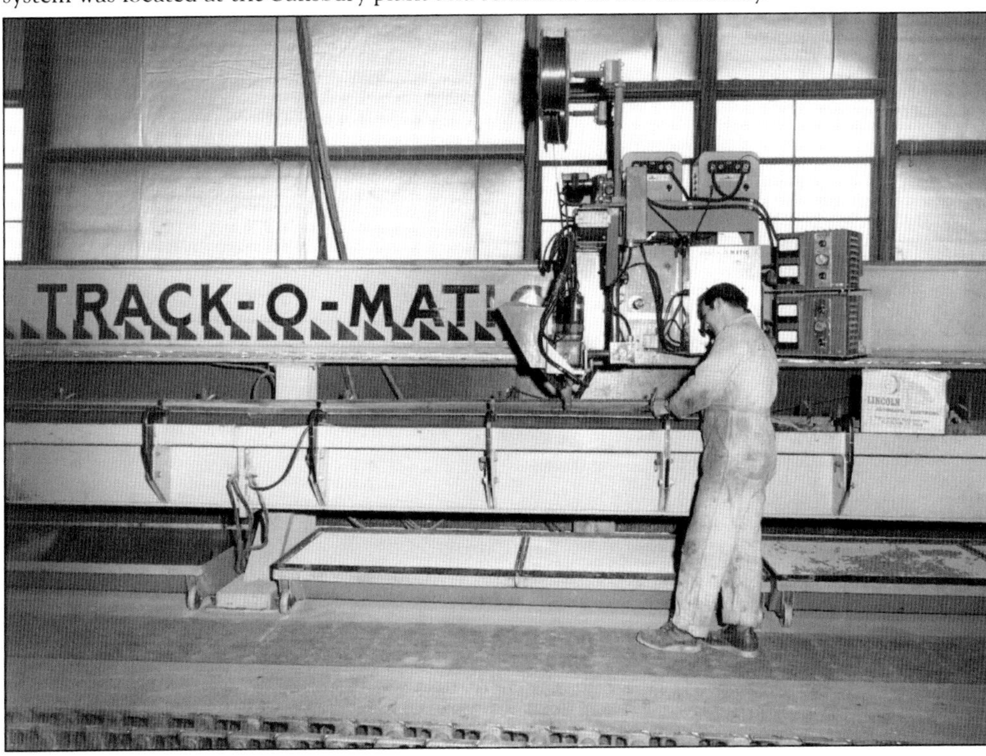

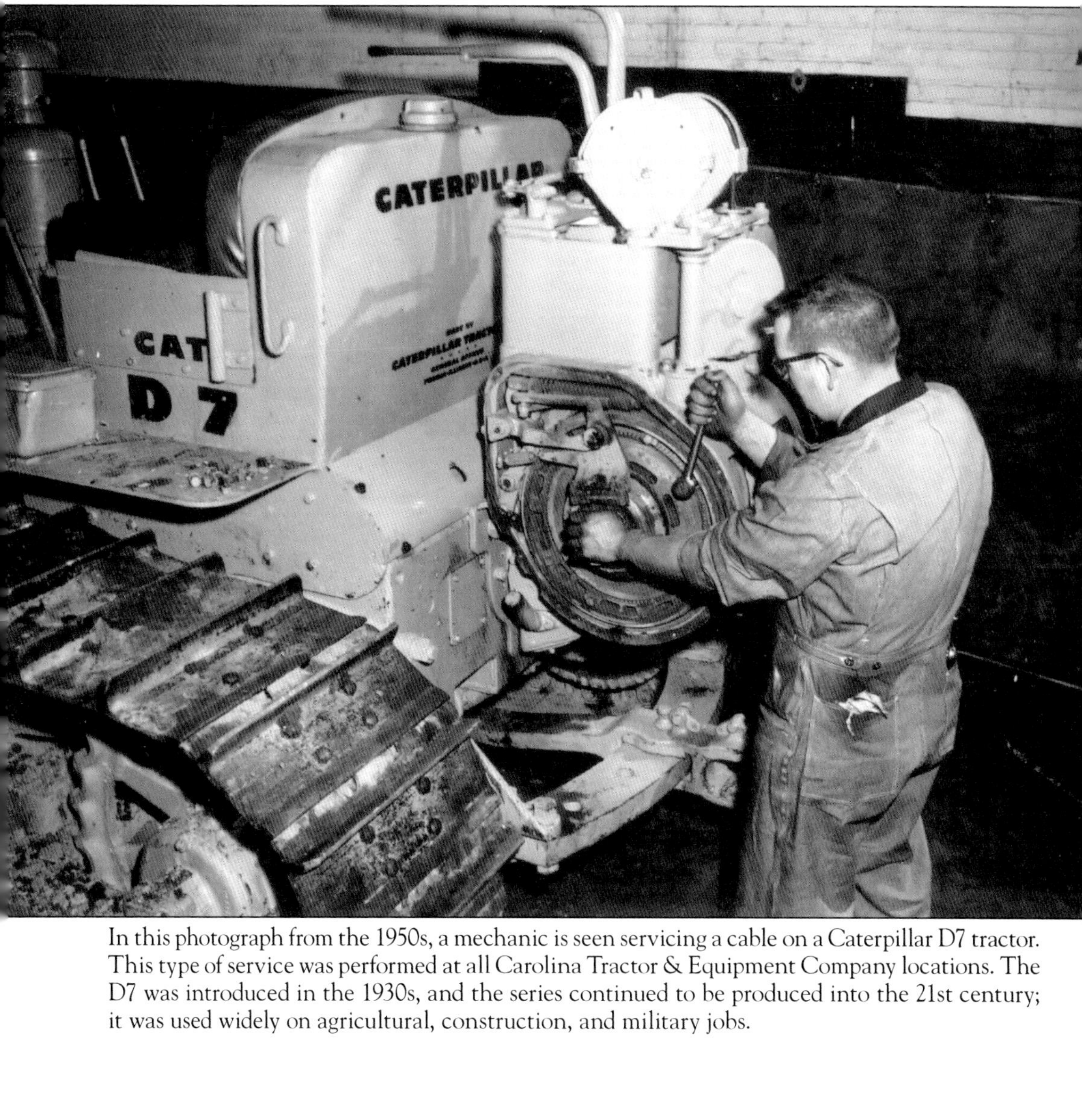

In this photograph from the 1950s, a mechanic is seen servicing a cable on a Caterpillar D7 tractor. This type of service was performed at all Carolina Tractor & Equipment Company locations. The D7 was introduced in the 1930s, and the series continued to be produced into the 21st century; it was used widely on agricultural, construction, and military jobs.

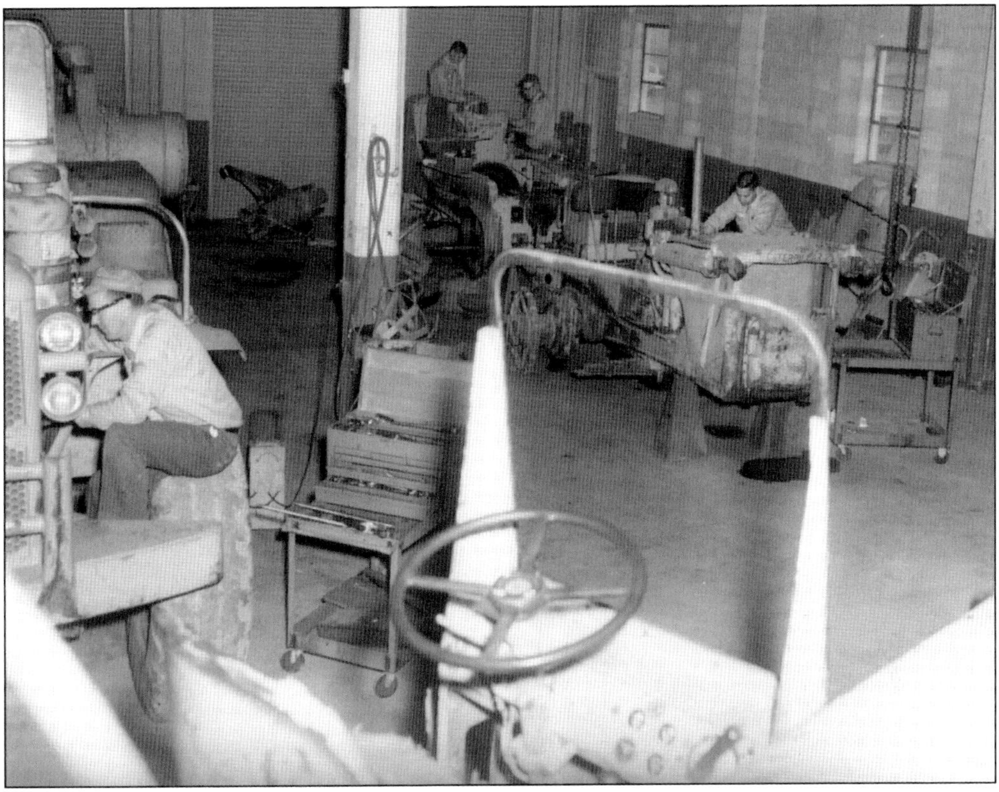

This Caterpillar DW10, which was manufactured from the 1940s through the 1950s, is being serviced in the shop at Carolina Tractor & Equipment Company. Although it was often advantageous to perform repairs or maintenance on equipment on-site to minimize time away from the job, it could be more cost-effective to bring the machines into dealers' own shops because the repair and service operations could run continuously, in addition to eliminating travel time sending mechanics to job sites.

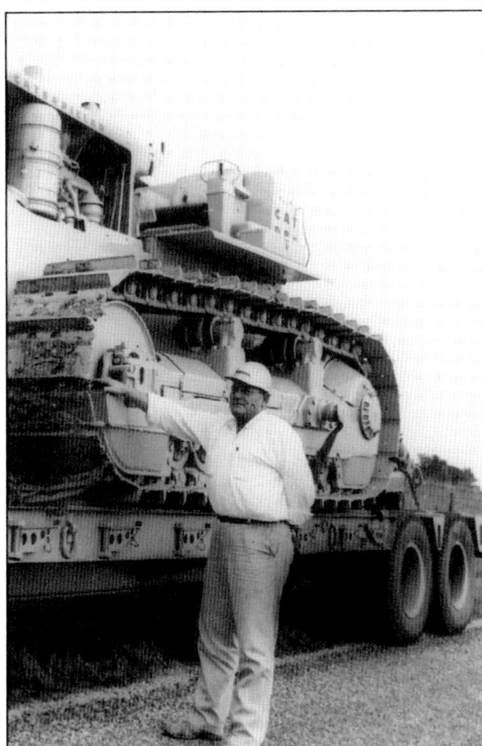

This new D8 tractor on a freight truck is being transported to a job site to move dirt in the late 1950s or early 1960s. With a blade that was 12 feet across, it was too wide to travel on roads with regulations that limited the width of vehicles to 10 feet. Sections of the equipment had to be moved separately and then assembled on-site. If a customer decided he wanted to sell or trade in the equipment in at a later time, a crew would have to come out to disassemble the machinery and transport it back.

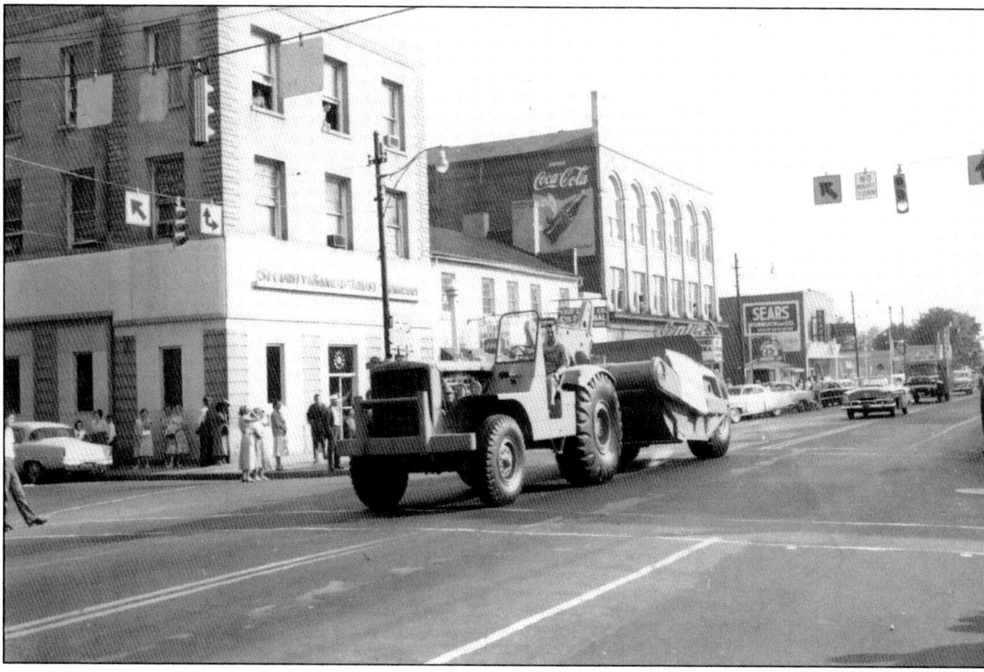

Whether in small towns or larger cities, nearly everyone loves a parade—especially children, who are often mesmerized by the giant equipment that goes rolling by. In these undated images, probably from the late 1950s or early 1960s, Salisbury's parade-goers watched the annual Safety Parade. Carolina Tractor & Equipment Company participated in the annual event that proceeded through the town. The equipment displayed a banner stating, "Safer Highways are built with Caterpillar."

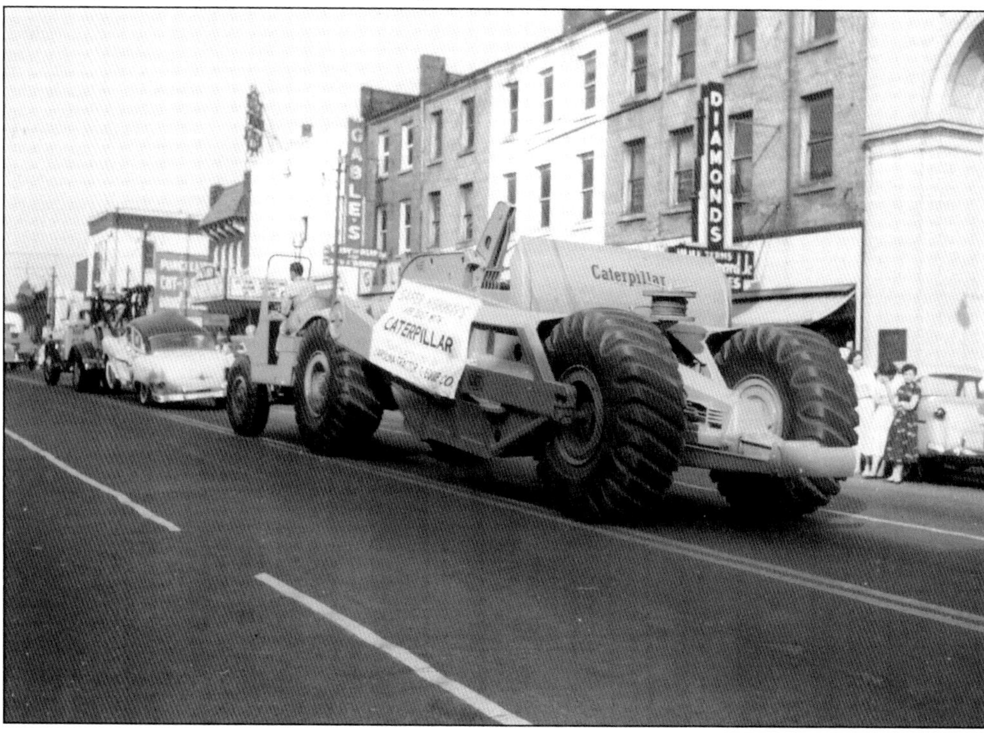

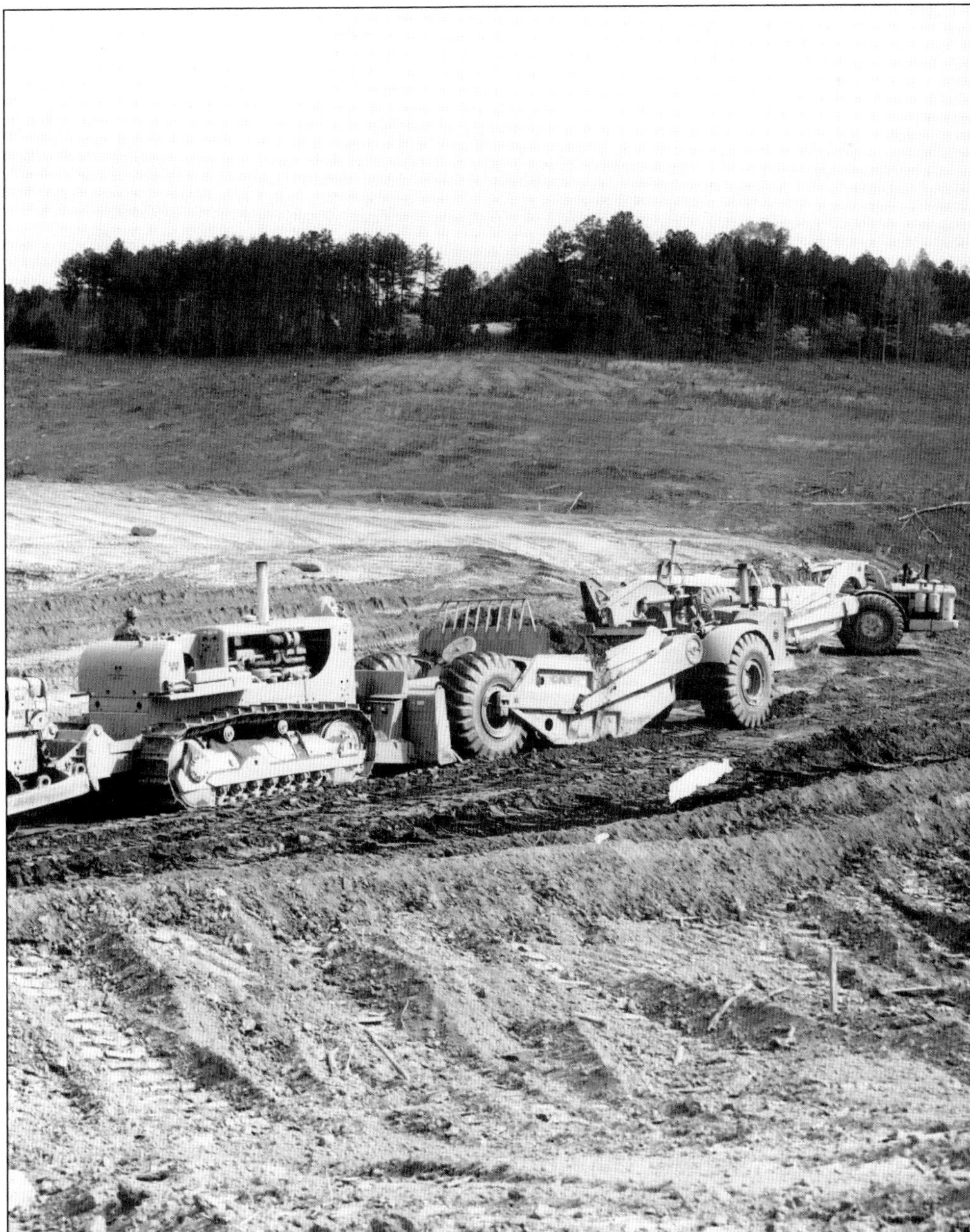

Depicted here are D9, D8, and DW21 machines, widely used during the post–World War II boom years on extensive interstate road construction projects. The separate components of the massive machines would be shipped to the job sites, where technicians and mechanics would assemble the equipment. This image shows work in North Carolina on what would become the corridor of Interstates 40, 77, and 85.

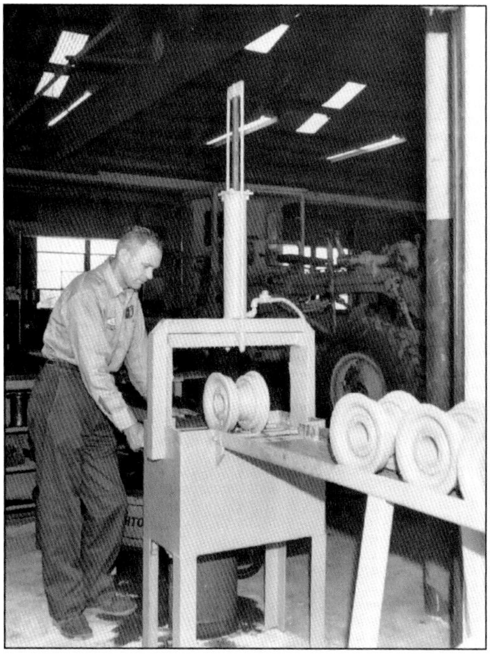

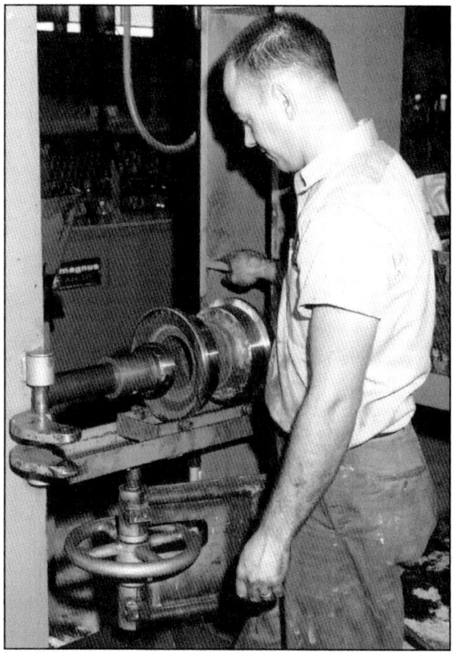

Over time, the rollers on tractors become worn from heavy use and must be rebuilt or replaced to allow the equipment to operate correctly. In these photographs, Carolina Tractor & Equipment Company employees work to rebuild rollers, which are then painted before they are reinstalled.

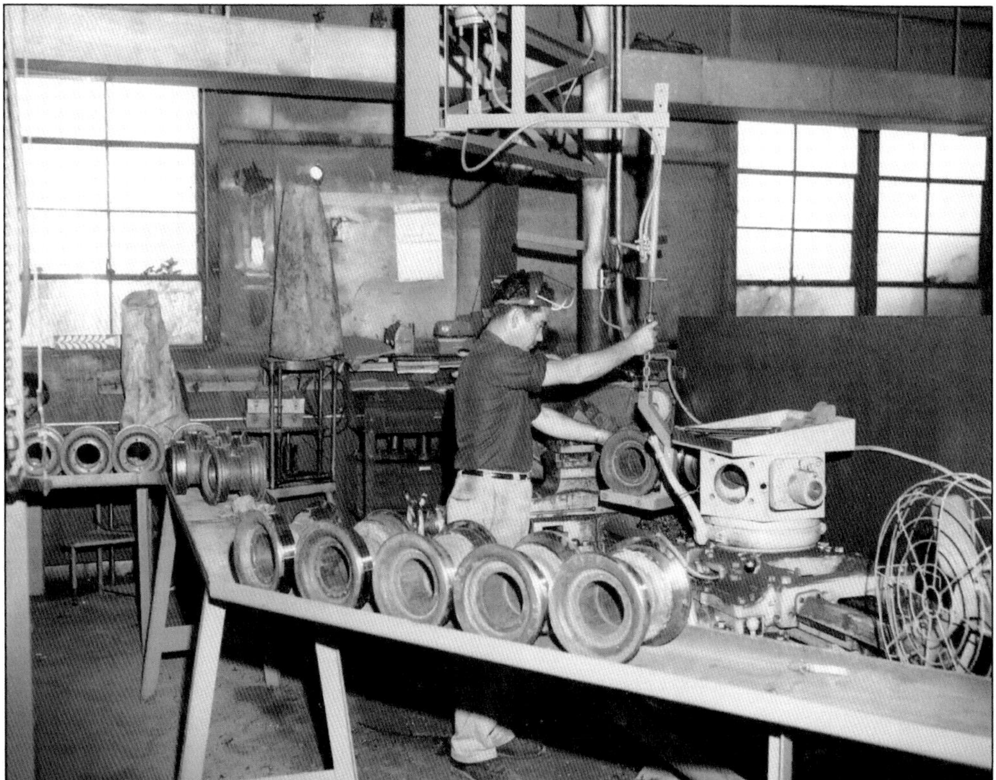

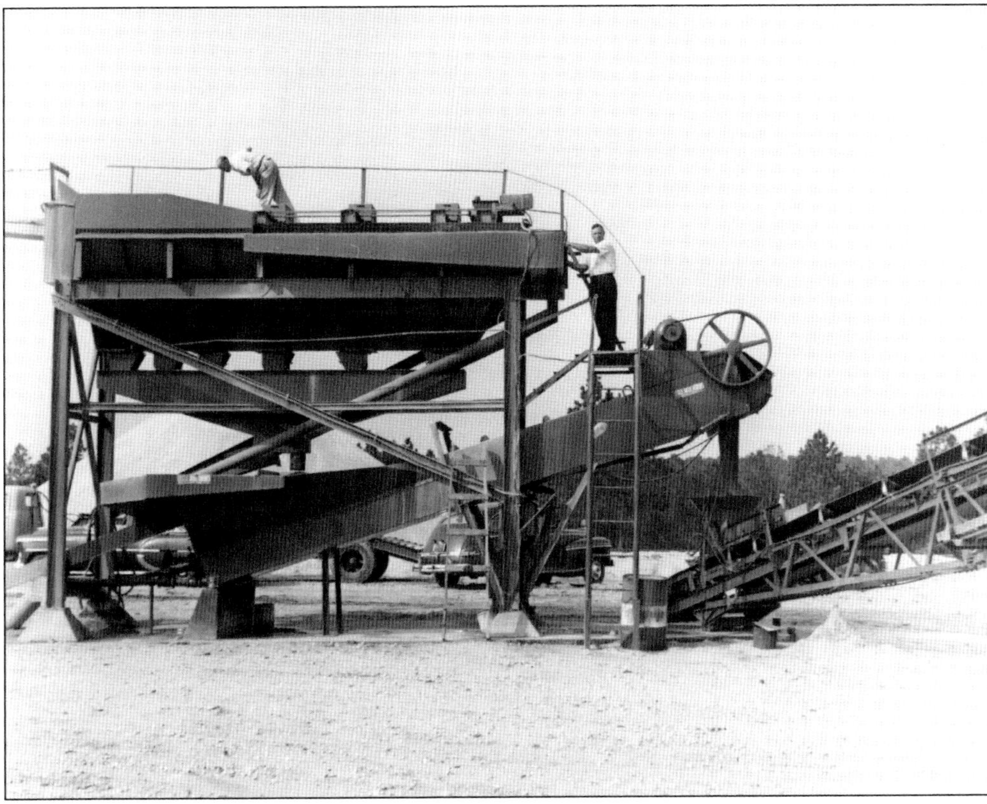

At this sand plant, workers sorted and graded the sand, then loaded it by conveyers onto trucks that would transport it to storage areas. Depending on the size of the particles, some could be used in metallurgy, but most of the sand went to highway construction projects.

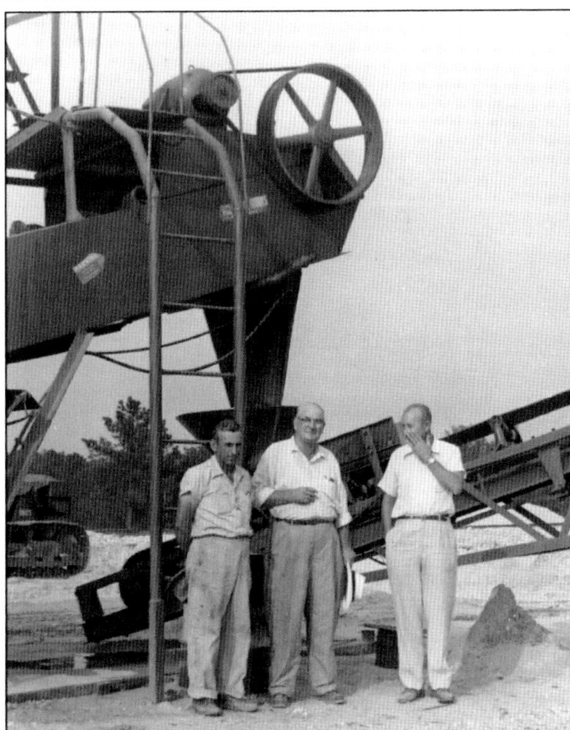

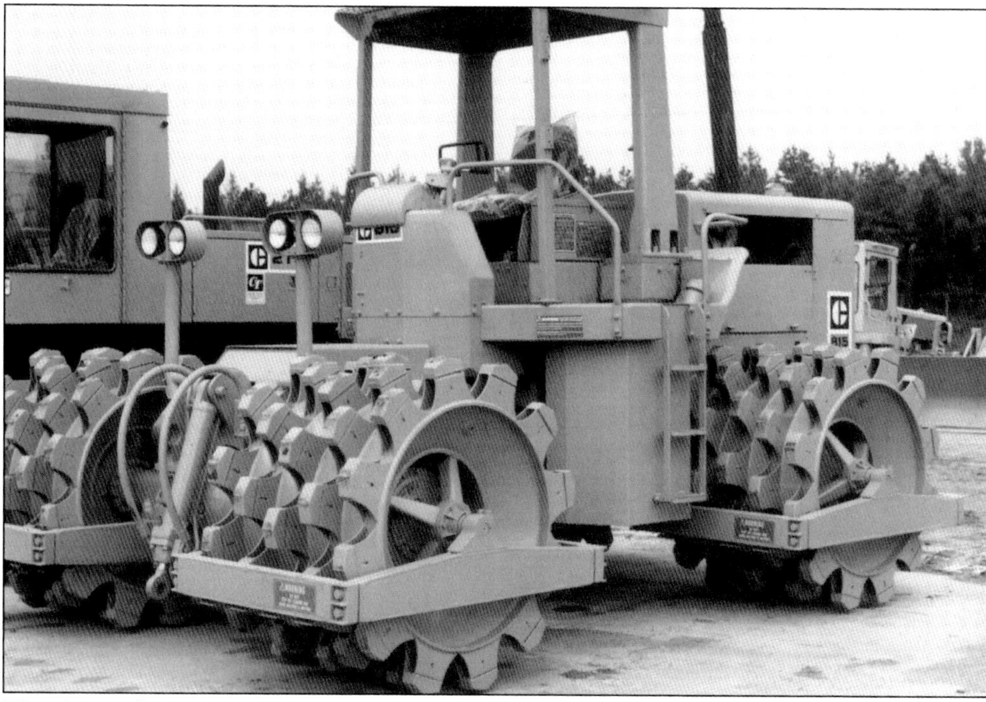

This Caterpillar 625 compactor was widely used during the post–World War II era when highway projects, funded by the federal government, provided employment for thousands of workers. The machinery vibrated to compact the earth as its rollers moved over the ground. Carolina Tractor & Equipment Company sold and serviced many of these compactors during this period of growth for the American economy.

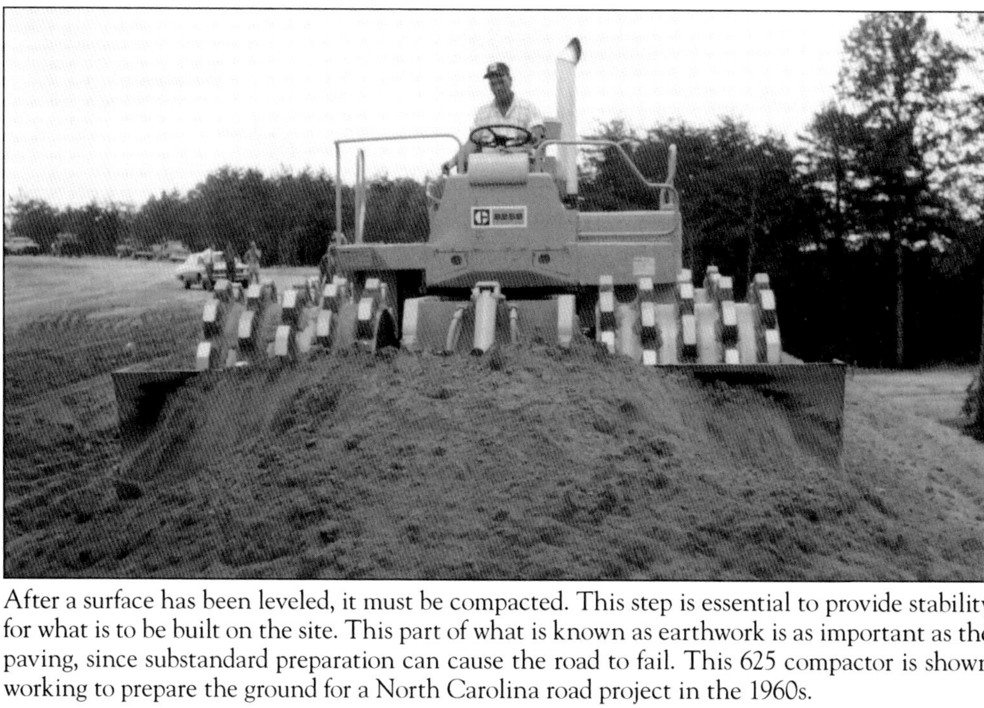

After a surface has been leveled, it must be compacted. This step is essential to provide stability for what is to be built on the site. This part of what is known as earthwork is as important as the paving, since substandard preparation can cause the road to fail. This 625 compactor is shown working to prepare the ground for a North Carolina road project in the 1960s.

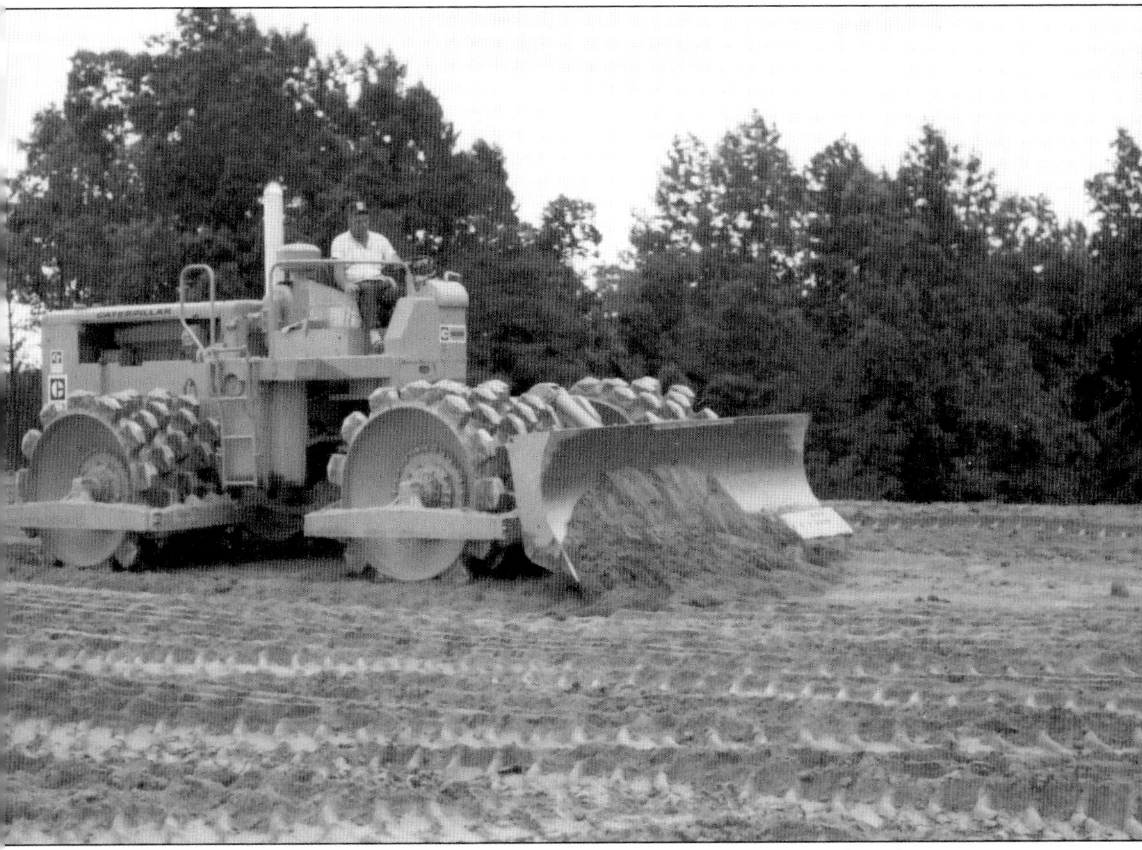

From small residential jobs to large highway projects, compactors are essential to the preparation of surfaces. This piece of equipment tamps down dirt so paving or other work can take place. The operator of this 625 compactor had to make sure he followed all the specifications set forth for this highway job under way during the 1960s. The government set the standards for the work and would send state inspectors to take measurements. If the work did not meet the standards, it would have to be redone.

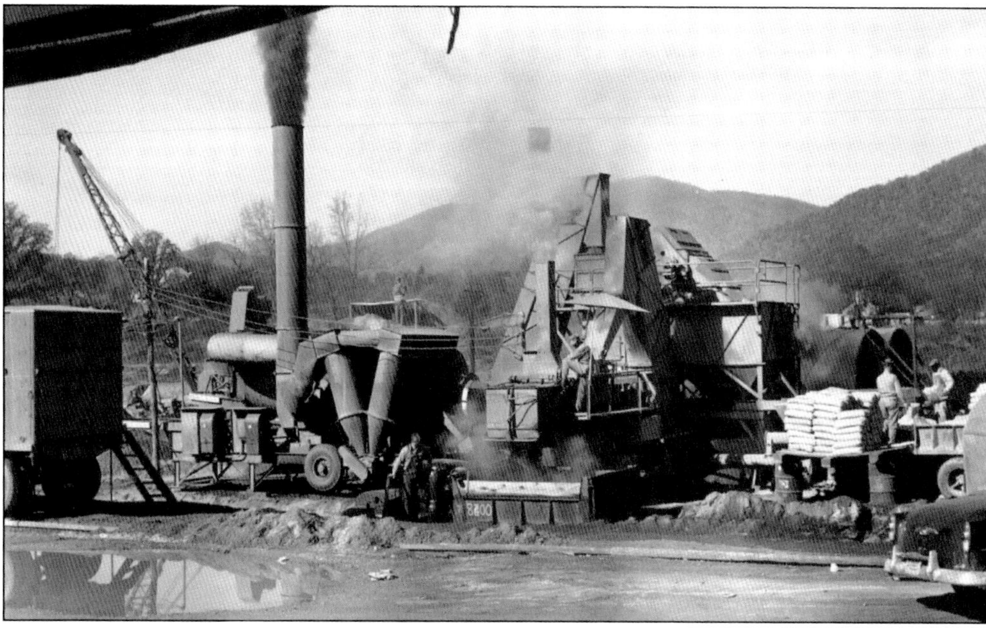

The images show one of the many asphalt plants in North Carolina during the 1960s. The plants operated Barber Green machines, which were sold by Carolina Tractor & Equipment Company in the 1960s. They did the work of making asphalt by crushing and combining stone, gravel, and sand into a mixture that would be dumped when finished into trucks that would transport it to job sites.

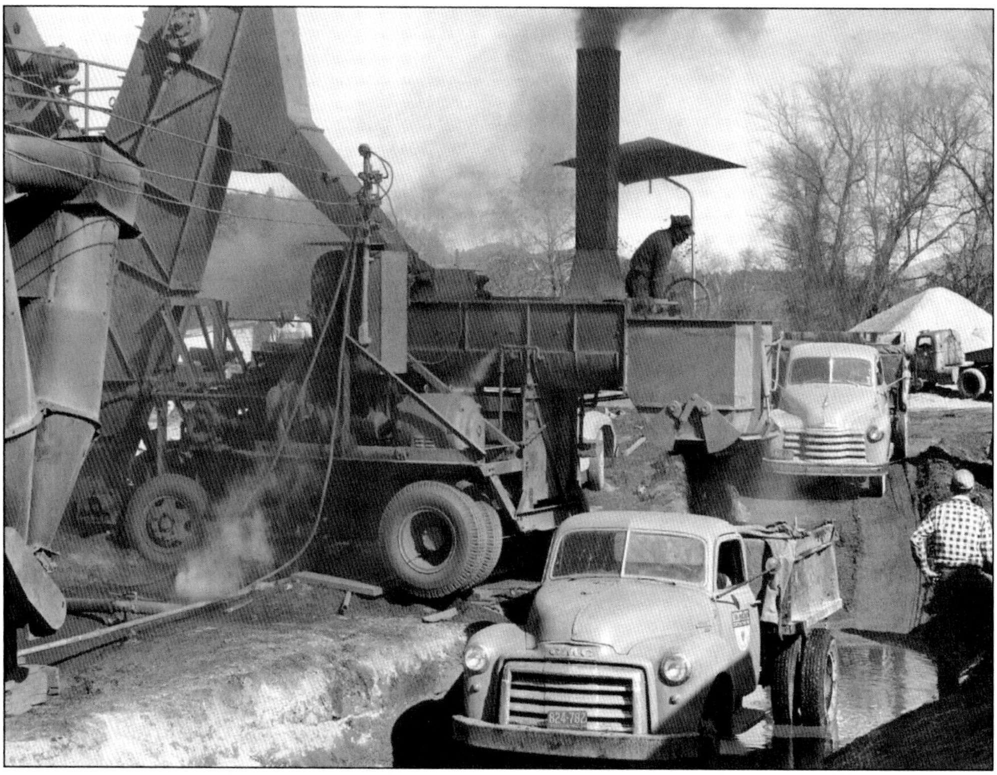

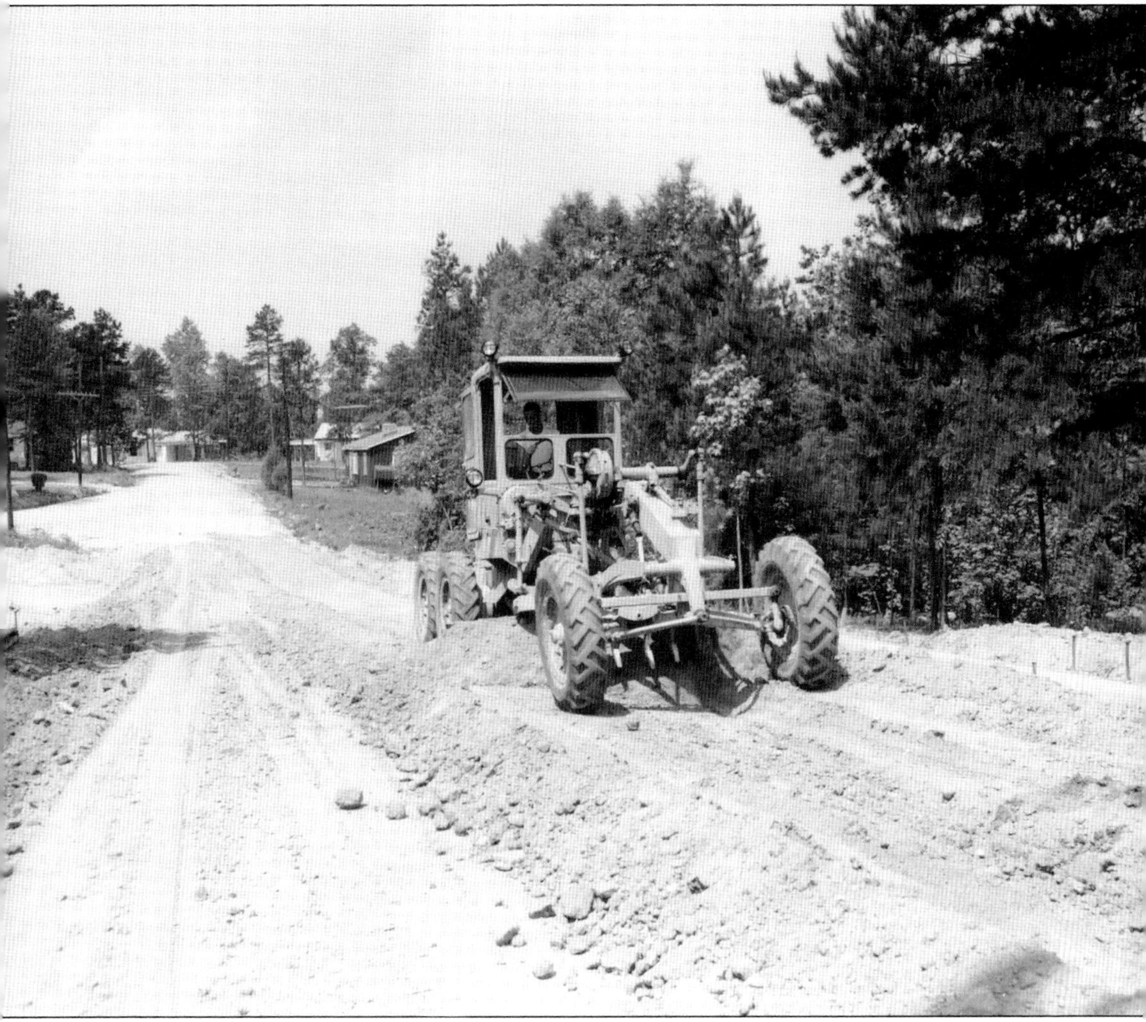

Residential roadwork is being done by this Caterpillar motor grader, seen here in the 1960s. The development of these homesites continued as people left farms in search of work in nearby towns, or returned from military service with a desire to put down roots.

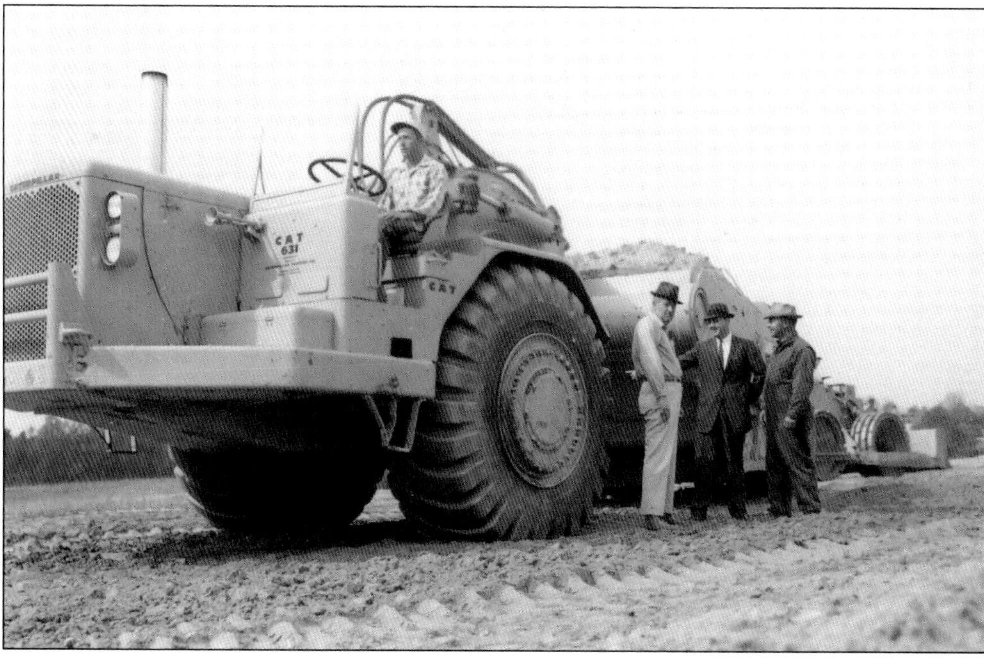

Pictured above, Harry Glover and Ed Weisiger Sr. are calling on customer A.V. Burton in this photograph from the 1960s; the operator is unidentified. When seen from a distance, it can be difficult to understand the enormous size of the equipment, but with people in view it becomes easier to see how massive the Caterpillar 631 really is. The motor scraper was introduced in 1960, and the 631 series remained in production for decades.

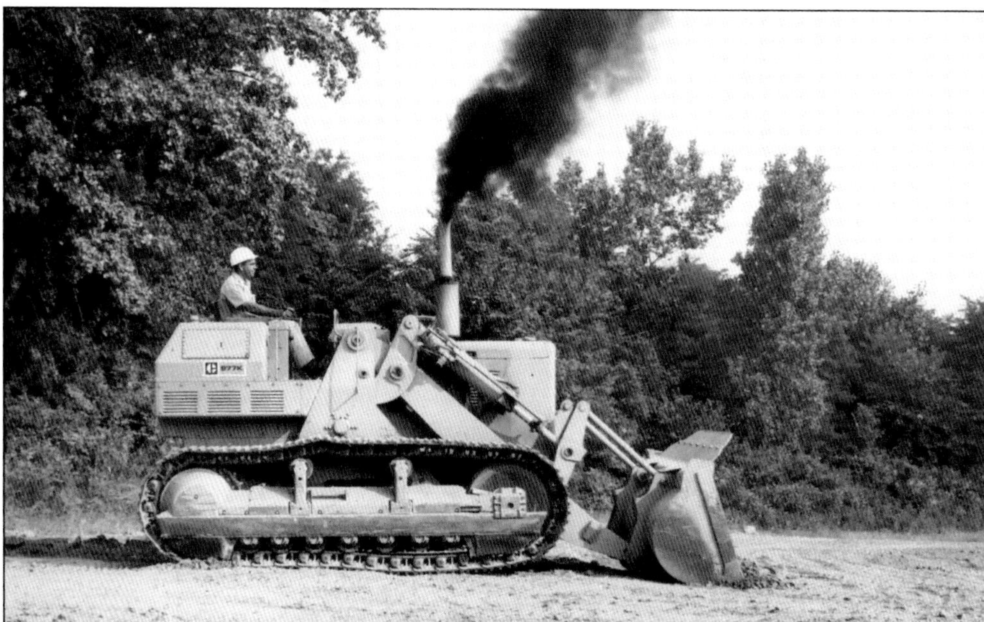

This 977 tractor on a customer's rural job is just beginning work for the day, as seen in this 1960s-era photograph. The telltale black soot that is visible is generated because there is excess fuel in the engine when it is started. Shortly after the motor is started, the soot disappears.

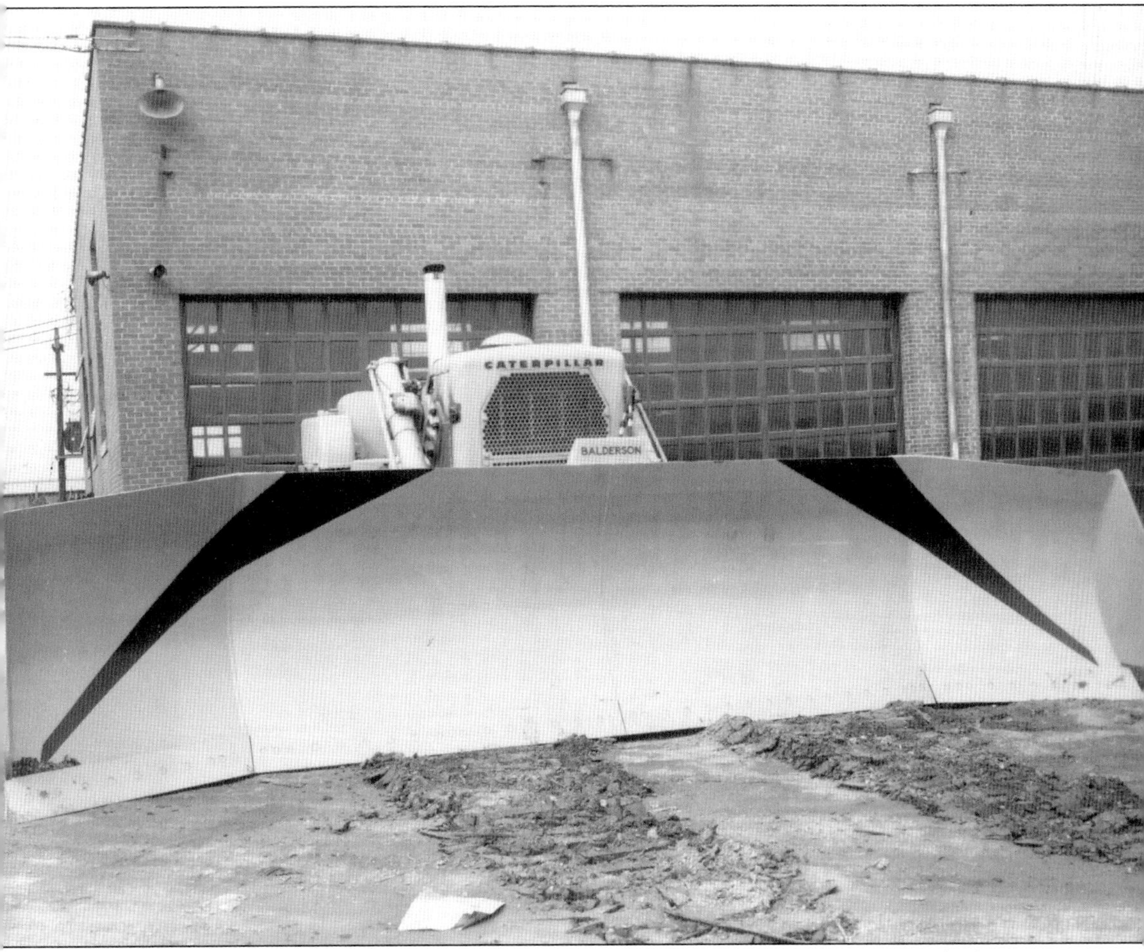

Duke Energy has evolved from a very modest beginning in the early 1900s to become the largest utility company in the United States with the acquisition of Progress Energy in 2011. Duke Energy began when its three founders created the Catawba Power Company, a South Carolina corporation. The company's first plant went online as Catawba Hydro Station, developed to produce electricity for Victoria Cotton Mills in Rock Hill, South Carolina. The relationship between Duke Energy and Carolina Tractor & Equipment Company goes back many years. Duke was certainly a champion of Carolina Tractor founder and owner L.M. Weisiger. Mr. Les was heard to ask, "Are they bigger than Duke Power?" Safe to say that Duke was a company that had earned the respect of Weisiger and thus was his basis of comparison. The track-type tractor in this image is a Cat D-9, 1960 vintage, equipped with a 45-cubic-yard coal blade. Compare that to the blades used today, which are 98 cubic yards.

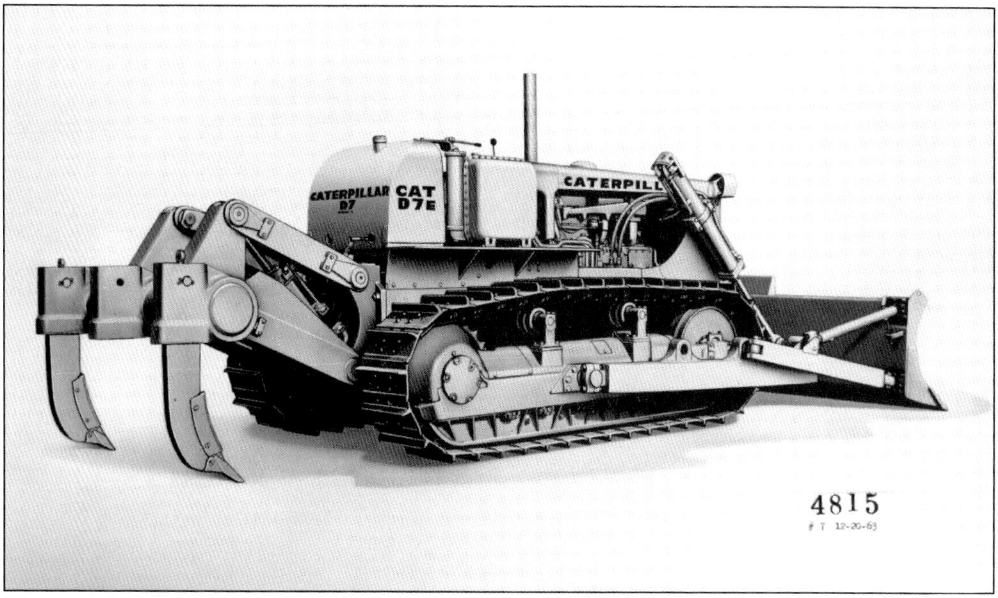

This artist's rendering of a Caterpillar D7E tractor is from 1965. By the time the drawing was made, the D7E had been on the market for nearly 30 years. It was introduced in 1938, and the company continued to produce upgraded models periodically. Carolina Tractor & Equipment Company sold this versatile and reliable machine widely.

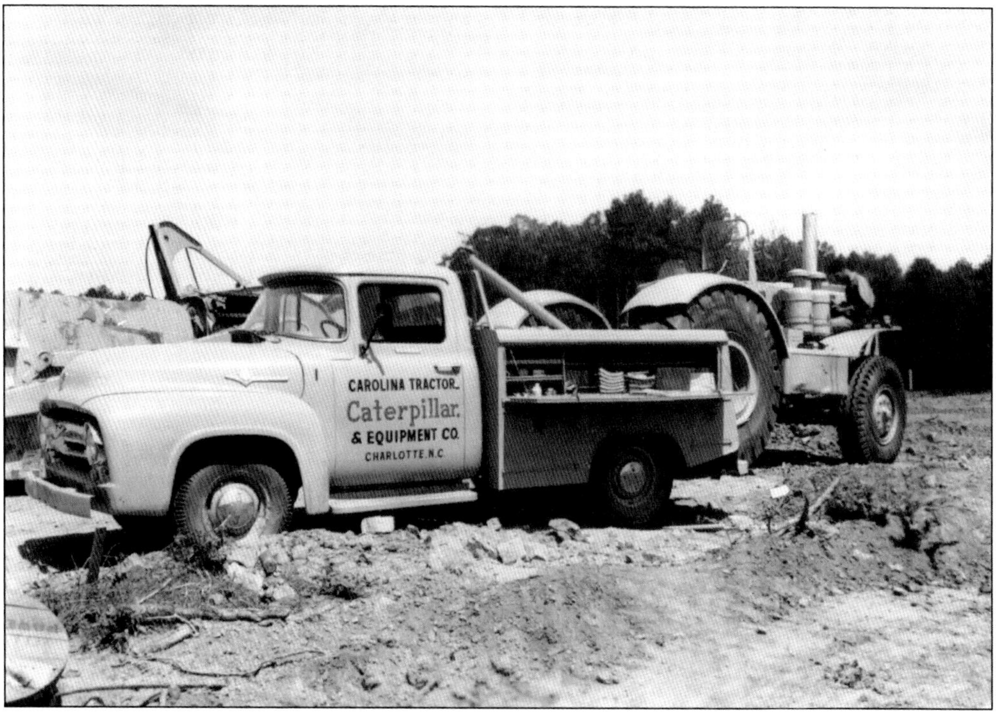

In this photograph that dates back to the mid-1960s from a field job in Charlotte, a DW20 scraper picks up dirt. In the foreground, one of the first Carolina Tractor & Equipment Company service trucks can be seen. It is one of a fleet that traveled to jobs for on-site maintenance and repairs on equipment that could not easily be brought to the shops.

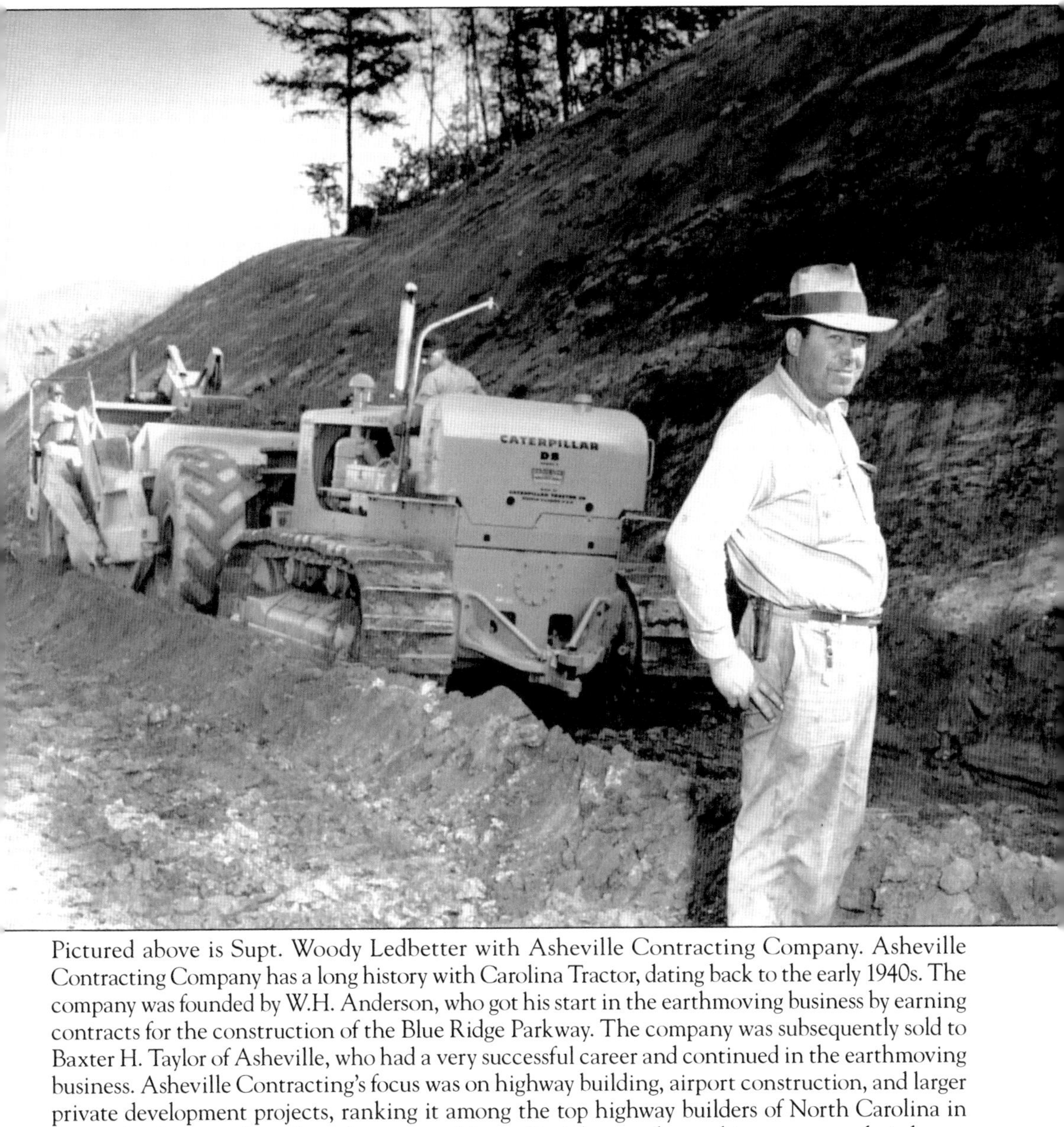

Pictured above is Supt. Woody Ledbetter with Asheville Contracting Company. Asheville Contracting Company has a long history with Carolina Tractor, dating back to the early 1940s. The company was founded by W.H. Anderson, who got his start in the earthmoving business by earning contracts for the construction of the Blue Ridge Parkway. The company was subsequently sold to Baxter H. Taylor of Asheville, who had a very successful career and continued in the earthmoving business. Asheville Contracting's focus was on highway building, airport construction, and larger private development projects, ranking it among the top highway builders of North Carolina in terms of mileage and number of contracts. Most of its jobs were located in western and piedmont North Carolina, South Carolina, and eastern Tennessee. The building of Interstate 40 in North Carolina and Tennessee afforded the opportunity to grow the company, which Taylor did.

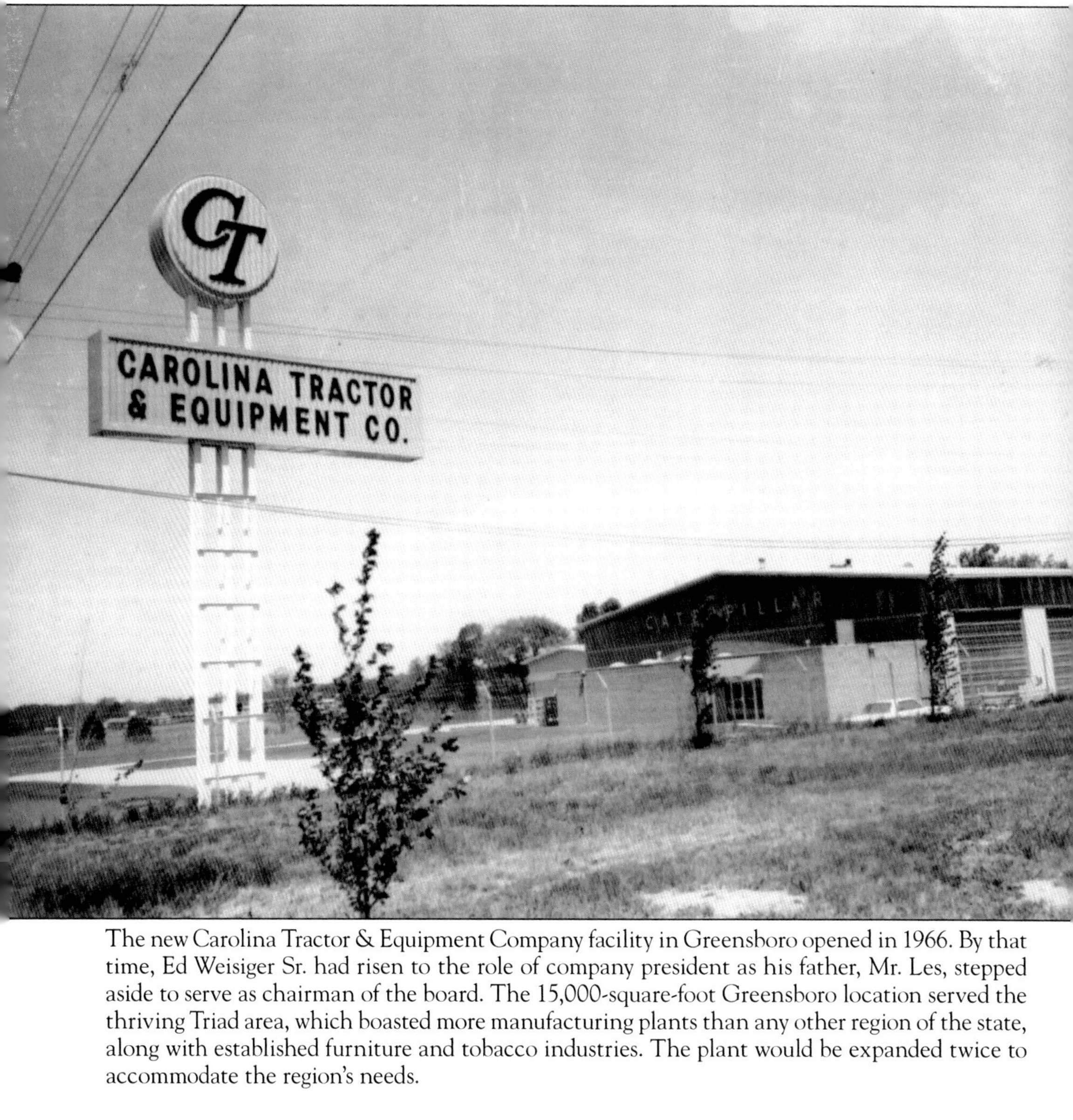

The new Carolina Tractor & Equipment Company facility in Greensboro opened in 1966. By that time, Ed Weisiger Sr. had risen to the role of company president as his father, Mr. Les, stepped aside to serve as chairman of the board. The 15,000-square-foot Greensboro location served the thriving Triad area, which boasted more manufacturing plants than any other region of the state, along with established furniture and tobacco industries. The plant would be expanded twice to accommodate the region's needs.

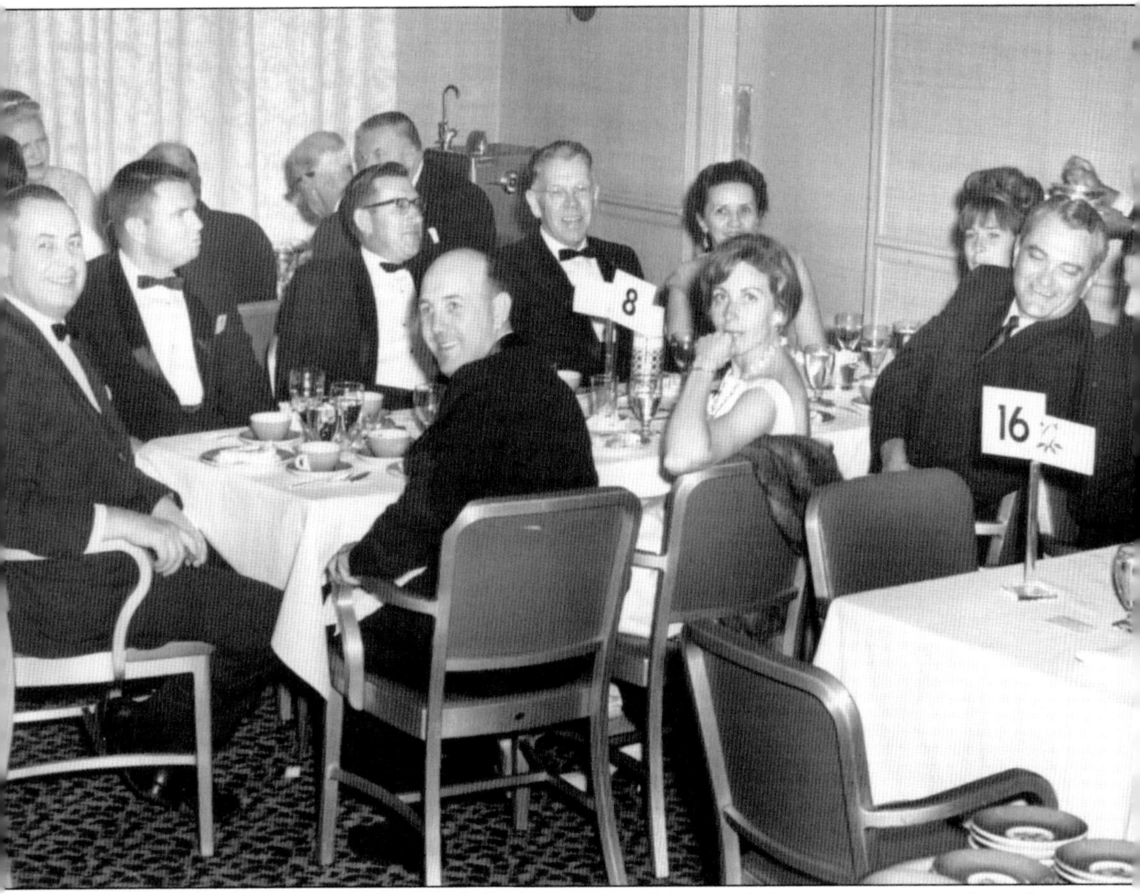

Members of the Association of General Contractors, or AGC, and their wives enjoy a formal evening banquet at the lavish Greenbrier Hotel in White Sulphur Springs, West Virginia. This occurred during another period of expansion for Carolina Tractor & Equipment Company, which opened a Greensboro facility in 1966.

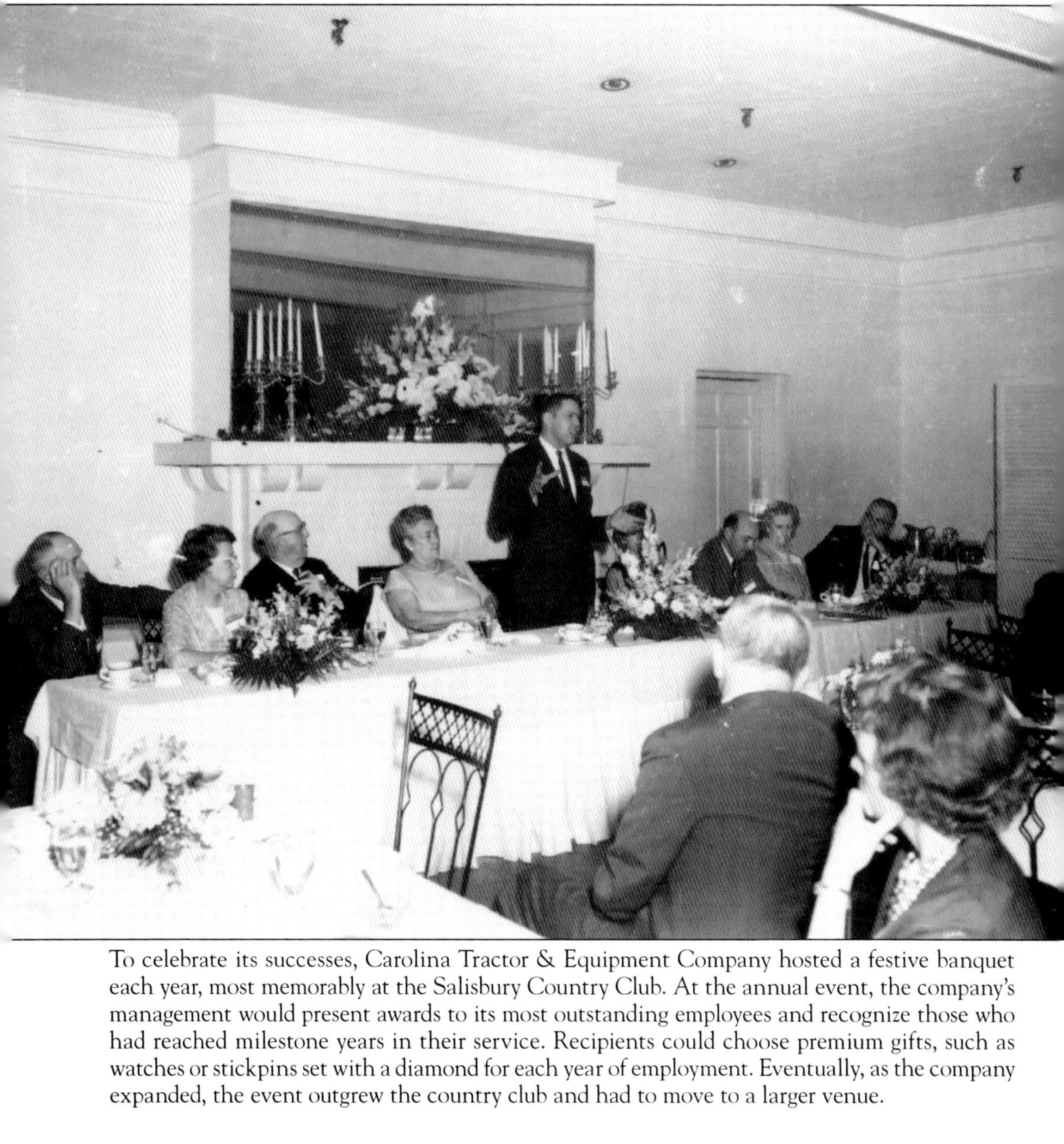

To celebrate its successes, Carolina Tractor & Equipment Company hosted a festive banquet each year, most memorably at the Salisbury Country Club. At the annual event, the company's management would present awards to its most outstanding employees and recognize those who had reached milestone years in their service. Recipients could choose premium gifts, such as watches or stickpins set with a diamond for each year of employment. Eventually, as the company expanded, the event outgrew the country club and had to move to a larger venue.

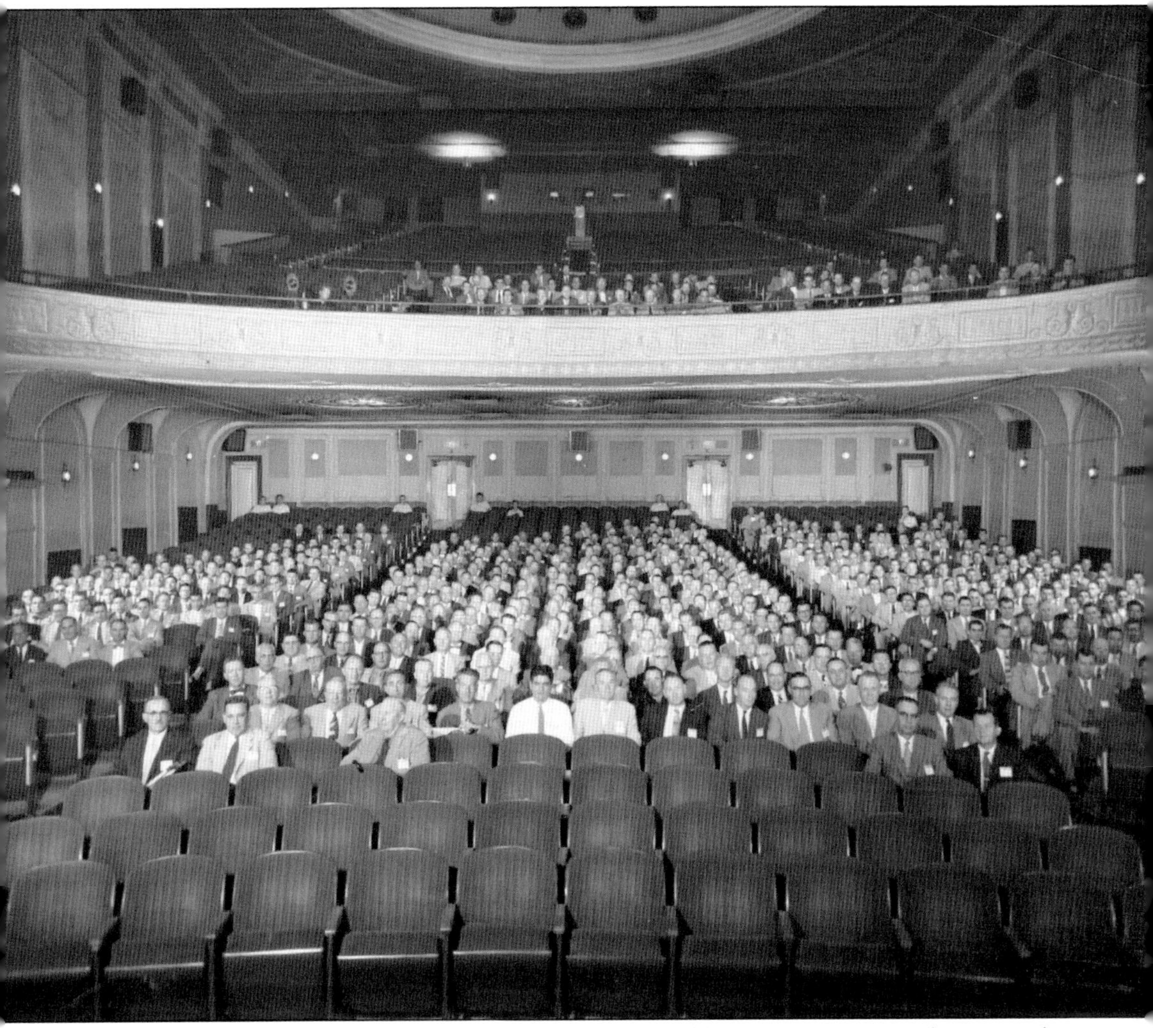

Annually, dealers from across the United States would attend business meetings at the national headquarters for Caterpillar, Inc., in Peoria, Illinois, but every 5 to 10 years, those who represented the brand internationally would attend as well, traveling from as far as Japan and South Africa. Larger than the other meetings typically held in hotels, gatherings such as this one would be held in theaters that could accommodate them.

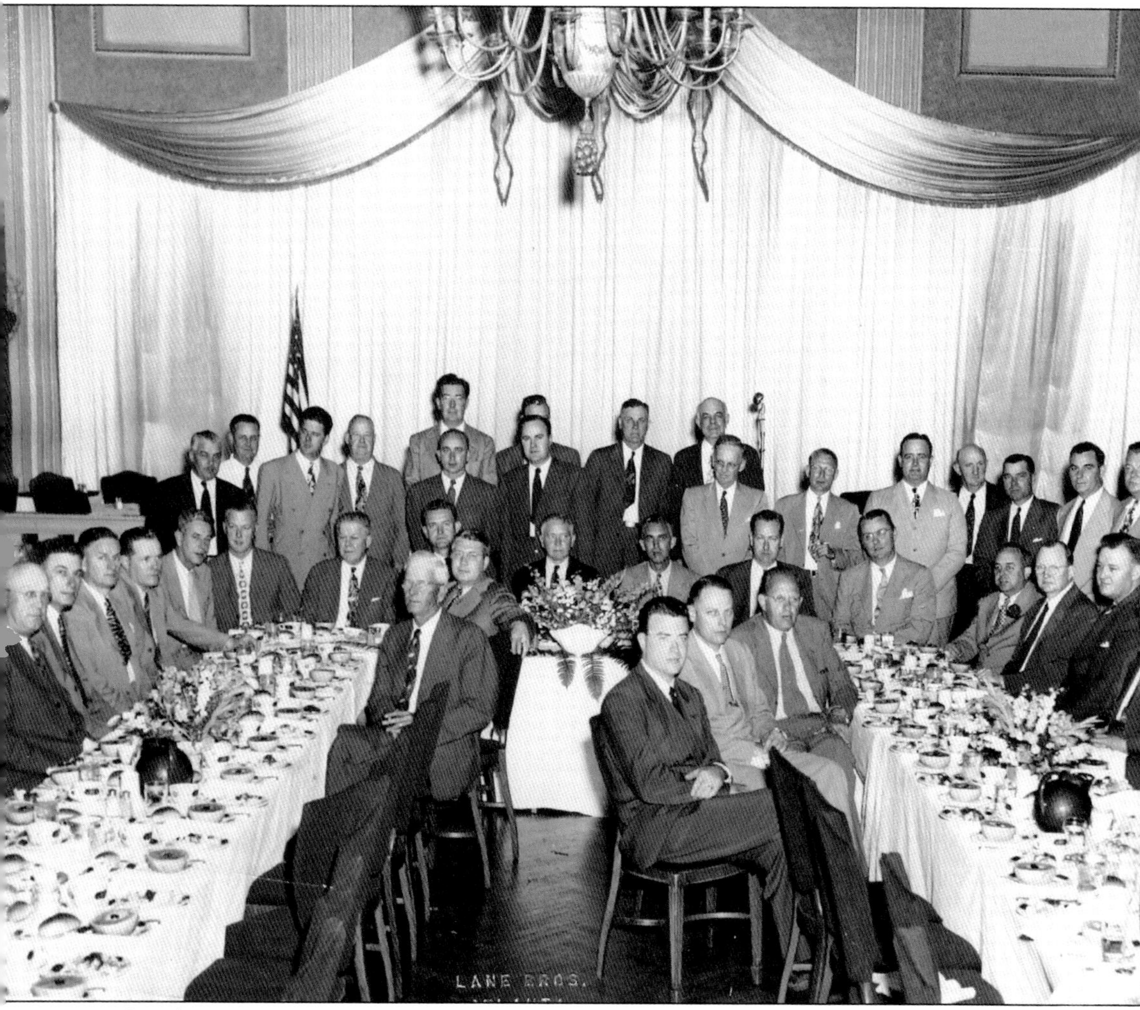

This photograph of Southeastern Caterpillar dealers was taken at an annual business meeting and banquet in Atlanta, Georgia. Mr. Les (back row, fourth from right) attended along with his esteemed colleagues. Others in attendance included J.I. Davis, Gordon Fowler, a Mr. Kelly, Pete Bussell, Fred Habercorn, Ben Lease, Tom Benbo, DeWitt Thompson Sr., Roger Stribling, Don Yancey, Caterpillar vice president of sales Gale Spain, Frank Ross, Lamar Burford, a Mr. Harris, Henry Howard, Nolan Harvey, Lou Douer, L.D. Yancey, Bud Cram, and Harry Toothacker.

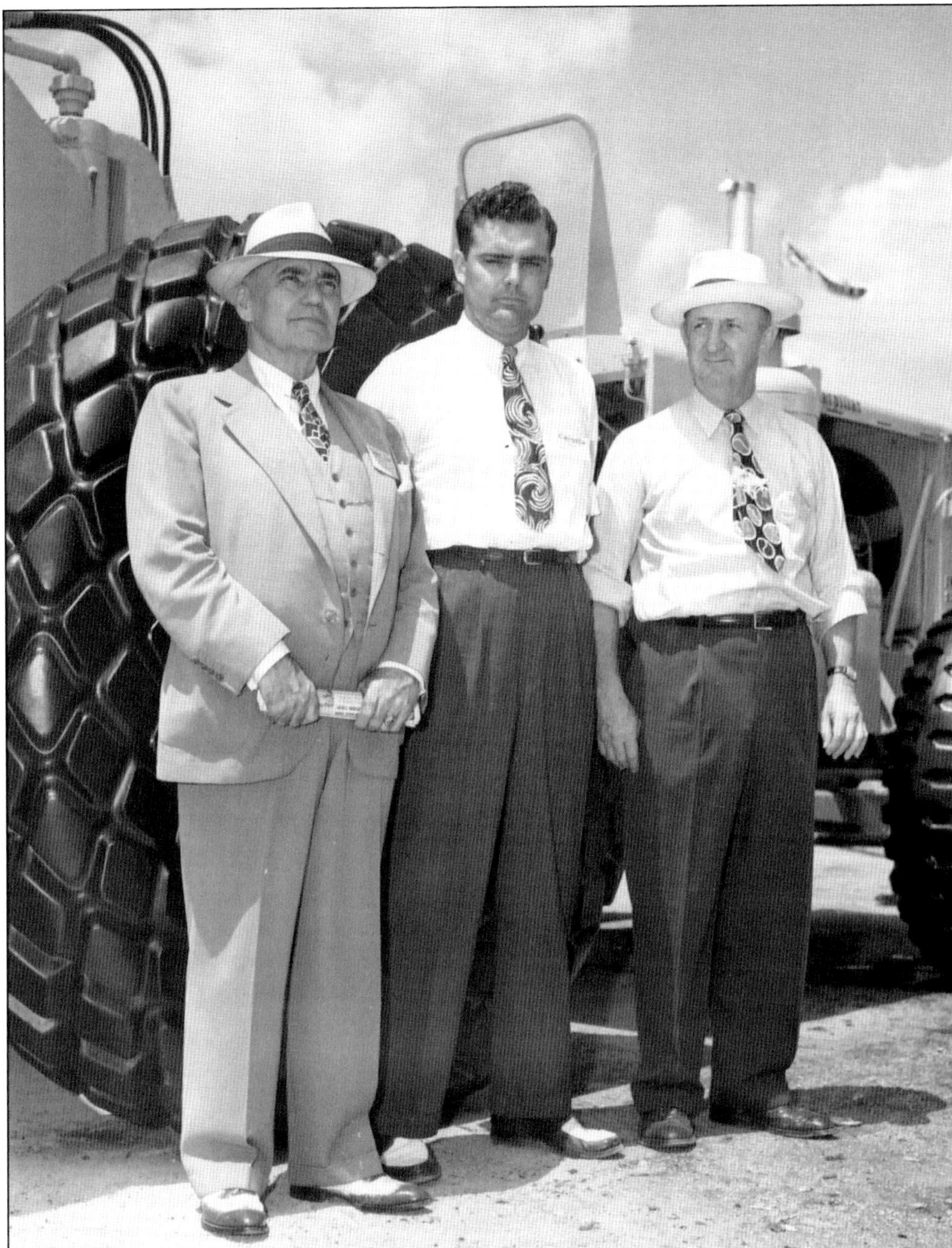

The DW20 pictured was introduced in the 1950s and was one of the first four-wheel, self-propelled, rubber-tired scrapers. The size of this DW20 tractor tire, taller than two of the three men standing in front of it, shows just how massive the machinery can be. This photograph depicts, from left to right, dealer J.C. Alban, his son Jim Alban, and L.M. "Mr. Les" Weisiger attending a Caterpillar convention in the late 1960s.

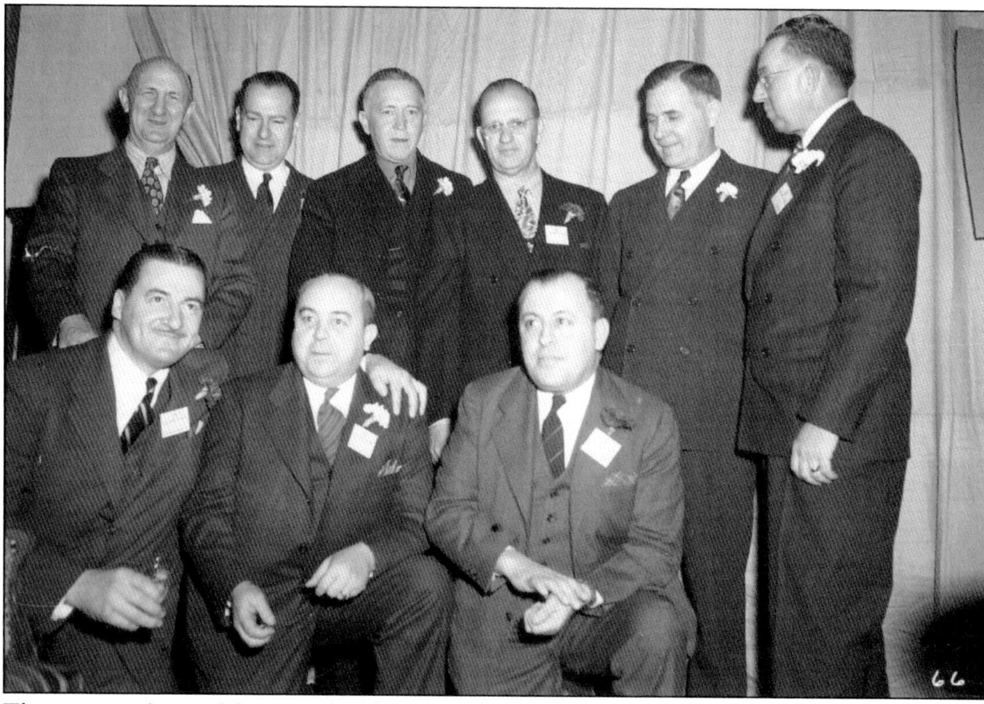

The portrait above of distinguished businessmen depicts the Southeastern Caterpillar dealers at their annual meeting. Mr. Les is shown, top left, at the gathering that was held in Boca Raton, Florida. Also in attendance are, from left to right, (first row) Bill Ziglar, Nolan Harvey, and unidentified; (second row) L.M. Weisiger, Bob Harris, Jeff Hunt, Harry Toothacker, J.D. Pittman, and unidentified.

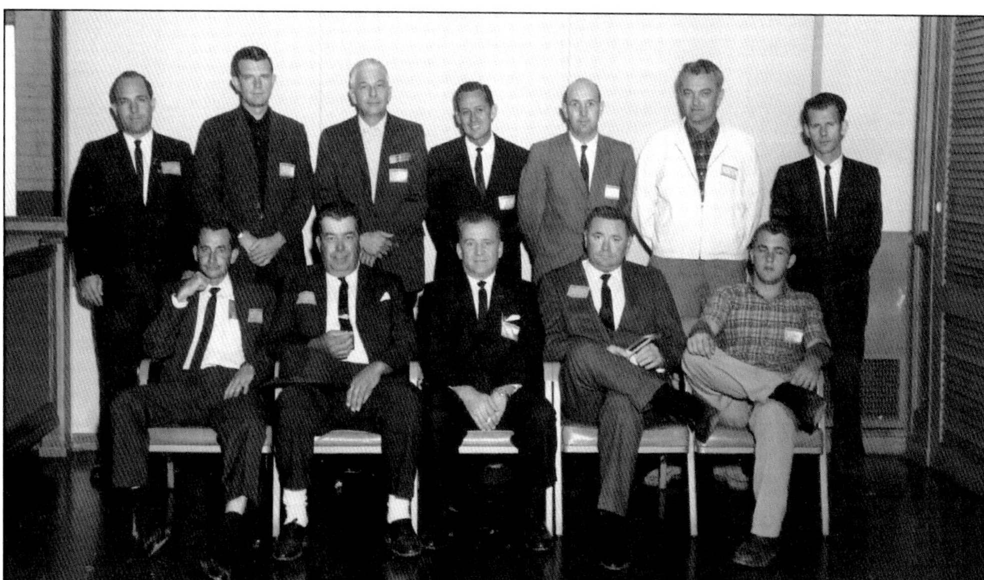

Factory visits, like this one pictured above, allowed dealers to take customers to see new equipment and talk to engineers. The attendees of this trip were from Asheville Contracting. By the 1960s, Carolina Tractor purchased their own plane to send customers on trips like these.

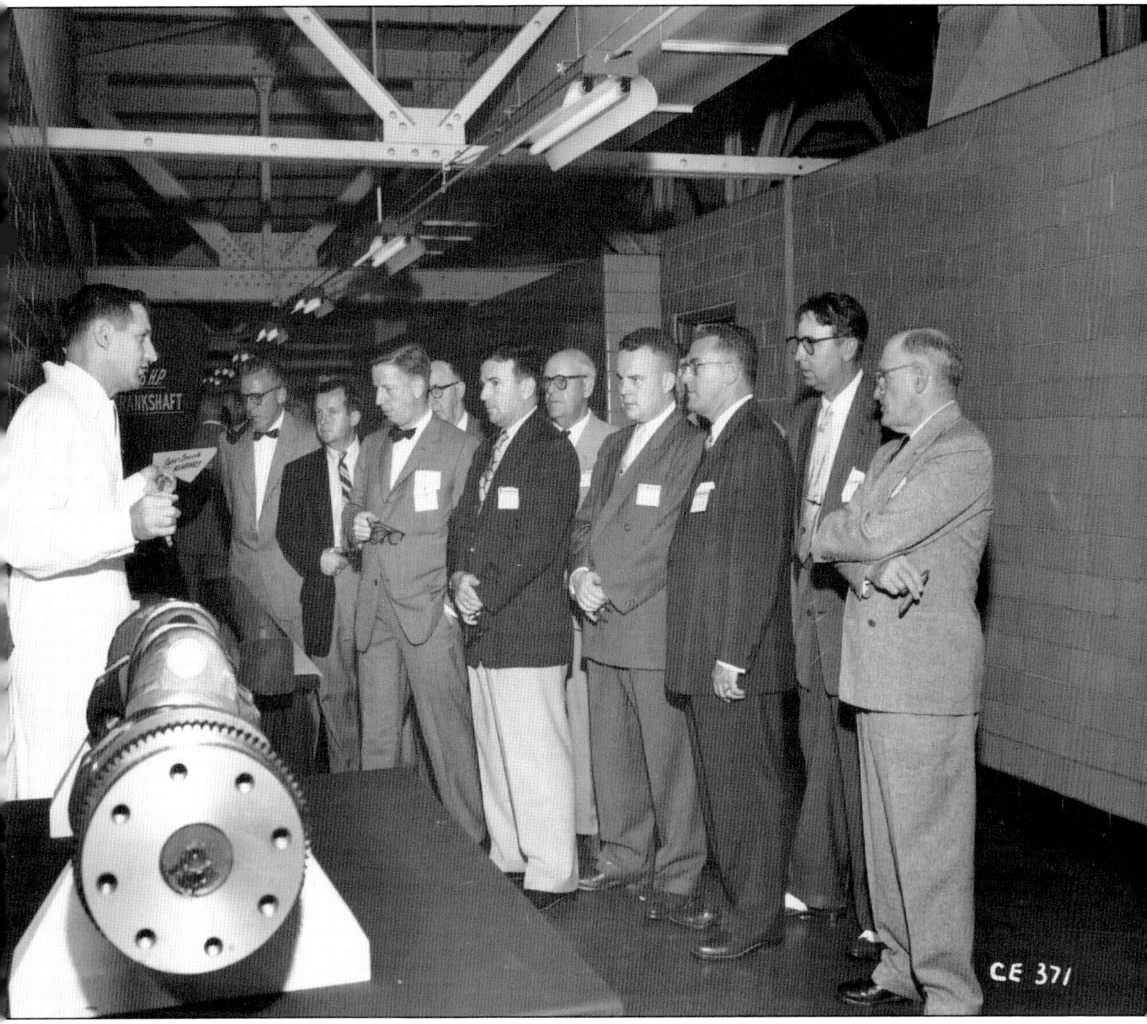

At a meeting of Caterpillar tractor dealers at the company's headquarters in Peoria, Illinois, the men toured the plant, where they could view the machinery on display, such as this new crankshaft. The photographer's notes from this event list the guests as, from left to right, E.H. Smith, unidentified, K.D. Beatie, L.M. Weisiger, D.D. Arnold, Carl Langley, W.A. Norris Jr., J.F. Baron, Peck Carlton, and R.L. Harrison.

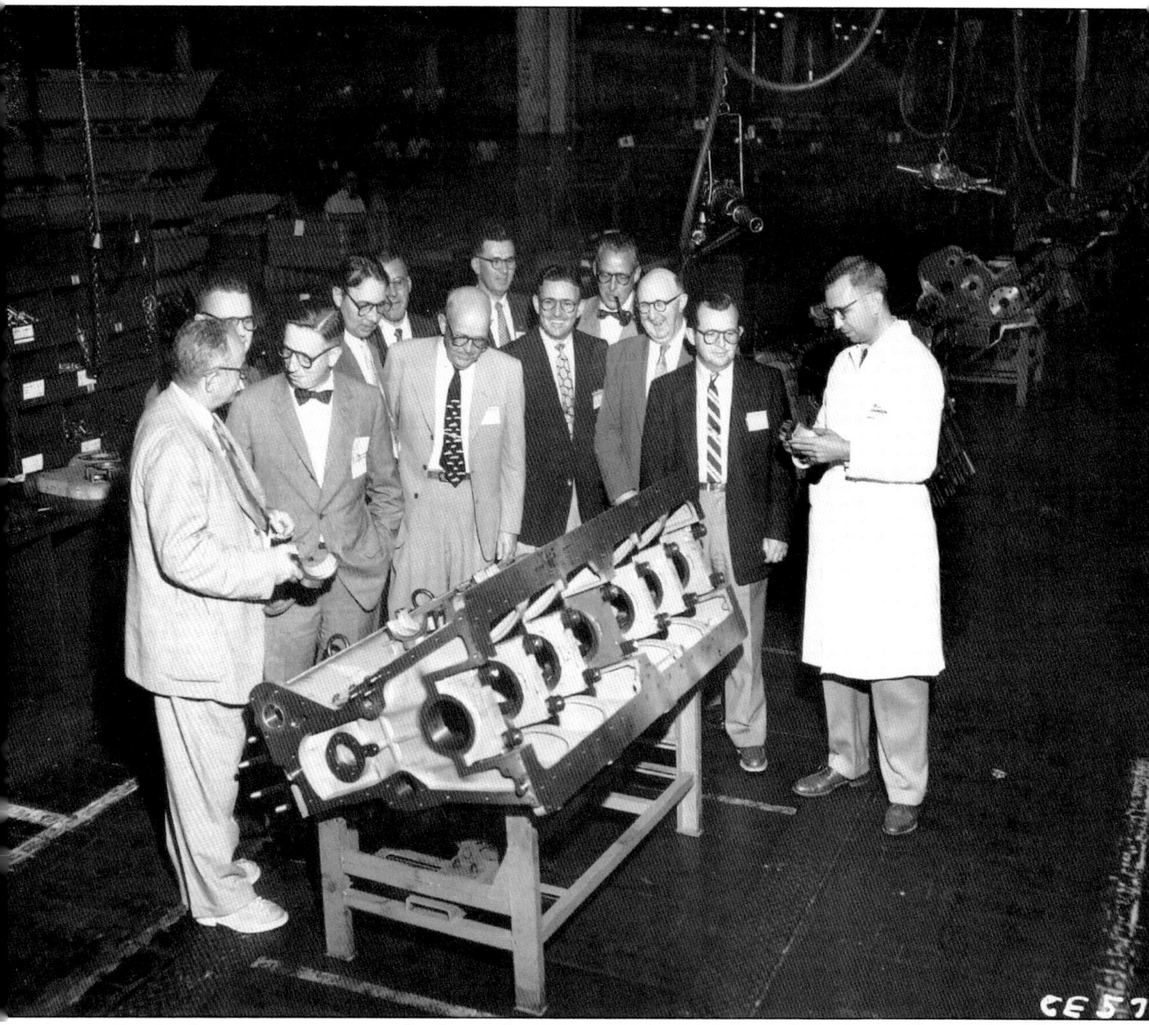

On display is a new engine, which a technician in a white lab coat describes to the visiting dealers during a Caterpillar factory tour. Included in this 1955 photograph are Bill McCoy, Peck Carlton, Carl Langley, Ed Smith, and L.M. "Mr. Les" Weisiger, who is third from right. These tours not only familiarized the businessmen with new products, they trained the attendees on the sales and service techniques to bring back to their individually owned dealerships.

Three

The 1970s–Forward

In the 1970s, North Carolina's economy shifted away from its steadfast agriculture toward manufacturing. Replacing the days of tobacco and textiles was a new era—technology. Caterpillar continued to introduce new models of construction machinery to the market, and as a result, Carolina Tractor continued to flourish.

In 1971, the company moved its Charlotte location to Statesville Road, chosen for its proximity to the booming Interstates 77 and 85 corridors for easy access. Combining the Salisbury and former Charlotte branches, the new facility most notably boasted state-of-the-art service bays that could provide repairs to large equipment, setting itself apart from its competition.

Escalating fuel prices were creating a worldwide gas crisis, and still the demand for machinery remained high, resulting in equipment shortages. Despite these unforeseen challenges, just as the company had done in the 1930s, Carolina Tractor maintained its profitability.

On July 11, 1980, Carolina Tractor marked a sad milestone with the passing of its longtime leader, Mr. Les. He had overseen tremendous changes and challenges throughout his tenure, and he left an enduring legacy that still lives on today.

Ed Weisiger Jr. became president of the company in 1991, representing the third generation of the family. In 1992, a new facility opened in Asheville. By 1995, Carolina Tractor was the seventh fastest-growing business and the 33rd largest in the state.

As the 20th century drew to a close, the company continued to assert its role as a market leader and met head on the unavoidable periods of economic uncertainty, both in the United States and internationally. From a small family business that grew into a major corporation operating in a new millennium, Carolina Tractor & Equipment Company remains committed to the growth and prosperity of North Carolina.

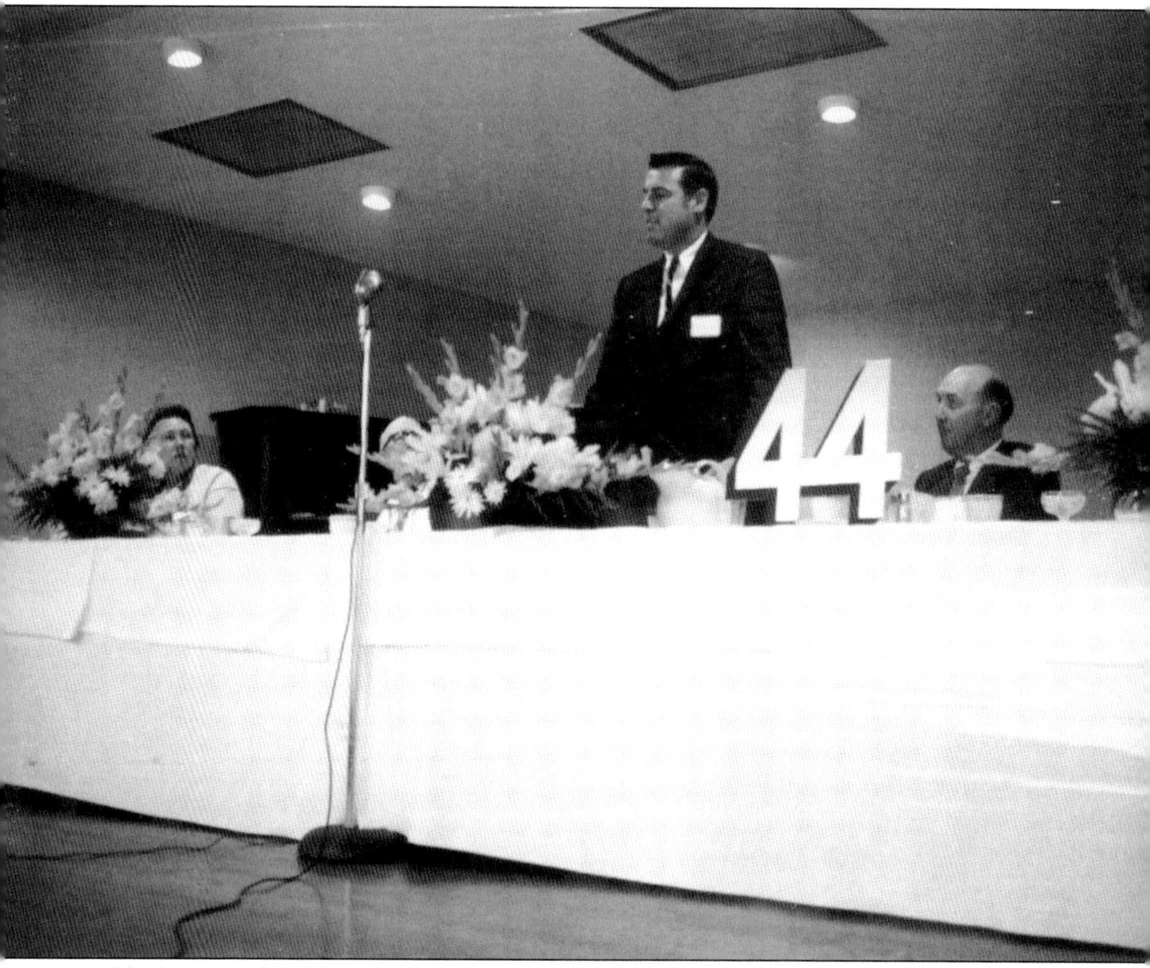

The large number 44 on the dais is a tribute to the anniversary Carolina Tractor & Equipment Company celebrated at its 1970 annual awards banquet in Salisbury. North Carolina's economy was beginning to move away from traditional agricultural and textile industries and toward the lucrative electronics, industrial, and chemical industries. Caterpillar expanded its product lines to meet the needs of its customers, but an economic downturn would soon be coming, bringing more challenging times with it.

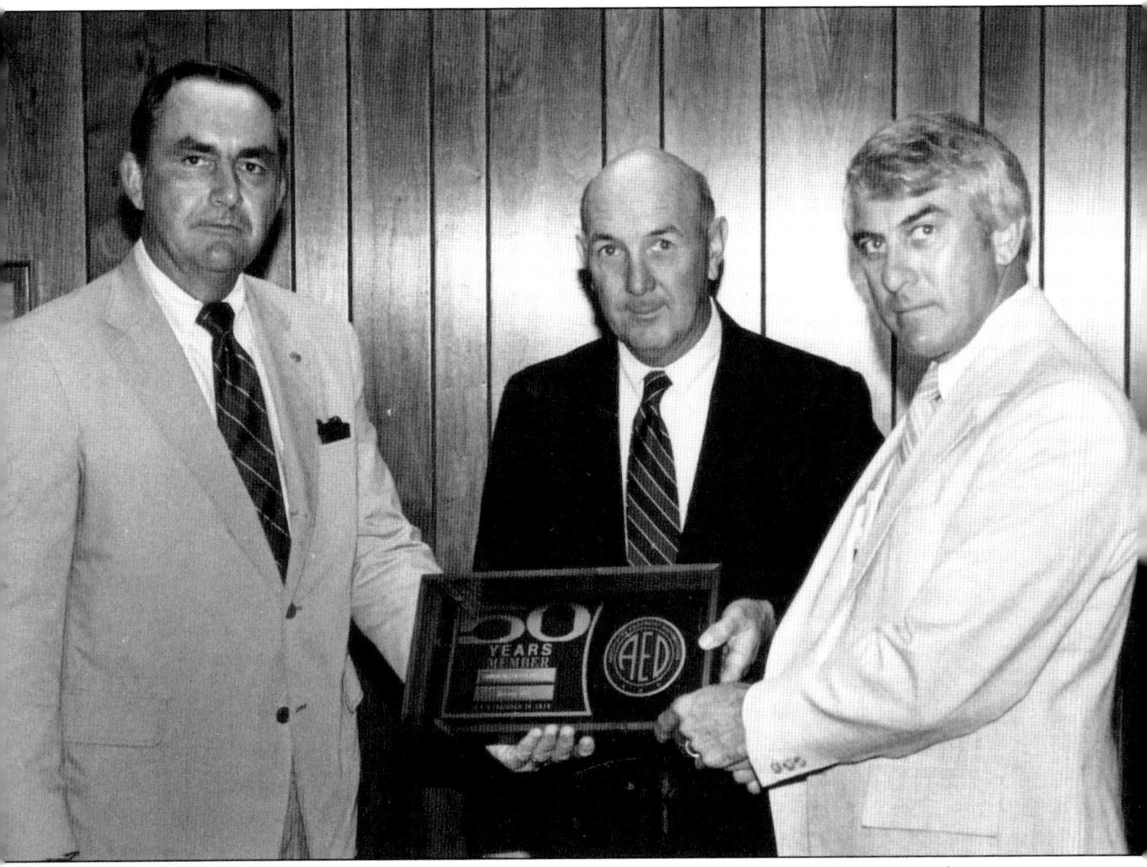

Ed Weisiger Sr. (center) is flanked by fellow members of the Associated Equipment Distributors, an international trade association. They are presenting an award to Carolina Tractor & Equipment Company, commemorating 50 years of success. Not only had the company survived the Great Depression years of the 1930s, it had remained profitable every year since 1932. And it continued to do so in the 1970s, when the United States suffered economic hardships brought about by the Mideast oil crisis and the resulting fuel shortages that caused the tax revenues that funded highway projects to drop.

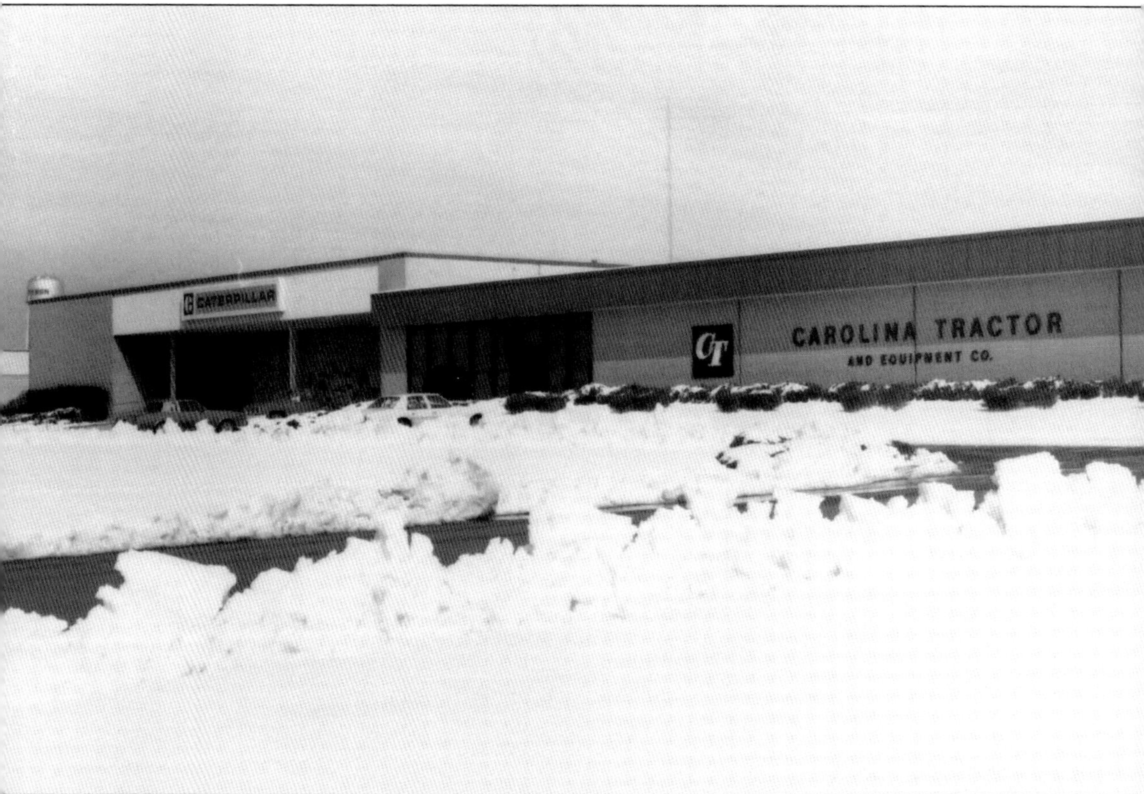

This early-1970s photograph of the Statesville Road facility shows the beginnings of what would grow to become a cornerstone of the region. It would offer 11 service bays, state-of-the-art technology, and an inventory of more than 50,000 parts. Within a few decades, this area would become fully industrialized and the facility would expand many times over.

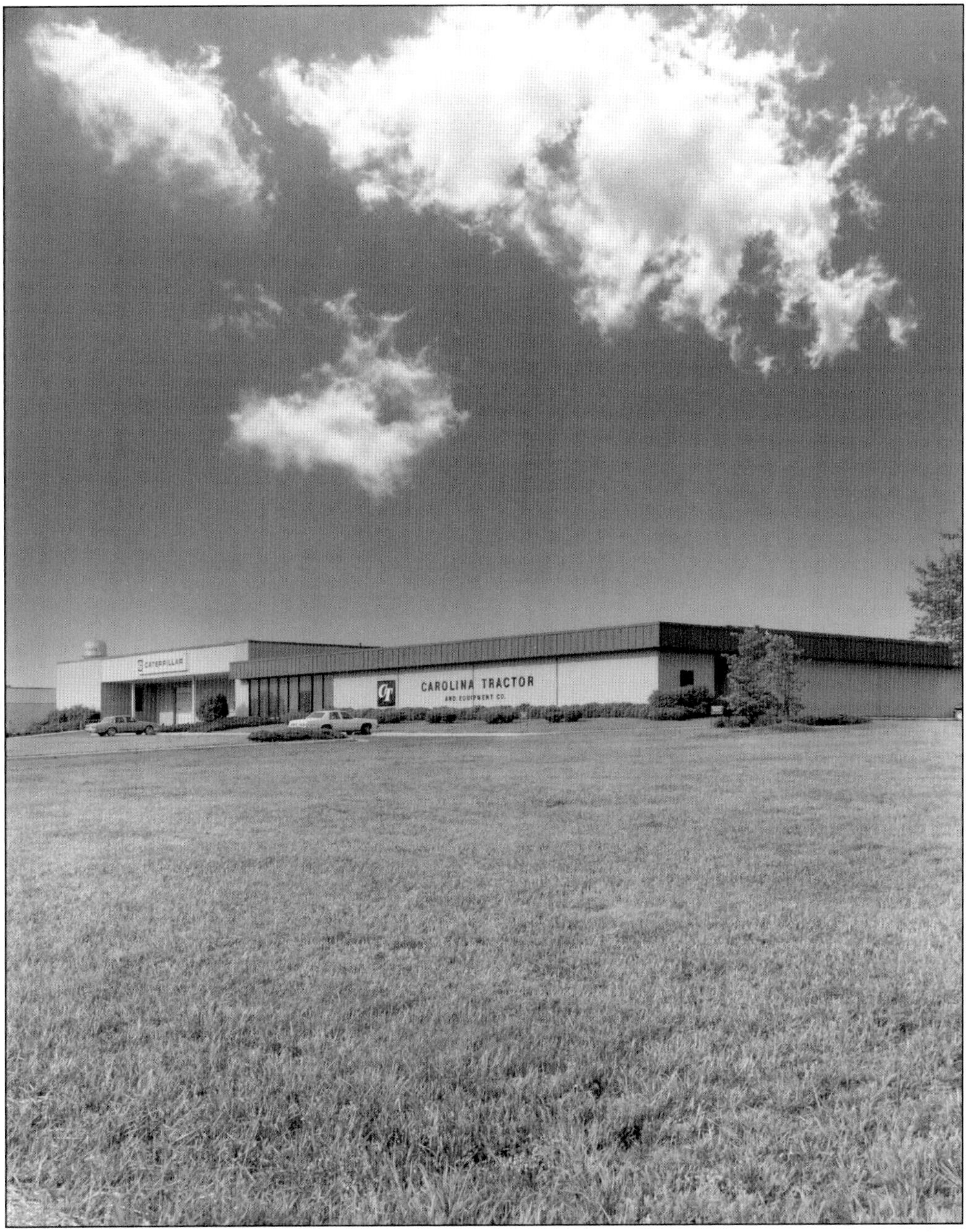

With a vision that would allow the company to build on its established reputation while expanding its reach, Carolina Tractor & Equipment Company opened a modern facility on Statesville Road in Charlotte in 1971. *Construction* magazine hailed it as "the most modern and complete heavy equipment sales, parts, and service facility on the east coast."

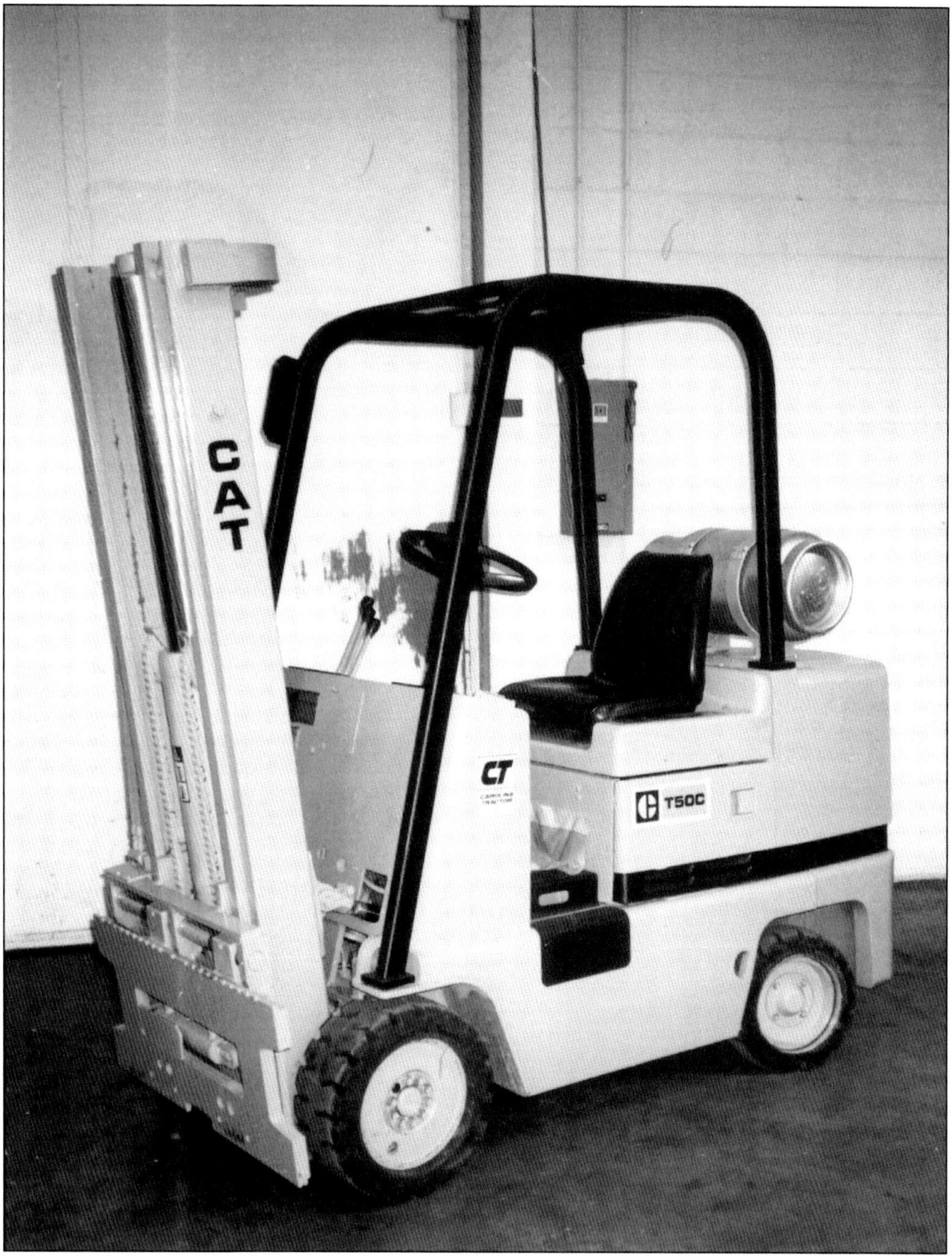

Lift trucks such as this one were nimble workhorses, especially for indoor warehouse use where they could easily maneuver among the aisles where parts were shelved. Early versions of lift trucks were fueled by gasoline, but modernization meant that by the 1970s, many newer models would be powered by propane.

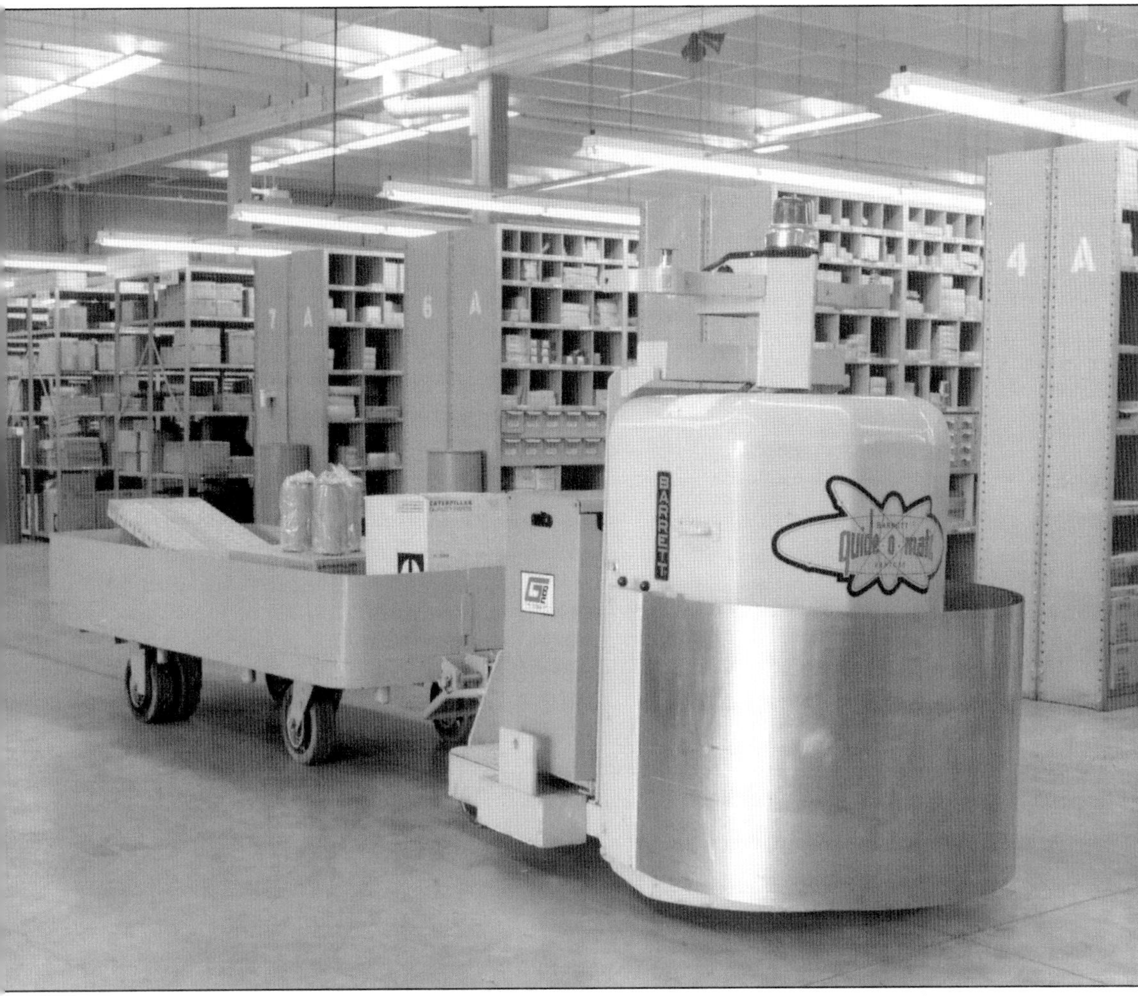

Sometimes, automation can create more problems than it solves. In the early 1970s, the company experimented with a system in which an unmanned cart traveled along tracks to move parts from the warehouse to the shops where mechanics worked on equipment. The cart was supposed to stop automatically if it encountered an obstruction, but one day in 1971, it malfunctioned and hit Mr. Les, who was in his mid-70s and suffered a severe broken shoulder as a result of the collision. The system was immediately abandoned.

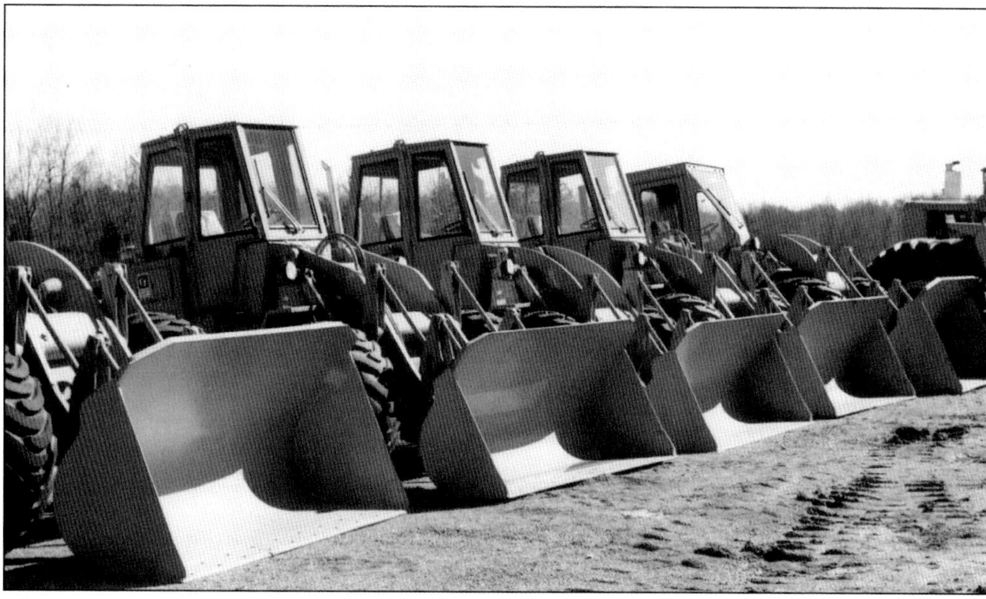

This row of equipment, shown in the yard at the Charlotte location of Carolina Tractor & Equipment Company in the 1970s, was shipped from the factory in pieces and then assembled on site, where technicians would provide field service once the work was under way.

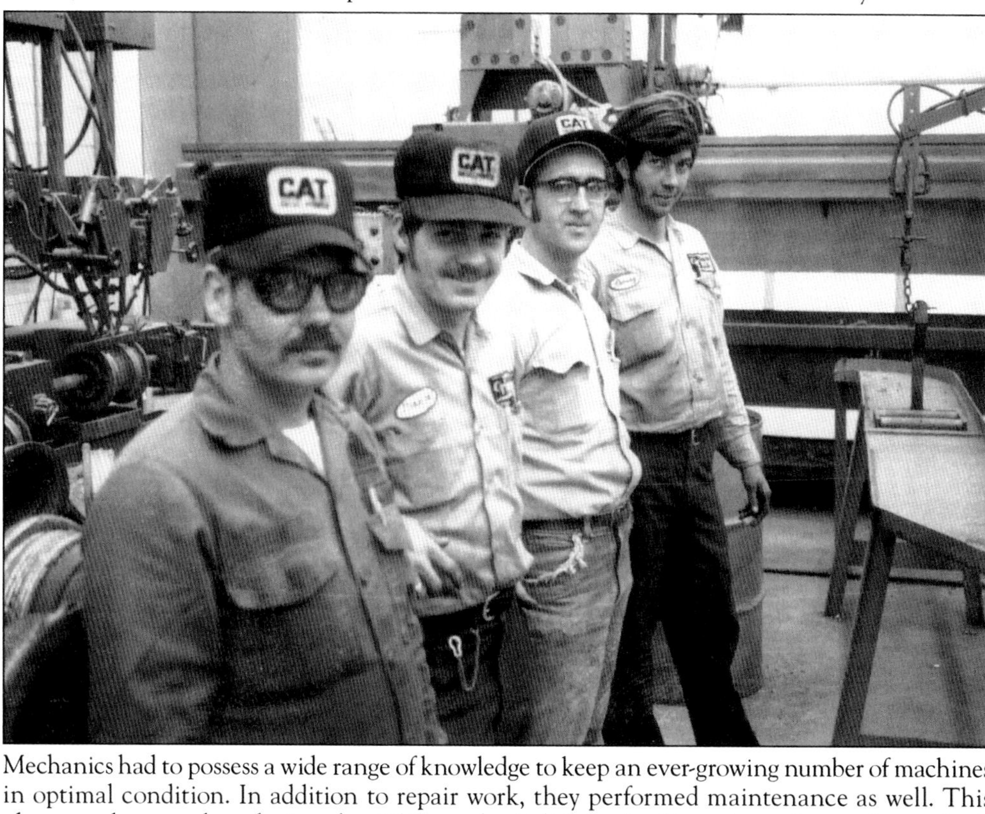

Mechanics had to possess a wide range of knowledge to keep an ever-growing number of machines in optimal condition. In addition to repair work, they performed maintenance as well. This photograph was taken during the 1970s at the Salisbury facility, where the workers rebuilt components of the equipment.

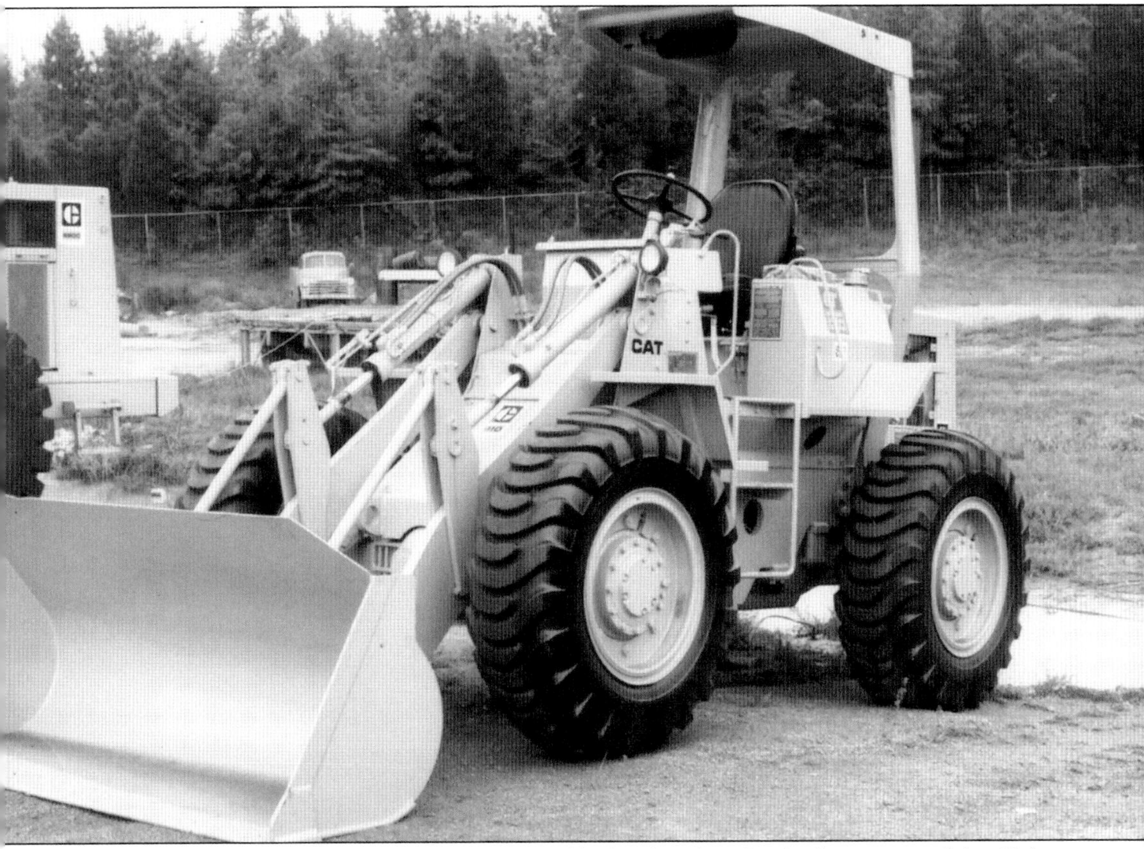

Although huge strides would be made in the world of technology by the latter part of the 20th century, much of the heavy equipment used on construction and farming projects remained largely unchanged, although models would be updated from time to time to improve efficiency. This reliable small loader from the 1970s was a popular machine sold by Carolina Tractor & Equipment Company.

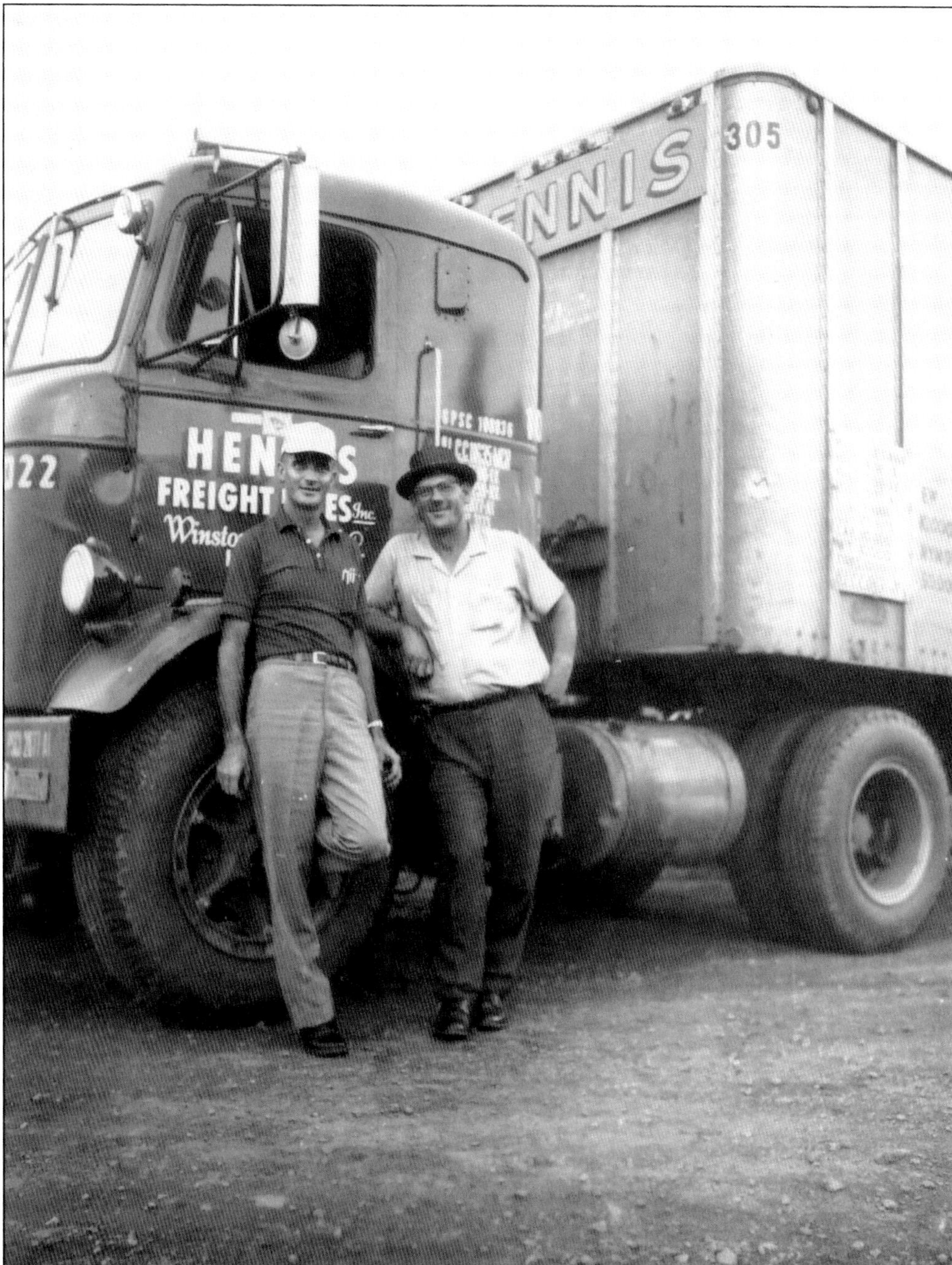

Without the trucking industry, goods cannot reach their markets. Engines manufactured by Caterpillar, Inc., of Peoria, Illinois, were in wide use across the entire country, not only in construction and engineering projects, but also in the transportation industry. This photograph, from the early 1970s, of trucks belonging to the Hennis company of Winston-Salem, show just a few of the countless examples where the engines sold and distributed by Carolina Tractor & Equipment played a pivotal role in the growth of the region where the company has been based since its beginnings.

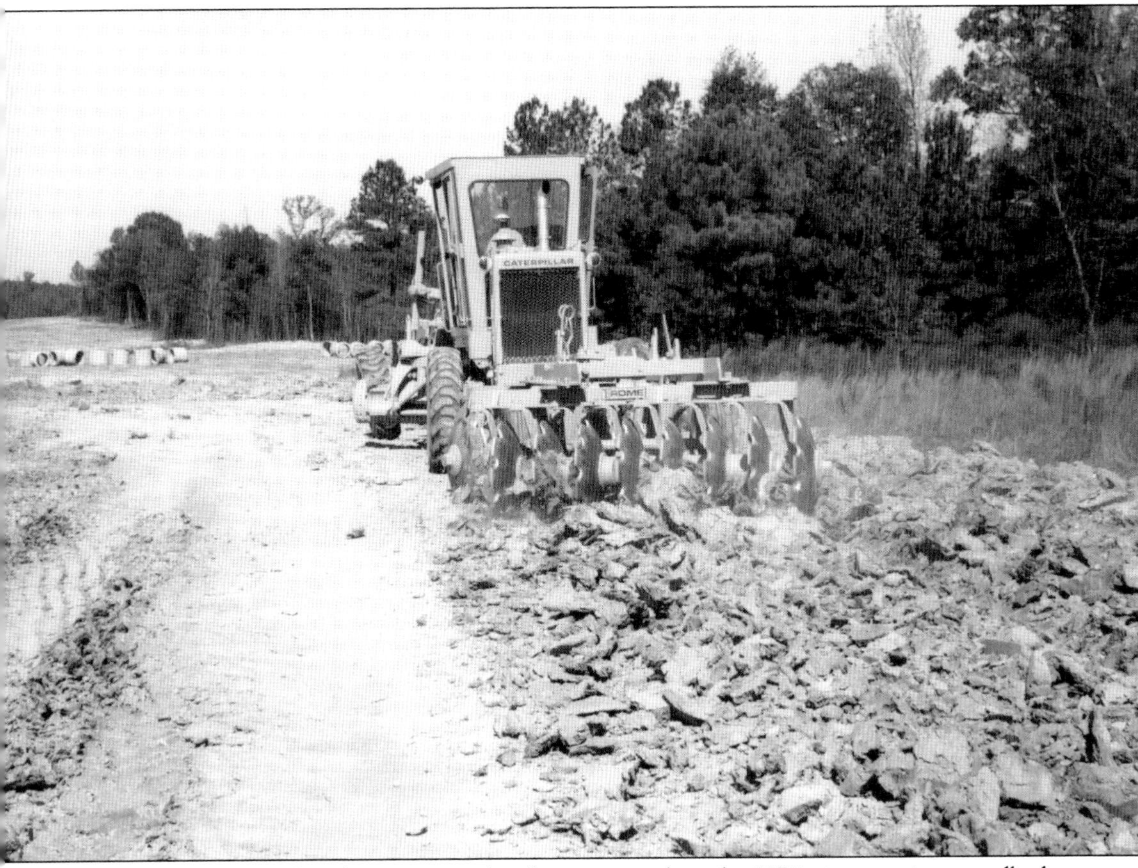

A trained eye can tell that this motor grader, shown on a job in the 1970s, is preparing a roadbed for the construction or expansion of an interstate project. The width of the area, scale of the work being performed, and the lack of development around the job site are sure signs that this cannot be residential development and can only be a highway job.

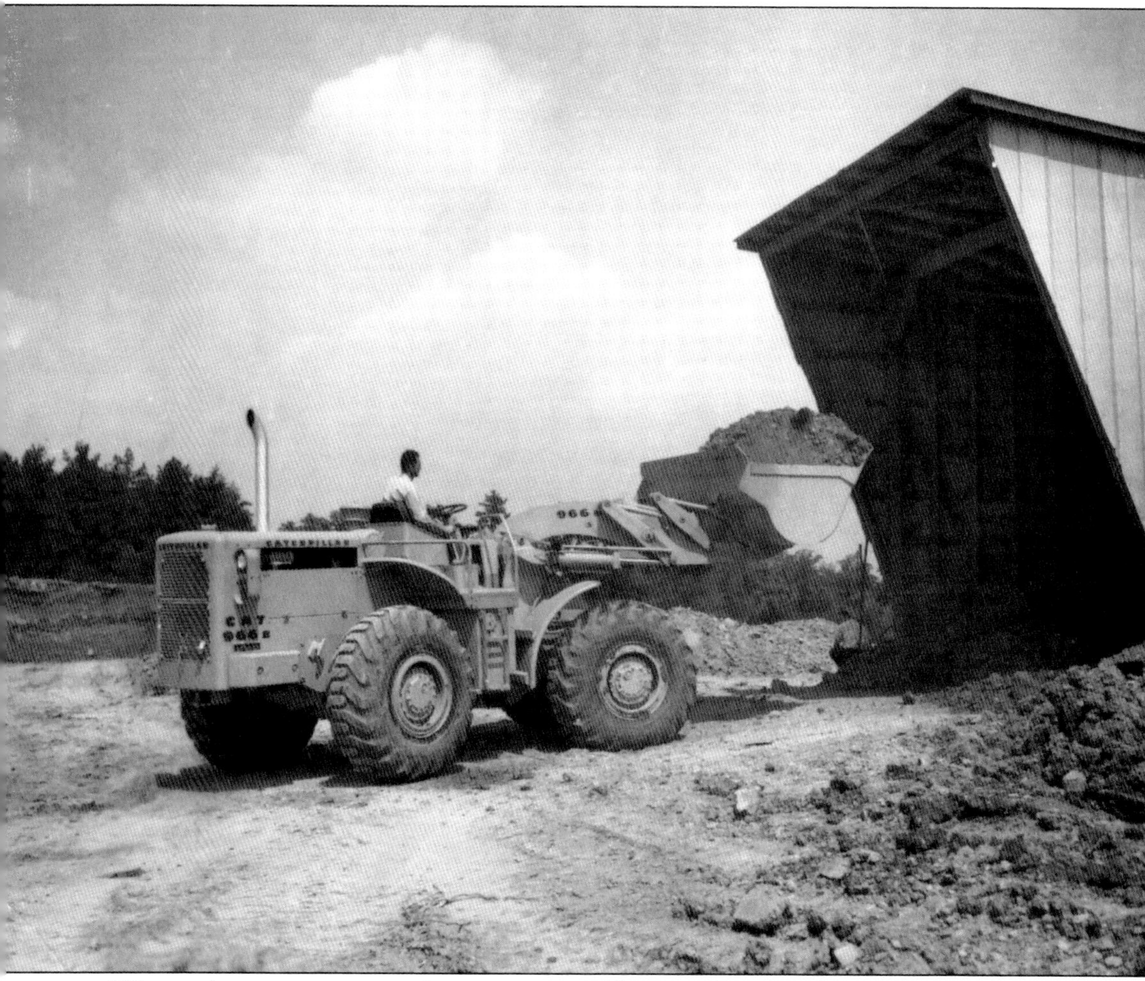

When military servicemen and women returned home to the United States after World War II, they needed housing, especially when they reentered the workforce, married, and started families. New housing developments meant an increased demand for bricks, which had to be manufactured to keep up with the pace of home building. This loader from Carolina Tractor & Equipment Company is seen working at a brick plant in the 1970s.

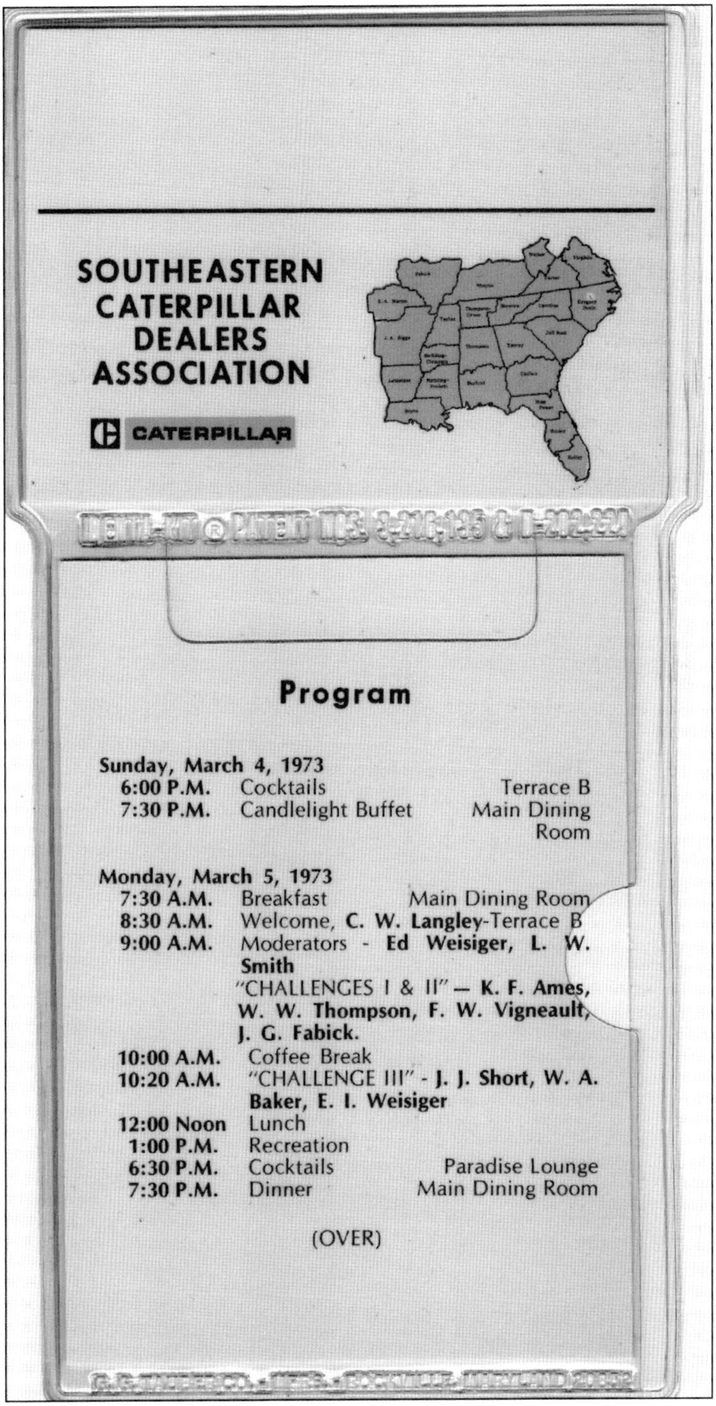

SOUTHEASTERN CATERPILLAR DEALERS ASSOCIATION

CATERPILLAR

Program

Sunday, March 4, 1973

6:00 P.M.	Cocktails	Terrace B
7:30 P.M.	Candlelight Buffet	Main Dining Room

Monday, March 5, 1973

7:30 A.M.	Breakfast	Main Dining Room
8:30 A.M.	Welcome, **C. W. Langley**-Terrace B	
9:00 A.M.	Moderators - **Ed Weisiger, L. W. Smith** "CHALLENGES I & II" — **K. F. Ames, W. W. Thompson, F. W. Vigneault, J. G. Fabick.**	
10:00 A.M.	Coffee Break	
10:20 A.M.	"CHALLENGE III" - **J. J. Short, W. A. Baker, E. I. Weisiger**	
12:00 Noon	Lunch	
1:00 P.M.	Recreation	
6:30 P.M.	Cocktails	Paradise Lounge
7:30 P.M.	Dinner	Main Dining Room

(OVER)

Ed Weisiger Sr. was elected president of the Southeastern Caterpillar Dealers Association and was a featured speaker at the meeting held in early March 1973. He discussed the challenges facing the industry, including the machine shortages that were resulting from worldwide demand for construction equipment, combined with price controls and other measures that were implemented in an attempt to curb inflation.

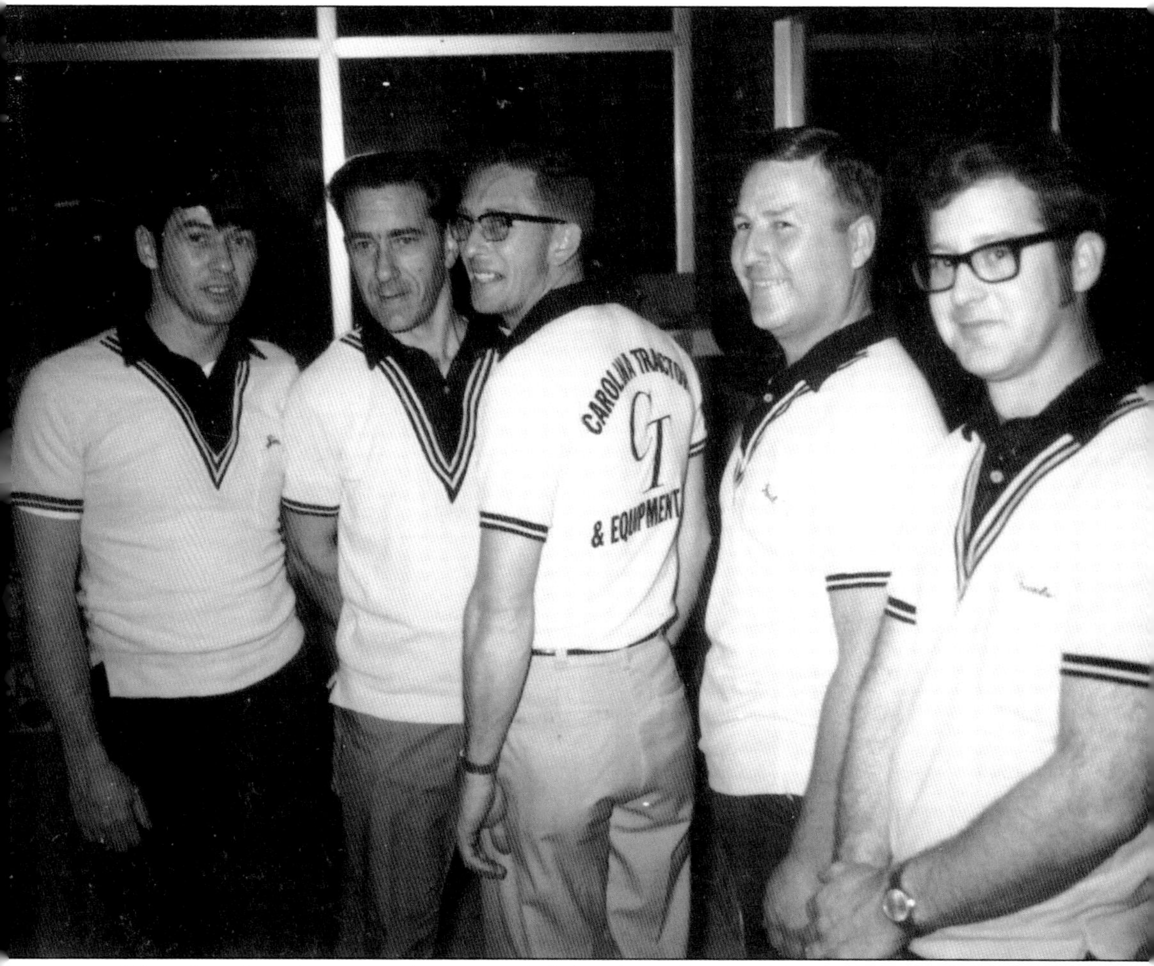

All work and no play can make anyone dull, but these Carolina Tractor & Equipment Company employees let off steam with bowling. In this photograph of bowling team members in the 1970s, the company name can be seen emblazoned on their shirts.

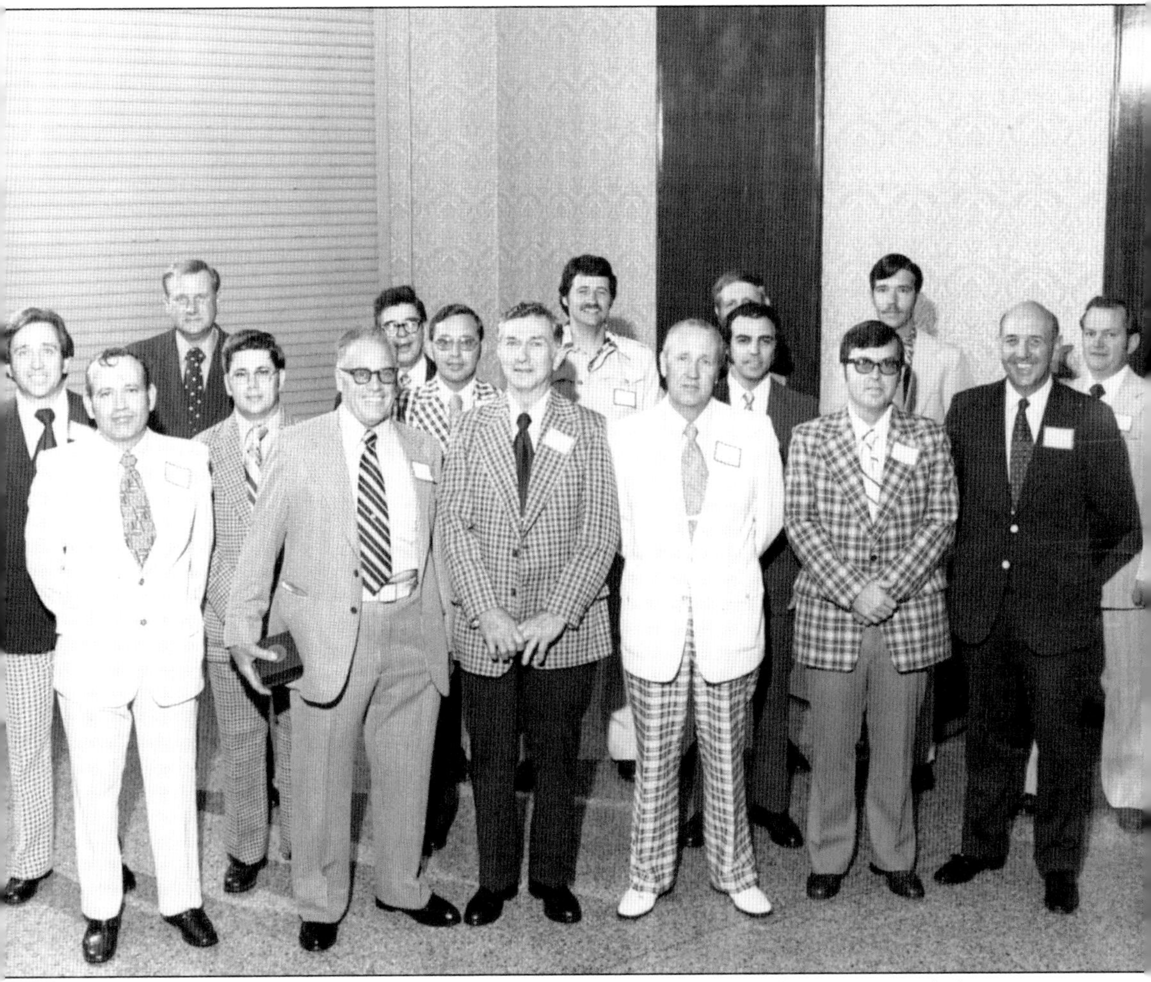

At the April 1975 Carolina Tractor & Equipment Company annual service awards banquet, employees were recognized for their years of dedication. The economy continued to be uncertain, as inflation reached dangerous levels. Economic instability meant that customers would see prices for equipment rise dramatically in the time between placing an order and taking delivery of their equipment. This group of honorees includes Howard N. Blankenship Jr., Floyd M. Blythe, Roy N. Brown, Kenneth H. Fondow, Thomas M. Fox, Thomas L. Gee, Arvin D. Hargett, Donald H. Owens, Daniel M. Pittilo, James T. Reynolds, Bobby L. Robinson, Fred C. Shepherd, Charles R. Starnes, Robert D. Fisher, Kenneth L. Wilcox, James R. Poole, John R. Brown Jr., Robert V. Osborne, Mitchell F. Houck, James T. Smith, and Paul W. Kepley.

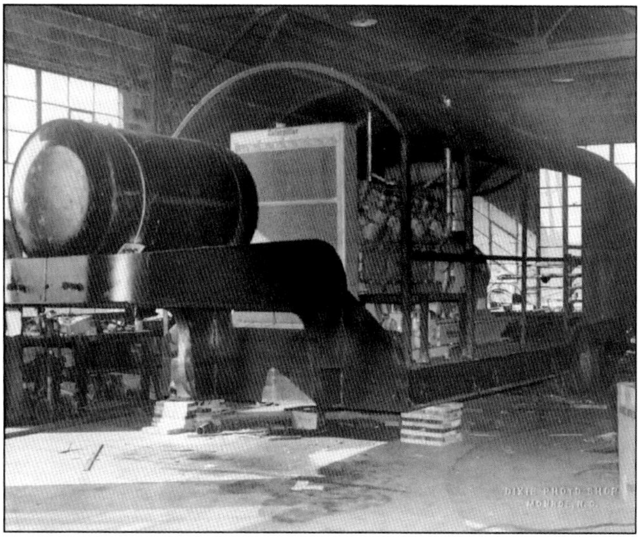

It has been said that "if the power goes out, you're out of business." Generators such as this one were critical power sources, and Carolina Tractor & Equipment Company provided the means to deliver them to job sites and customers who could be difficult to reach due to lack of roads.

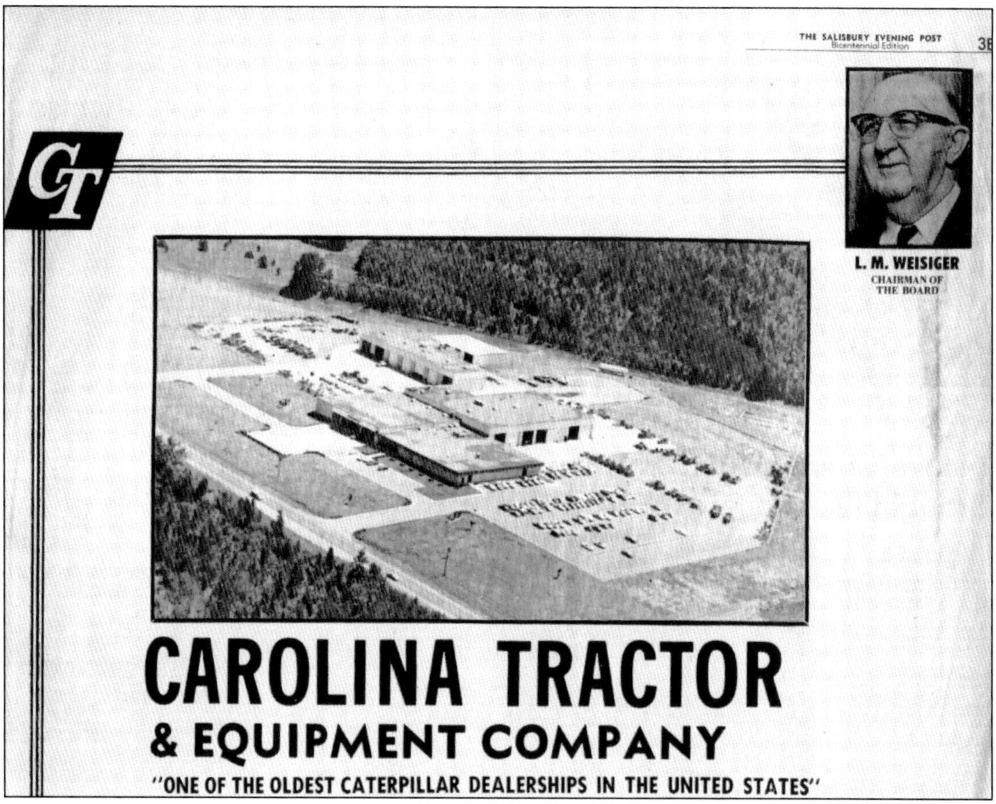

Carolina Tractor & Equipment Company is one of the oldest Caterpillar dealerships in the nation. Throughout its existence, it "has supplied the machines and know-how for the development of a better North Carolina since 1926," according to Ed Weisiger Sr. in a promotional news circular from 1976. When Mr. Les stepped aside to serve as the company chairman, Ed Sr. took over as president in 1965. Ed Sr. consolidated the family's ownership by purchasing outstanding stock in the company. In 1991, Harvard University graduate Ed Weisiger Jr. would be named company president as Ed Sr. took on the role of chairman.

Four

Our Employees

The people who work in the sales, parts, and service departments of Carolina Tractor are the front-line resources for customers, but behind the scenes there are just as many men and women who contribute to the company's success. Many employees and their families have been part of Carolina Tractor for three or even four generations.

From the company's beginnings, trained technicians have traveled to job sites when customers needed repairs or parts for their equipment in the field. From the days of cardboard tags to the age of microfilm to the modern era of barcode scanners, parts clerks have managed inventories of thousands of items valued at millions of dollars. Also, parts and supplies that once traveled by rail now reach their destinations in a fraction of the time, due to trucks that travel a network of modern highways.

In this chapter, readers will meet some of the many valuable and dedicated employees who contribute to the daily workings of Carolina Tractor, as these insiders share some of their favorite anecdotes and remembrances.

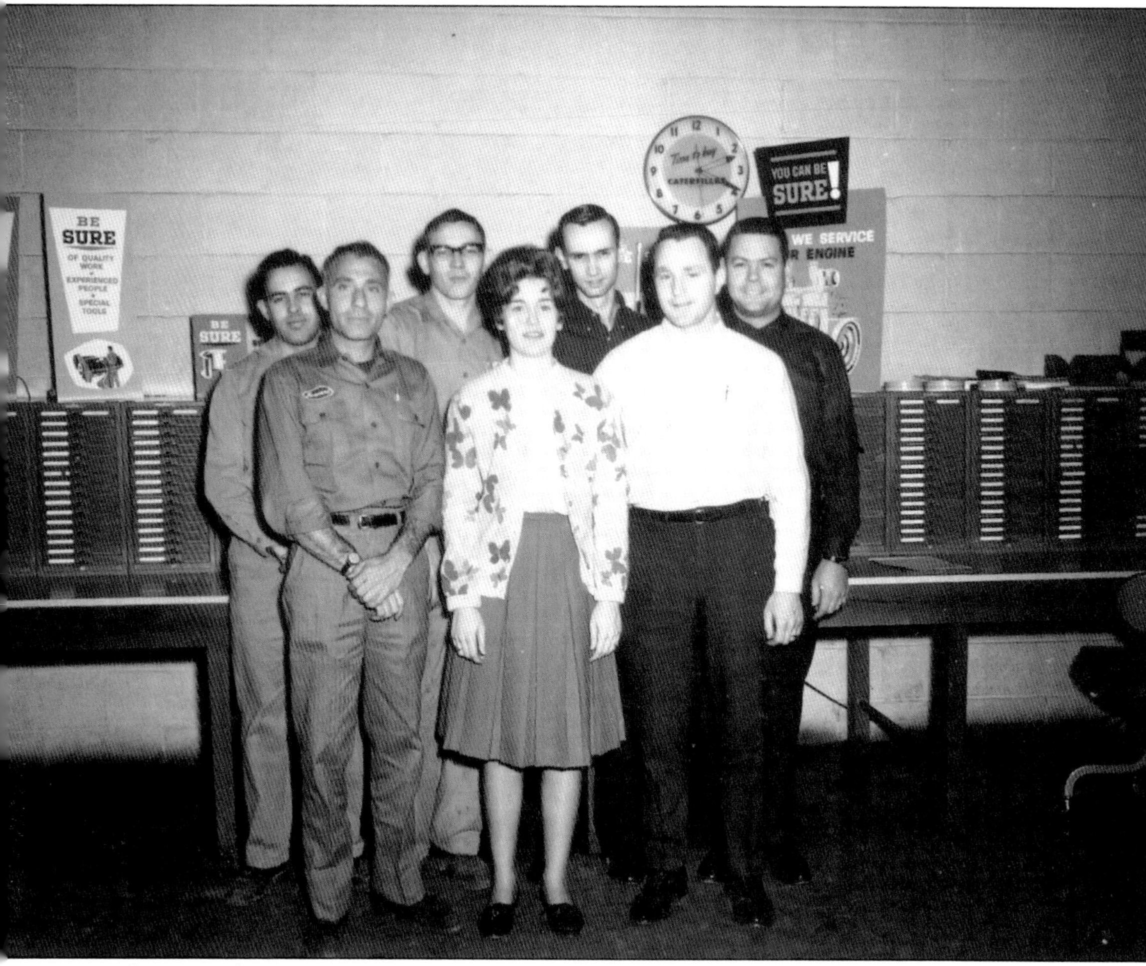

These Carolina Tractor & Equipment Company employees, pictured in the 1950s, worked at the Salisbury location, where they were responsible for accounting and managing the company's vast inventory of parts. The card system visible in the background was an improvement over old-fashioned record-keeping methods, but it still had a long way to go before the computerized age would begin to truly modernize these and other office functions.

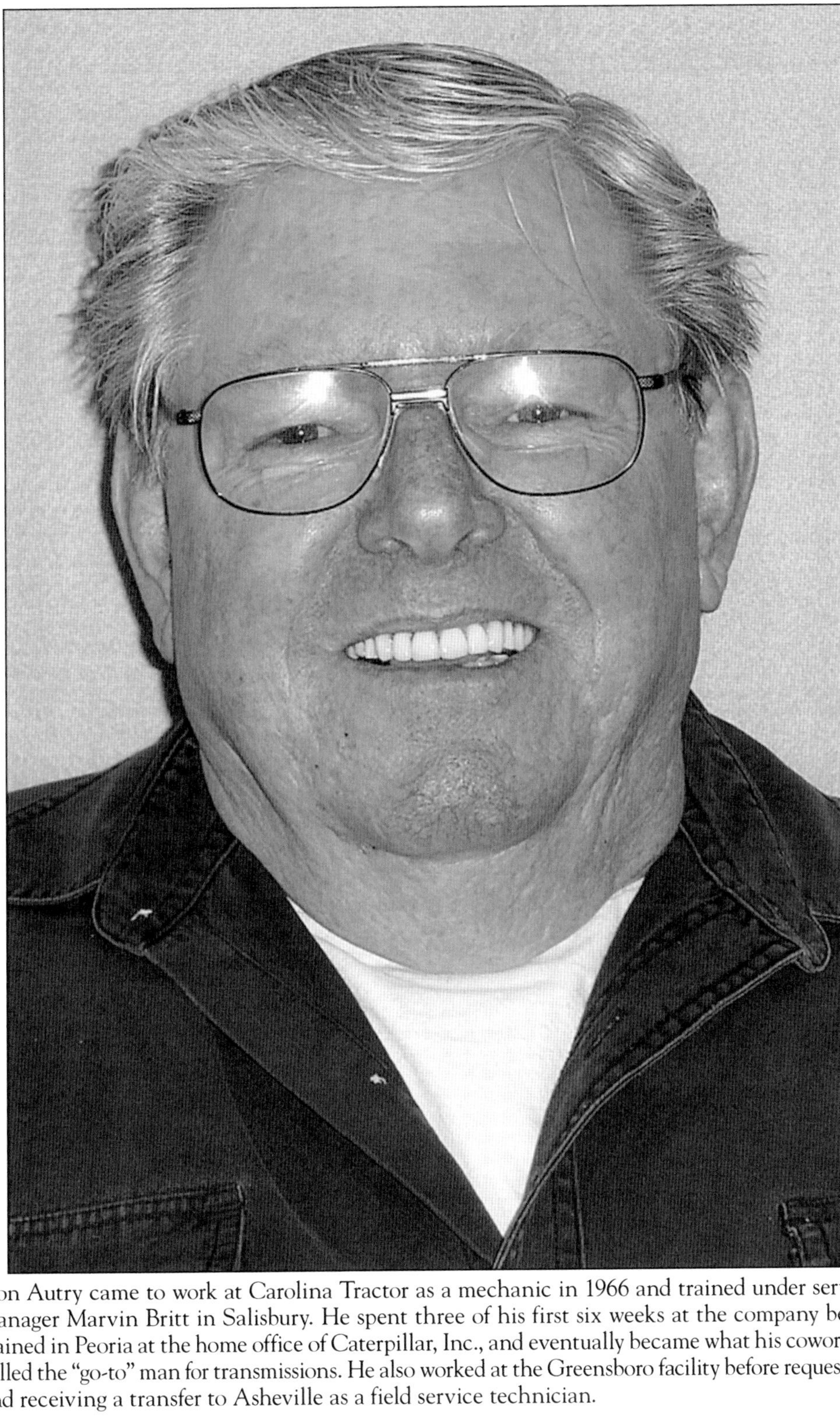

Don Autry came to work at Carolina Tractor as a mechanic in 1966 and trained under service manager Marvin Britt in Salisbury. He spent three of his first six weeks at the company being trained in Peoria at the home office of Caterpillar, Inc., and eventually became what his coworkers called the "go-to" man for transmissions. He also worked at the Greensboro facility before requesting and receiving a transfer to Asheville as a field service technician.

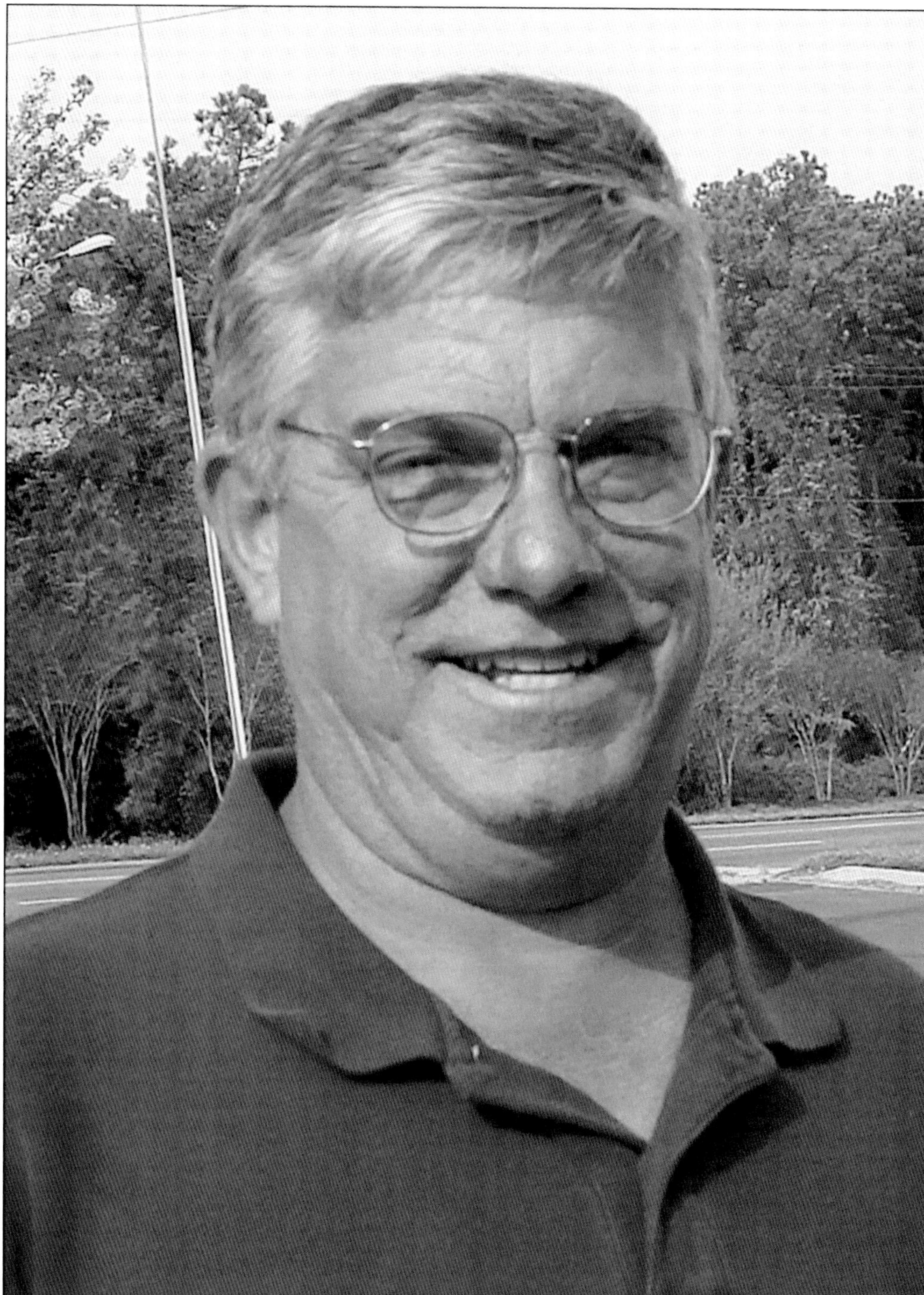

Ken Bickett was a student at North Mecklenburg High School when a teacher suggested that the young man who was working two part-time jobs apply for employment at Carolina Tractor & Equipment Company. Bickett took that advice and got hired as a shop clerk in 1970 while he was still in school. He graduated on a Friday and went to work full-time the following Monday. Over Ken's 35 years with the company, he worked in almost every division and department.

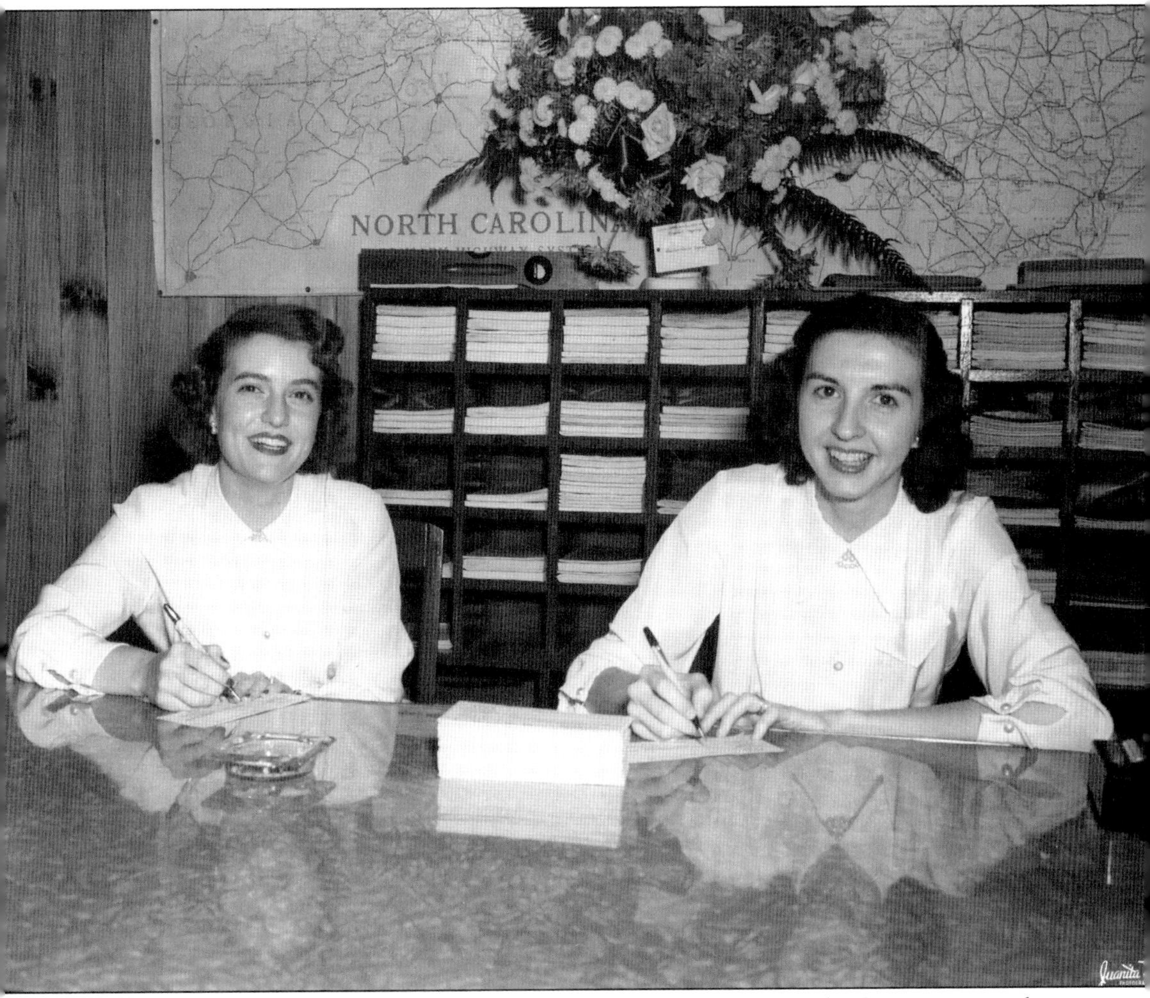

Pictured above are Jewel Wolfe Ziprik (left) and Frankie Bost (right). Frankie Bost was part of a generation of women who entered the workforce after World War II. Like countless others, she came from a rural background to work in an office setting. Mr. Les's brother Henry Weisiger interviewed and hired her to begin work at Carolina Tractor & Equipment Company in June 1946. Her responsibilities included answering the telephone, typing letters, and bookkeeping. When a coworker left for maternity leave, Frankie took over the job of invoicing and discovered she had an aptitude for the job; it was one she kept until she retired 53 years later.

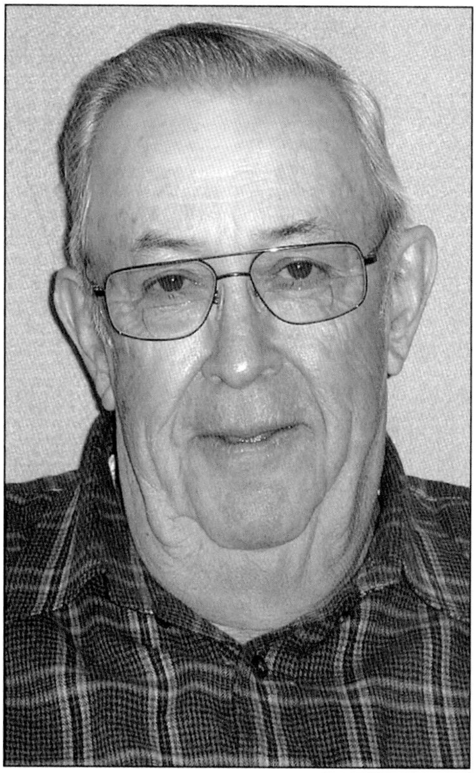

Glen Hollars had been an aircraft mechanic when he came to work as a welder at Carolina Tractor in 1963. He was one of the first to work on the Caterpillar 992 and spent many years assembling and servicing equipment on some of North Carolina's most ambitious construction projects, including building the Linn Cove Viaduct on the Blue Ridge Parkway and servicing the WLOS television transmitters atop Mount Pisgah near Asheville. Glen retired in 1998 after 35 years of service.

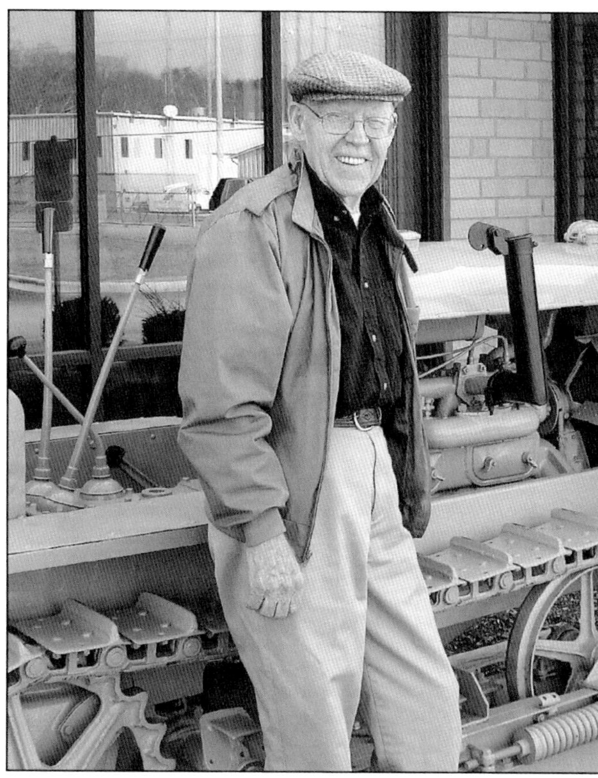

Red Kinsey had been an auto mechanic before coming to work at Carolina Tractor in 1958. He had not worked on heavy equipment before but learned on the job from his fellow shop mechanics. After developing expertise pressing out the shafts and brushings on the bottom rollers of bulldozers, he went on to become a specialist on the Caterpillar 933. After a 30-year career, Red retired from the company.

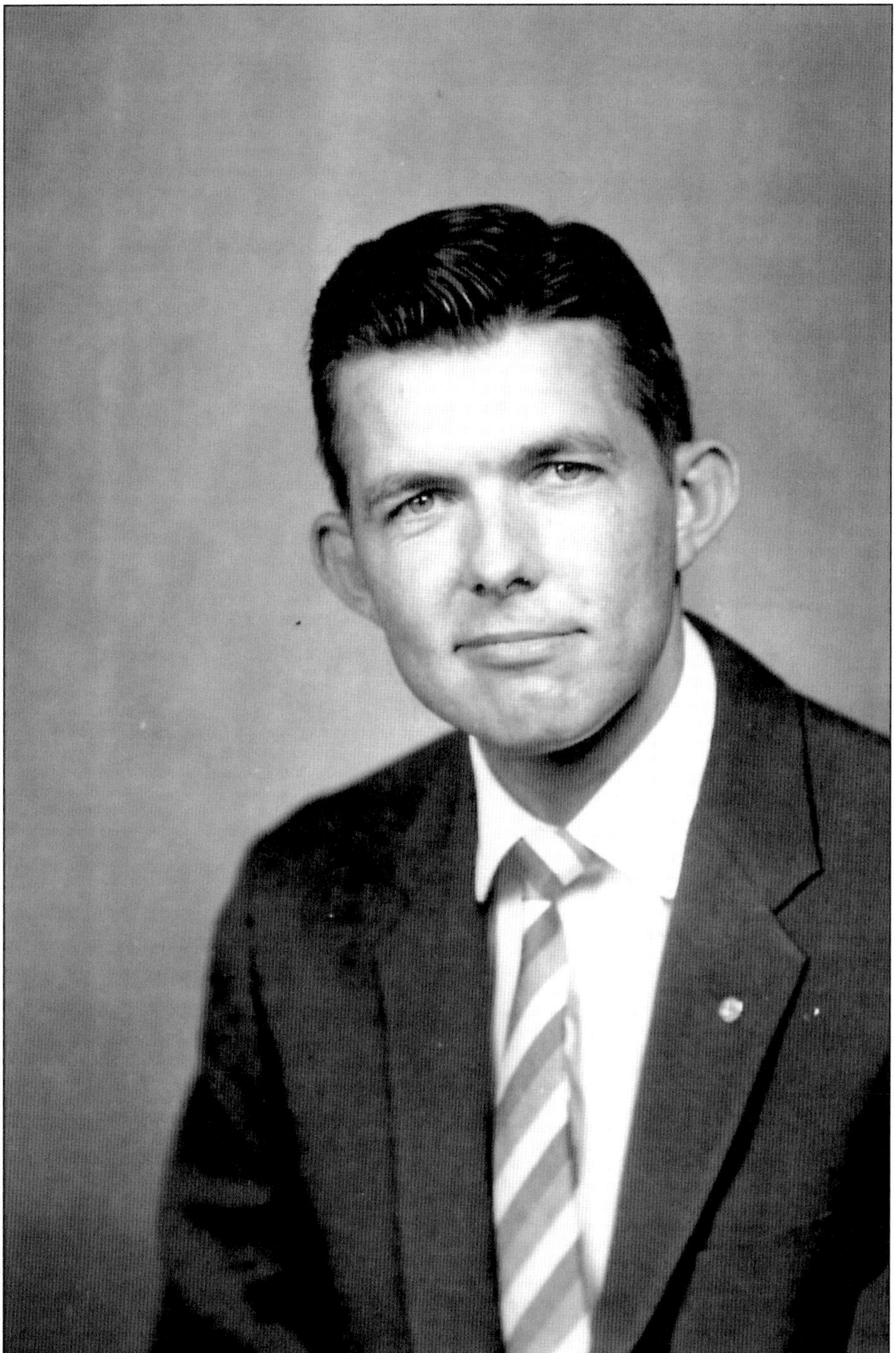

Ben Nine had been selling other brands of machinery in Tennessee, but he wanted to sell Caterpillar equipment, so he relocated to Salisbury and came to work for Carolina Tractor & Equipment Company in 1963. He became the territory salesman for eight western counties, then took over as Asheville sales manager, major accounts manager, and later mine and quarry manager, positions that were both challenging and rewarding. After serving 50 years in the industry, he retired in 2013.

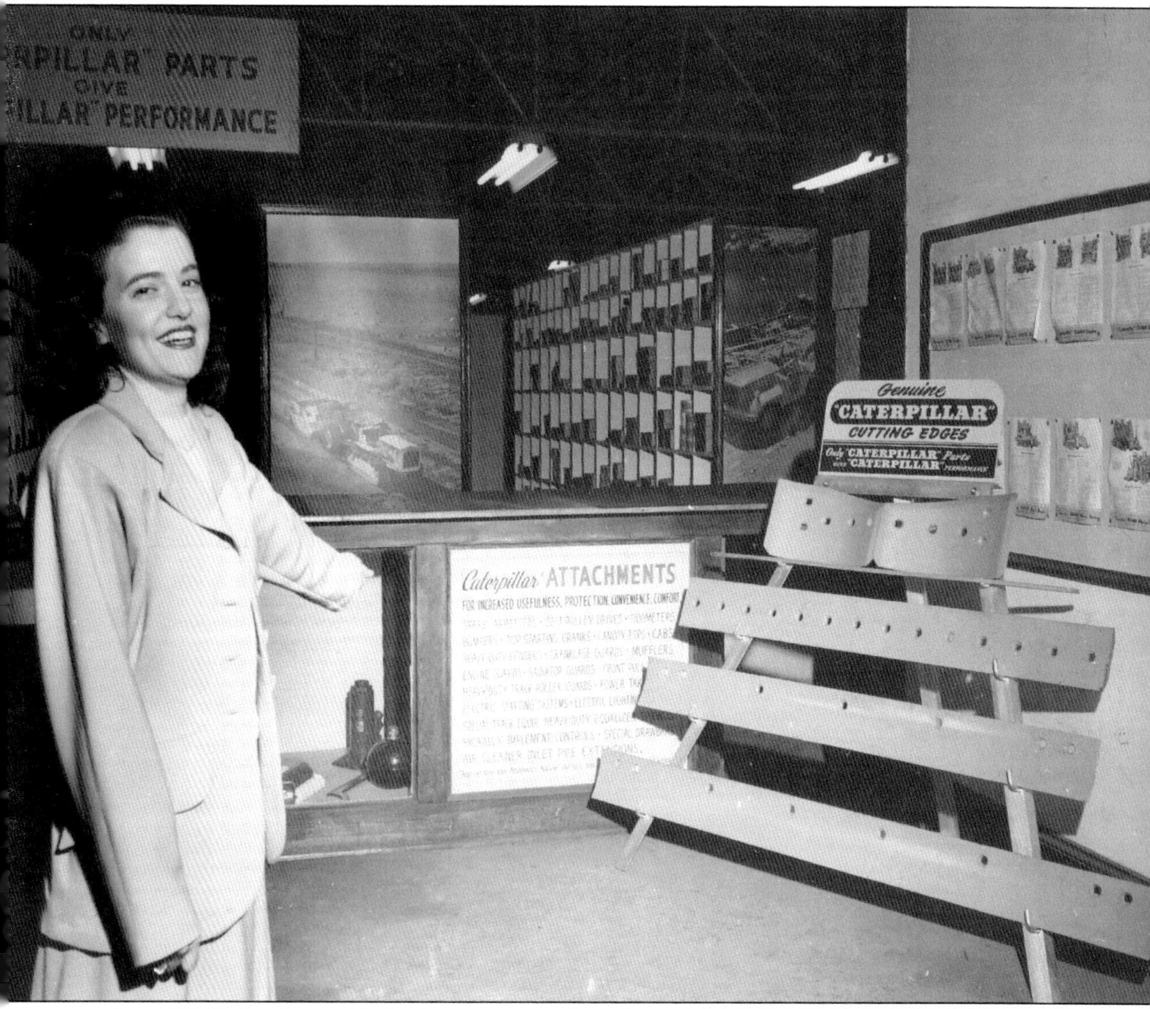

Jewel Wolfe Ziprik was Mr. Les's secretary, and staff sometimes joked that she could do everything at the company except fix the machinery. In addition to her office duties, she was entrusted by Mr. Les with the management of open house events and Christmas parties.

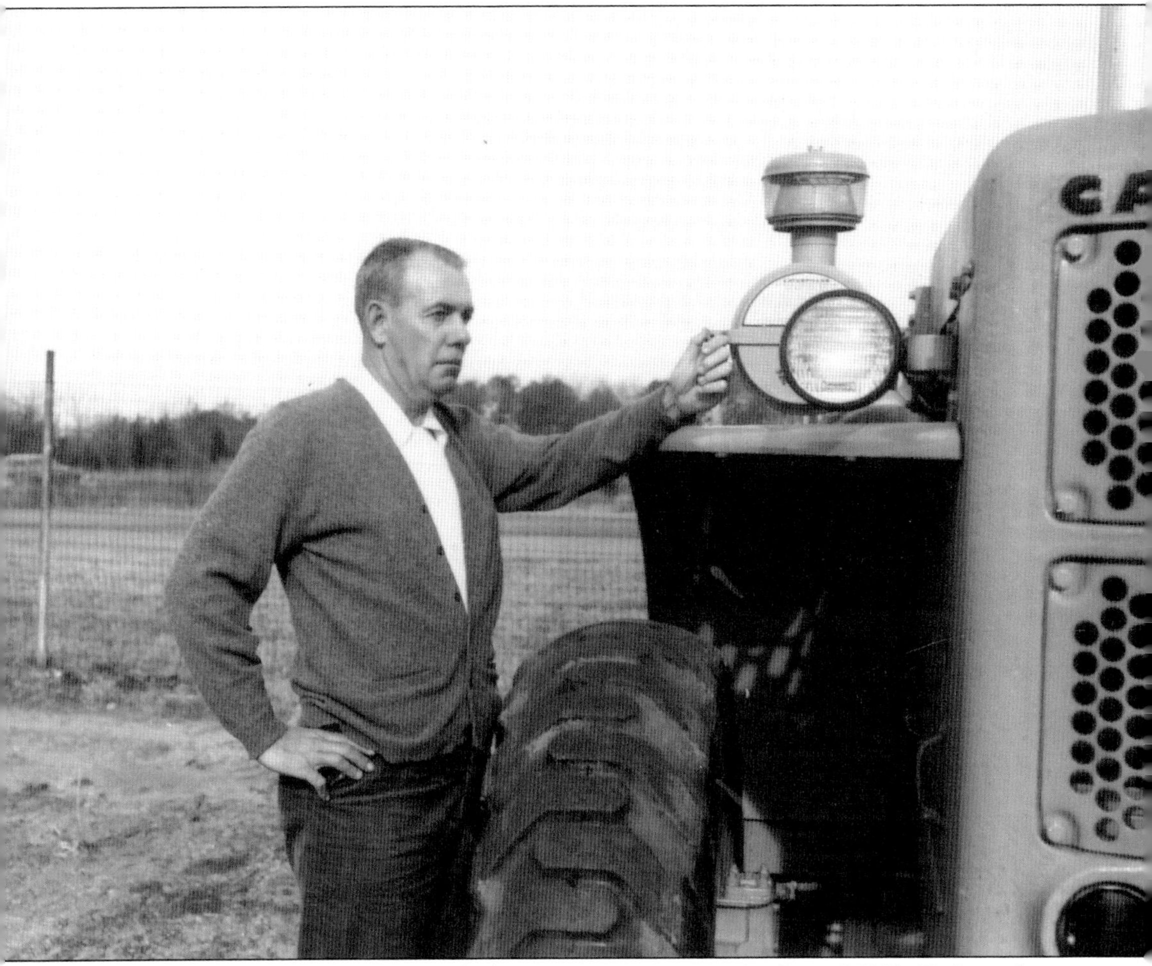

Tom McCormick had become a parts and sales service representative by the mid-1960s. Earlier in his career, he had worked on one of the most challenging jobs with Ransomed Shuping. In the 1940s, the two men had to drive a crane and boom on two trucks through treacherous mountain roads from Salisbury to a job site in Tennessee. McCormick also traveled to Greenland to troubleshoot surplus military equipment that was being used to build an airport in the 1950s.

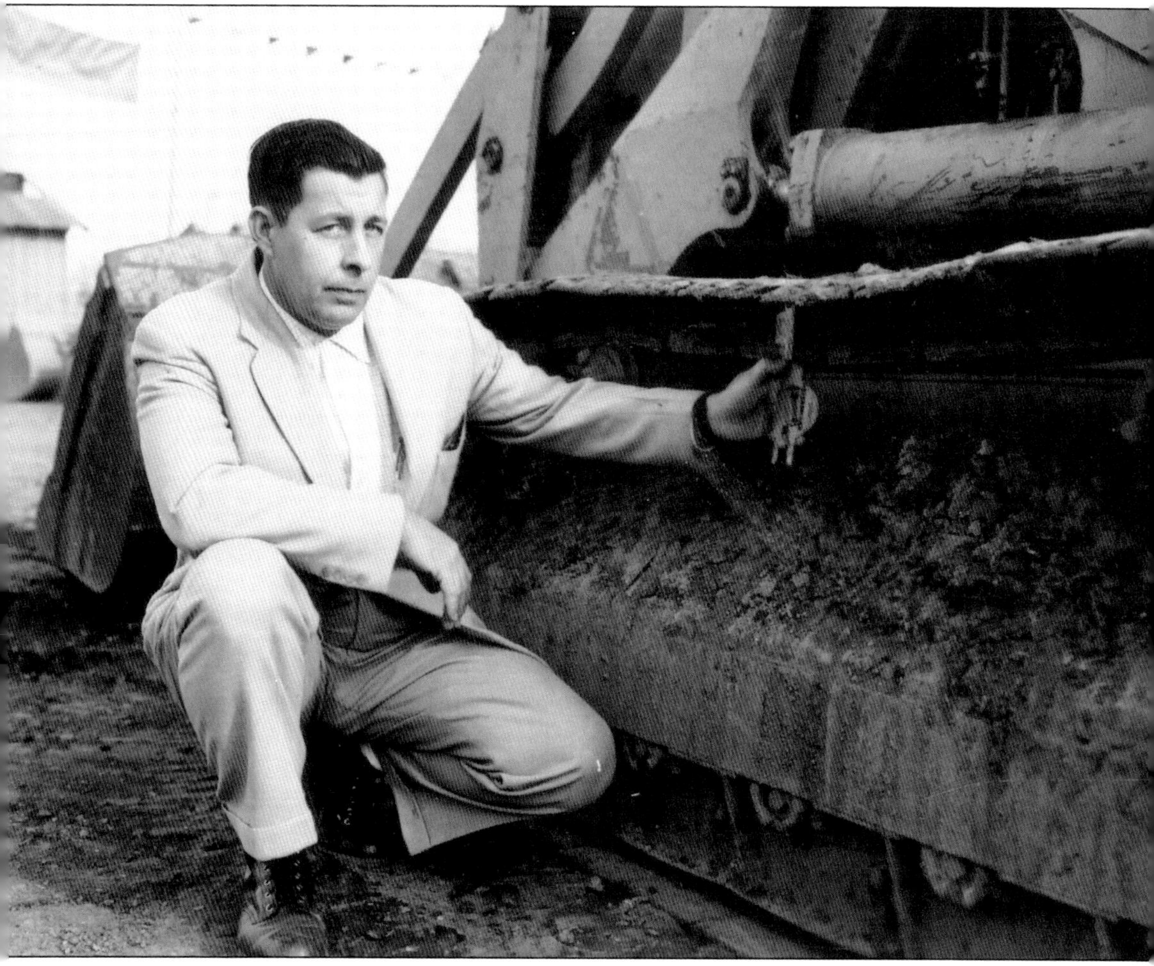

PSSRs, as they came to be known, were not confined to working at a desk, or even indoors. They braved the elements year-round as they traveled to customers' job sites, often located in remote areas that were difficult and dangerous to access. This PSSR is inspecting and measuring equipment in the field.

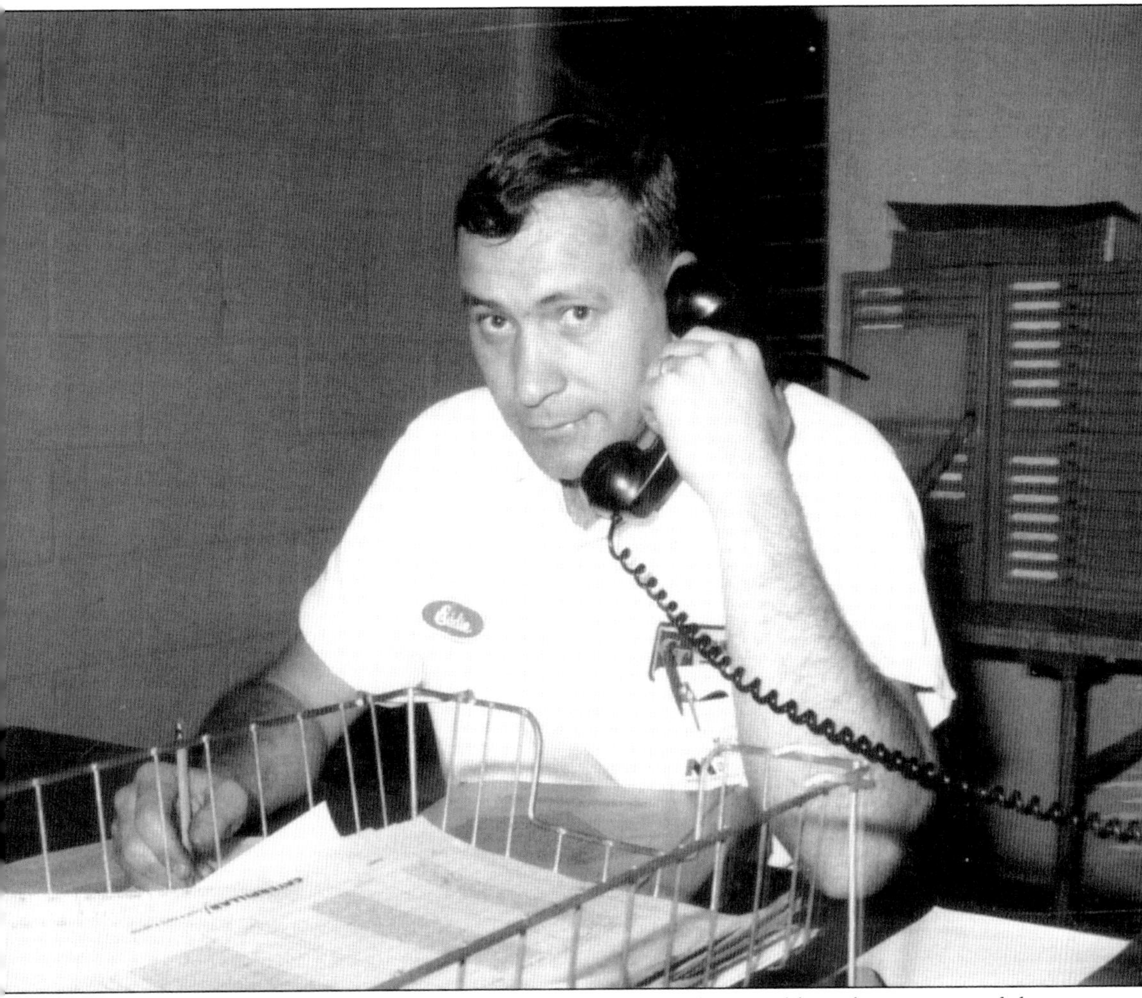

Eddie Hensley is at work in the 1960s, using a card system that would track inventory of the thousands of parts needed to keep Carolina Tractor & Equipment Company running as well as keep customers up to speed on their jobs. At the time, the system was considered modern. During that decade, the North Carolina Department of Transportation's budget essentially doubled, which drove the demand for the heavy equipment needed for highway and road projects.

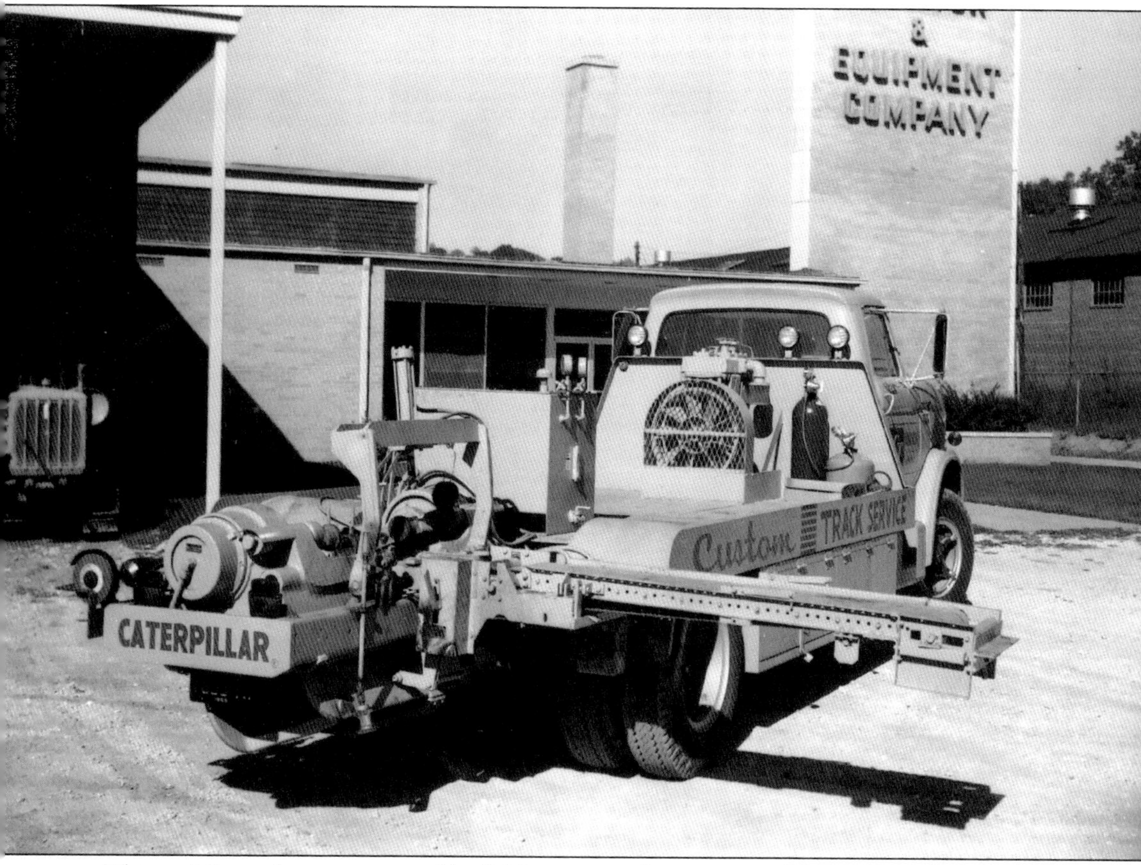

This mobile track press, operated by field service technicians, would travel to job sites to change pins and bushings on equipment in the field. This equipment is shown at the Asheville facility, which serviced a region known for its challenging terrain, remote job sites, and hazardous travel required to reach the customers.

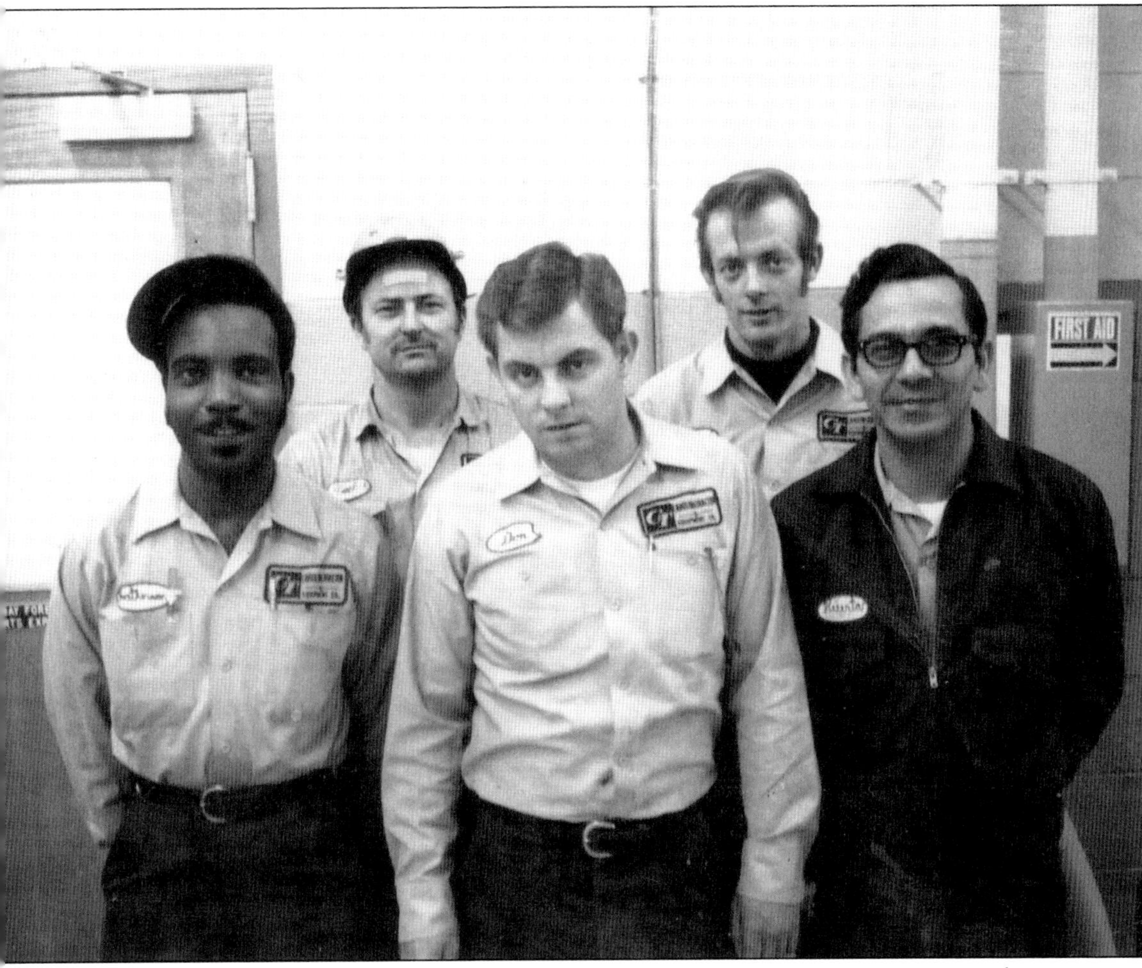

No one was more essential to the operation of Carolina Tractor & Equipment Company than its fleet of technicians. In the early years, many came to work at the company from their small hometowns, where they had often learned basic skills on farm machinery. As the company grew, it provided on-the-job training to its workers, who had to keep pace with a growing number of machines to service as well as the technology that continued to evolve.

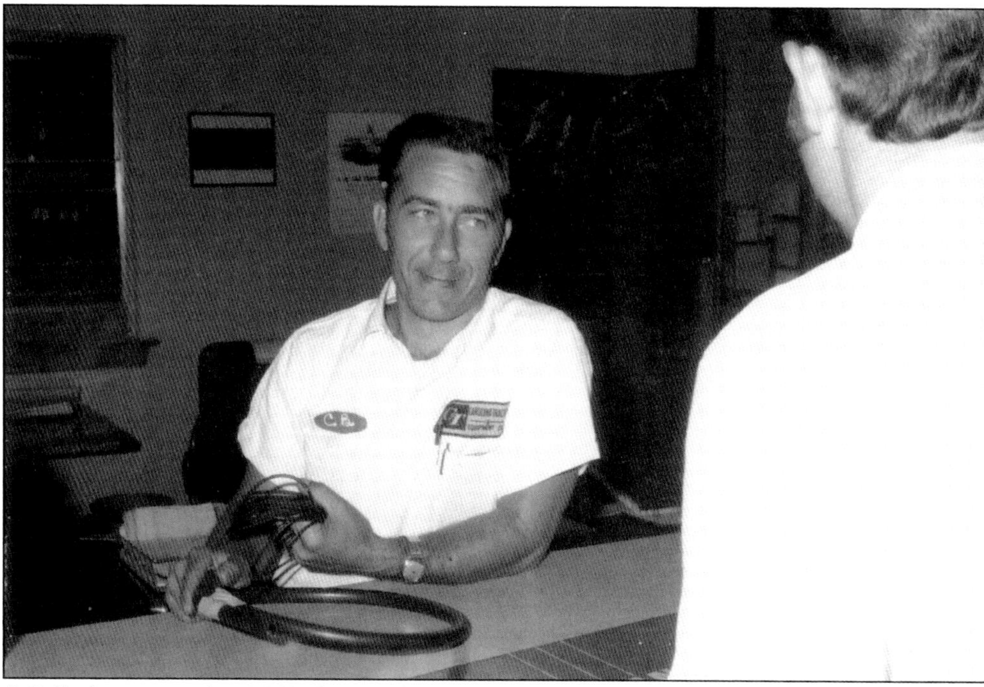

C.B. Early was another PSSR for Carolina Tractor & Equipment Company. In this photograph from around 1969, he draws upon his experience to consult with a customer who is visiting the parts department.

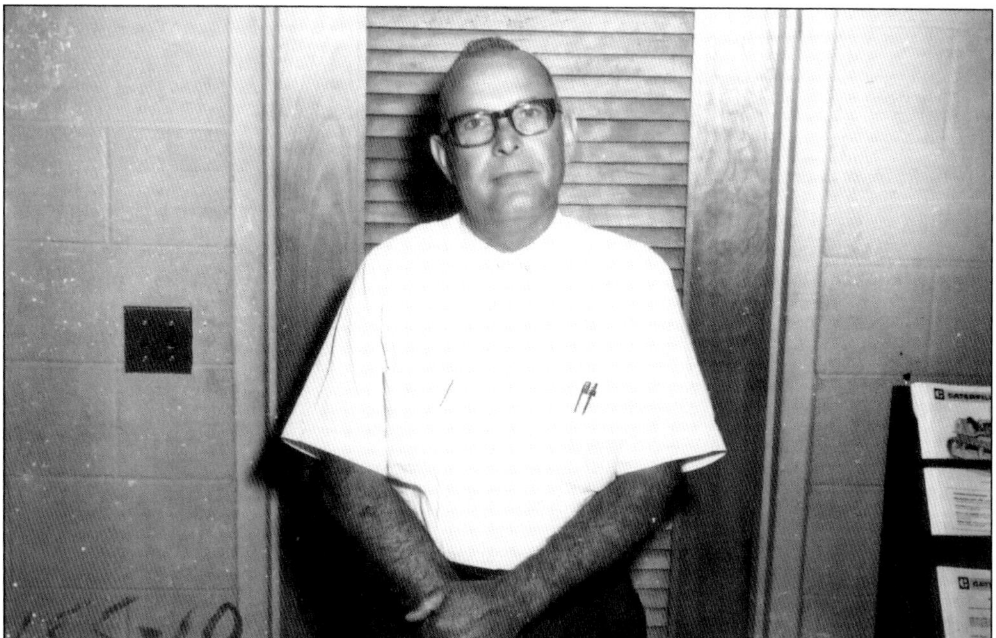

Walt Bailey began his career working in the parts department in the warehouse but became one of Carolina Tractor & Equipment Company's hardworking parts and service sales representatives. They worked not behind desks but in the field, where they traveled to customers' job sites to provide everything from advice to technical support.

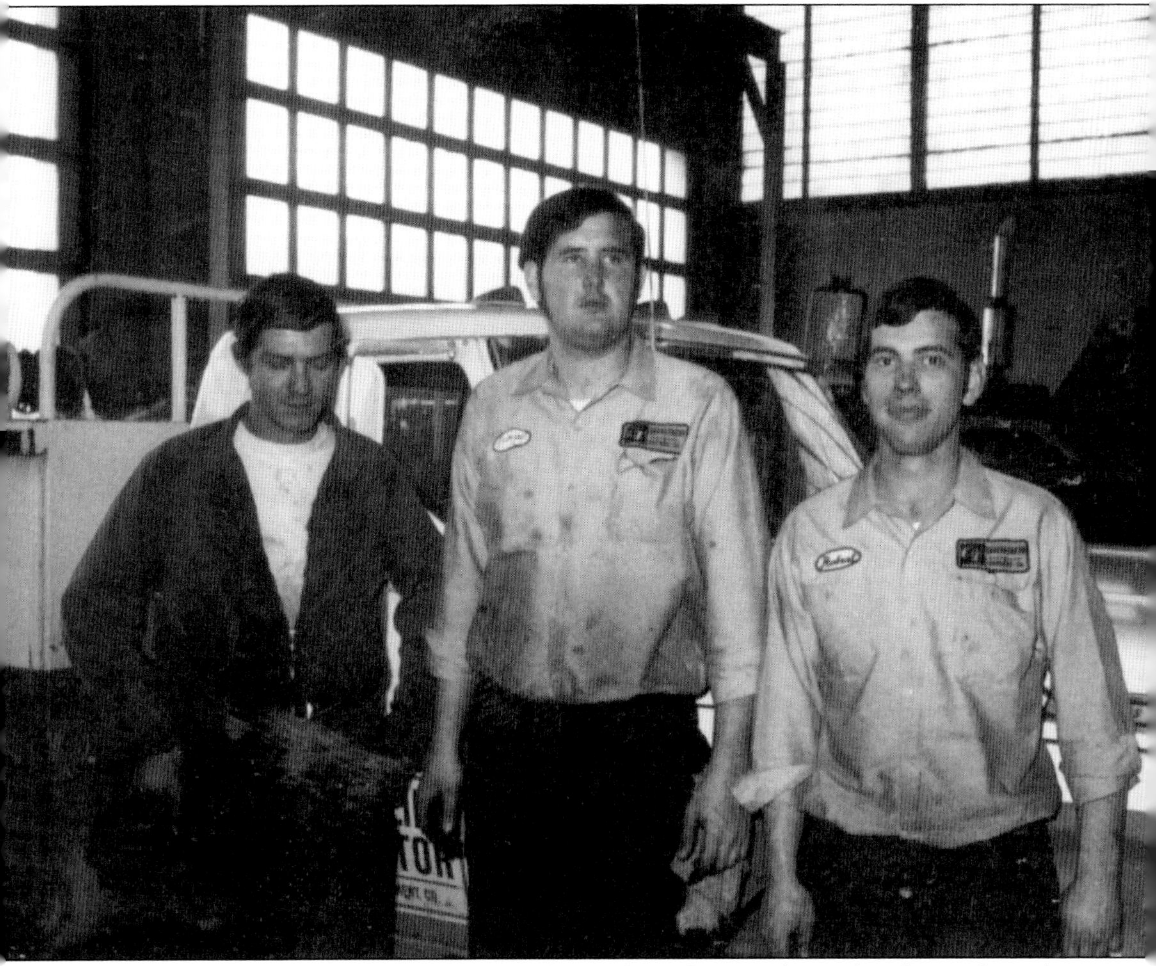

Carolina Tractor & Equipment Company provided uniforms for its workers, who often performed dangerous tasks in harsh conditions. Regardless of weather, steel-toed boots were a necessity on the job, and heavy coats in winter protected the workers who spent long hours outdoors. Service department workers on the job in the service bays took a moment from their tasks to be photographed in this image. From left to right, they are Mike Reeves, George Wright, and Bob Roland.

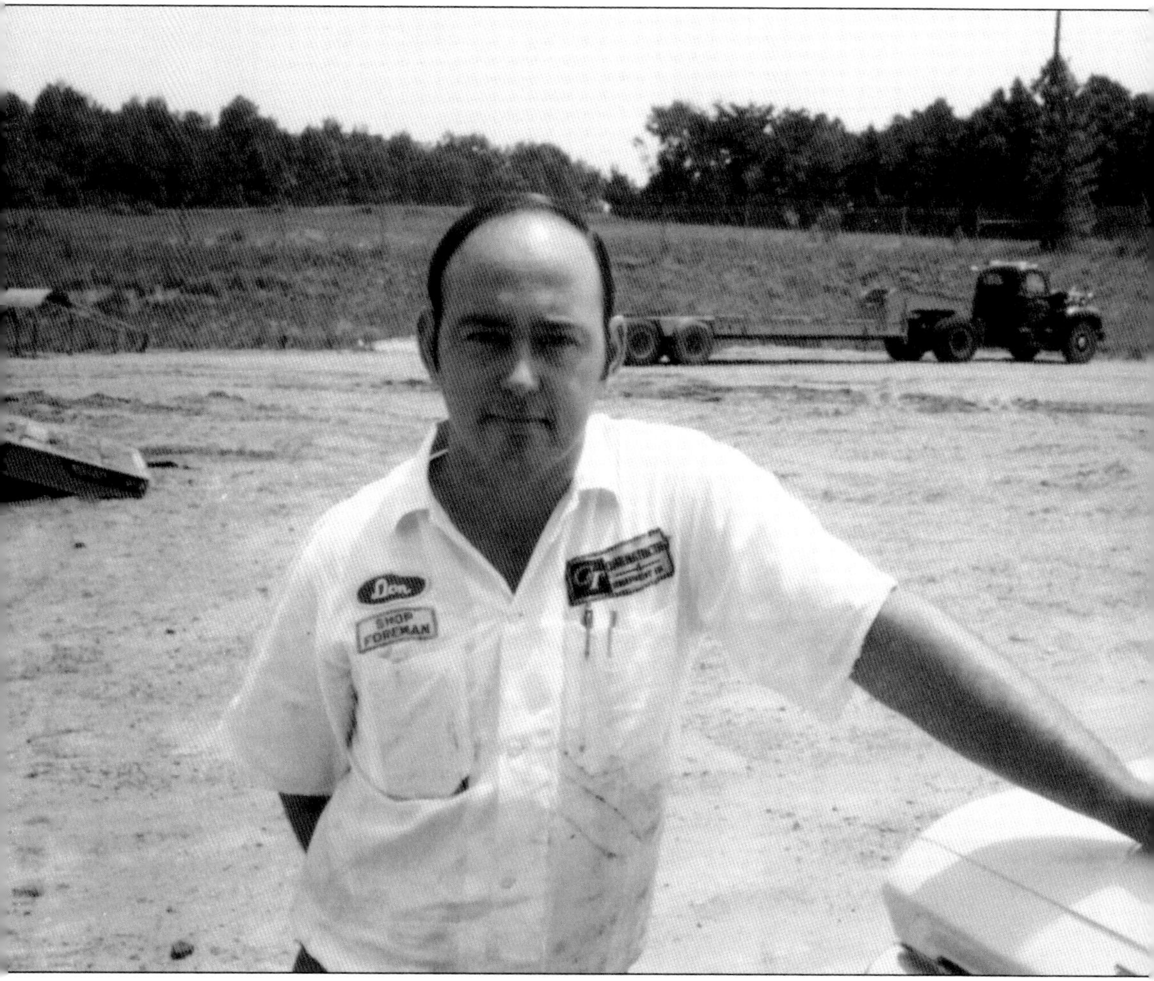

Don Lester came to work as a mechanic at Carolina Tractor & Equipment Company's Salisbury facility in 1966 and trained under Marvin Britt. He then moved to Greensboro, where he worked as a field mechanic. He eventually became shop foreman.

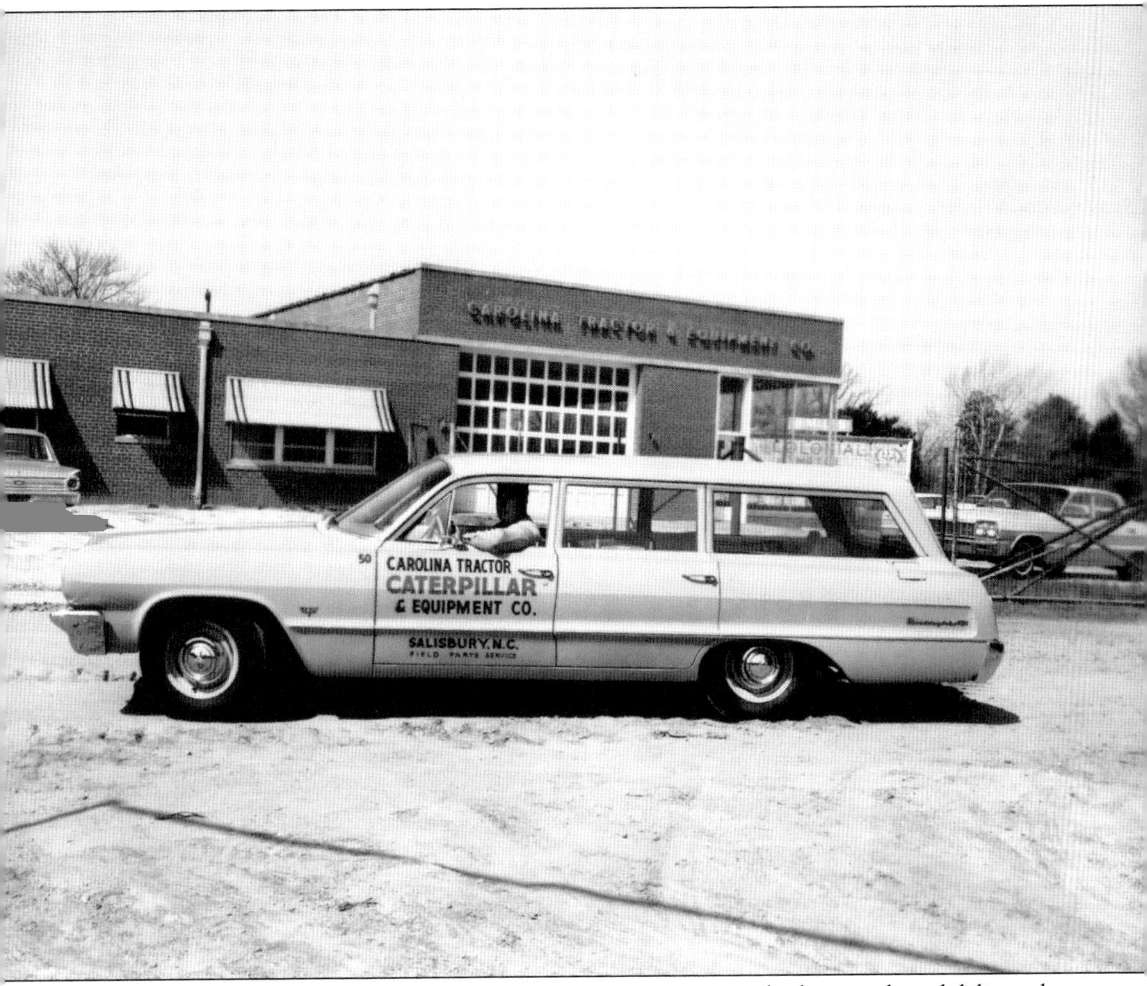

Carolina Tractor & Equipment Company service representative made the rounds and delivered parts in a station wagon during the 1960s. Although trucks were needed to haul bigger parts and gear, when a customer needed a filter or other small item, the station wagon could leave the plant and arrive at the job site quickly.

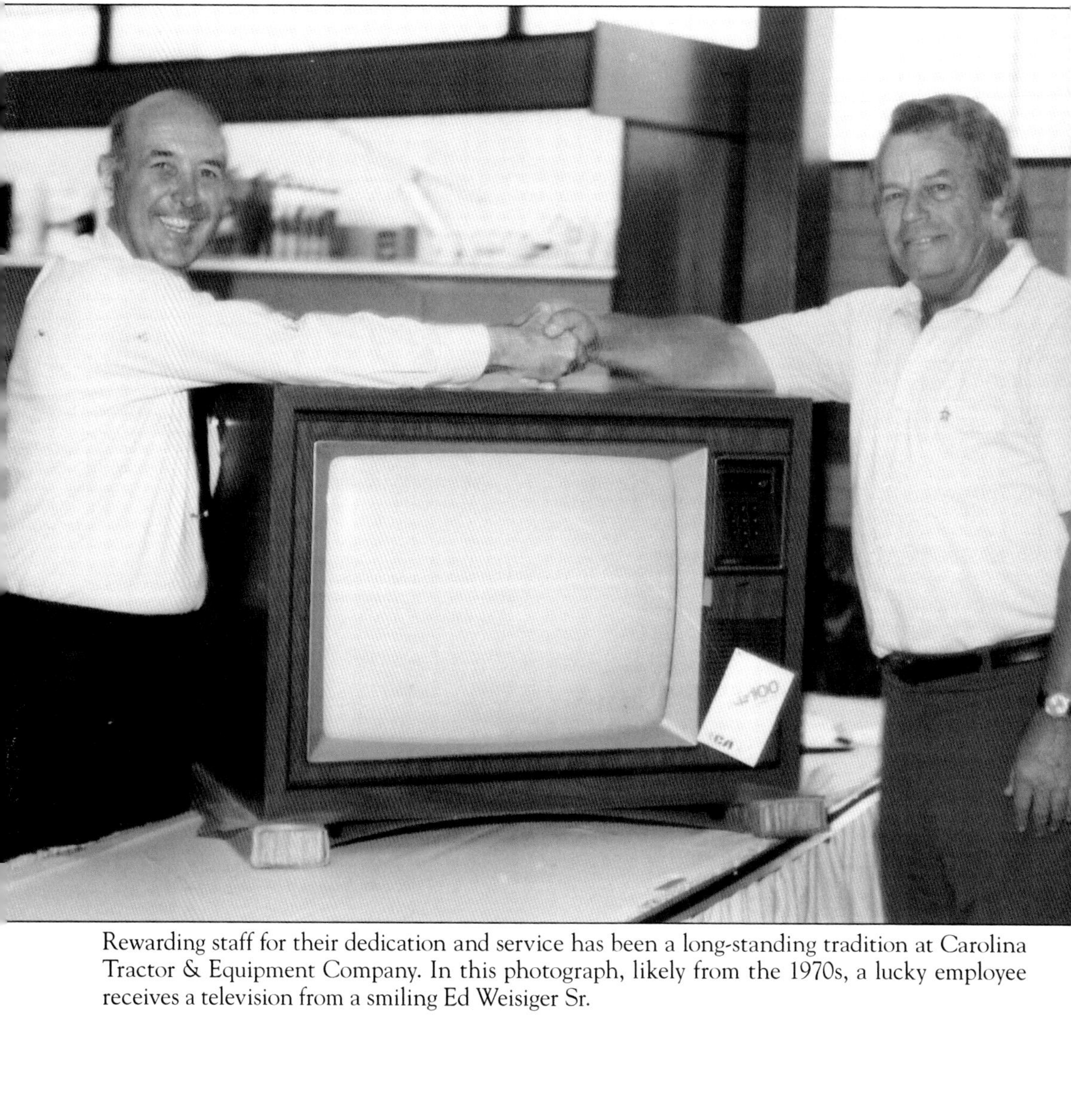

Rewarding staff for their dedication and service has been a long-standing tradition at Carolina Tractor & Equipment Company. In this photograph, likely from the 1970s, a lucky employee receives a television from a smiling Ed Weisiger Sr.

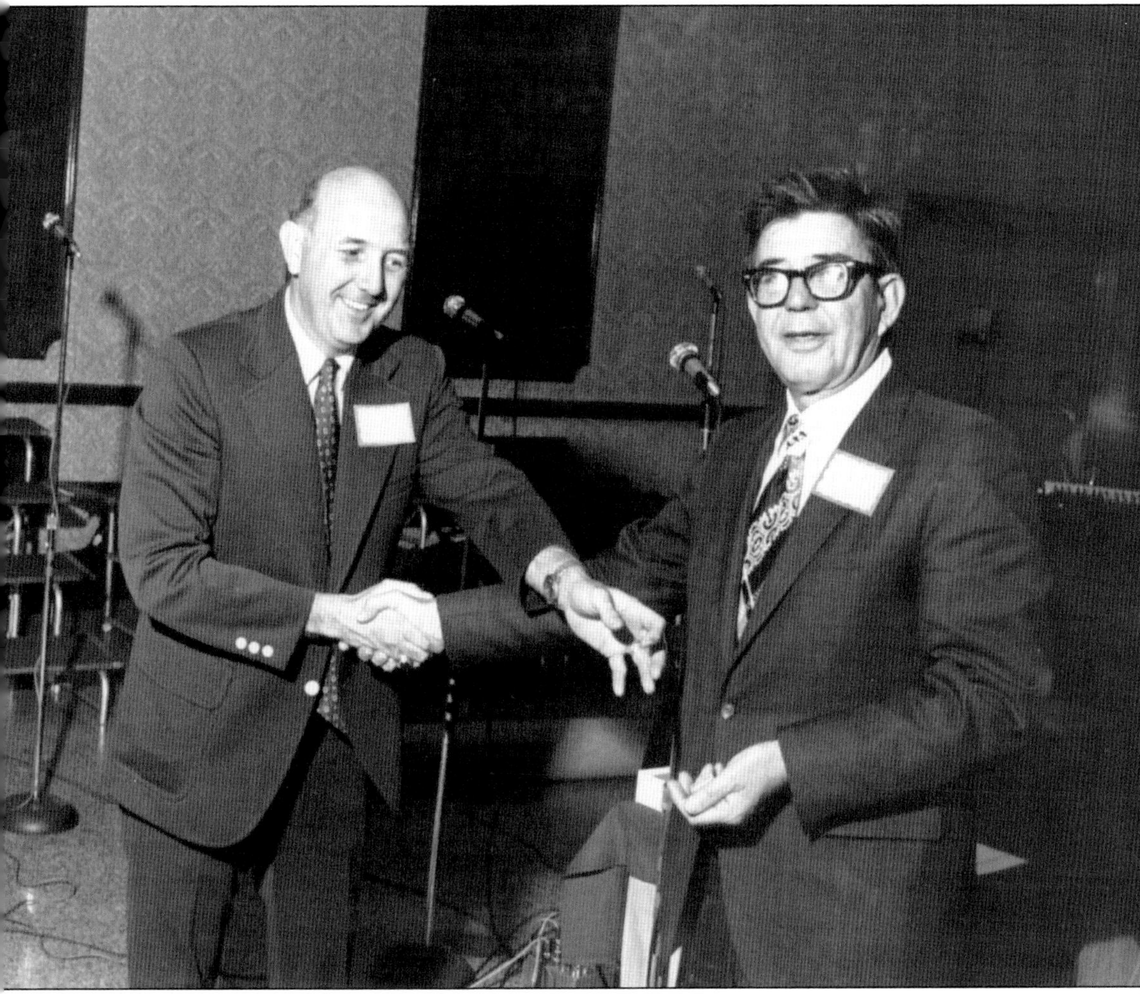

Carolina Tractor & Equipment Company president E.I. "Ed Sr." Weisiger is shown presenting a service award to the company's executive vice president, Robert V. Osborne, at the annual service awards banquet in 1975. Osborne was recognized for 20 years of employment with the company and received a tie tack embellished with three jewels.

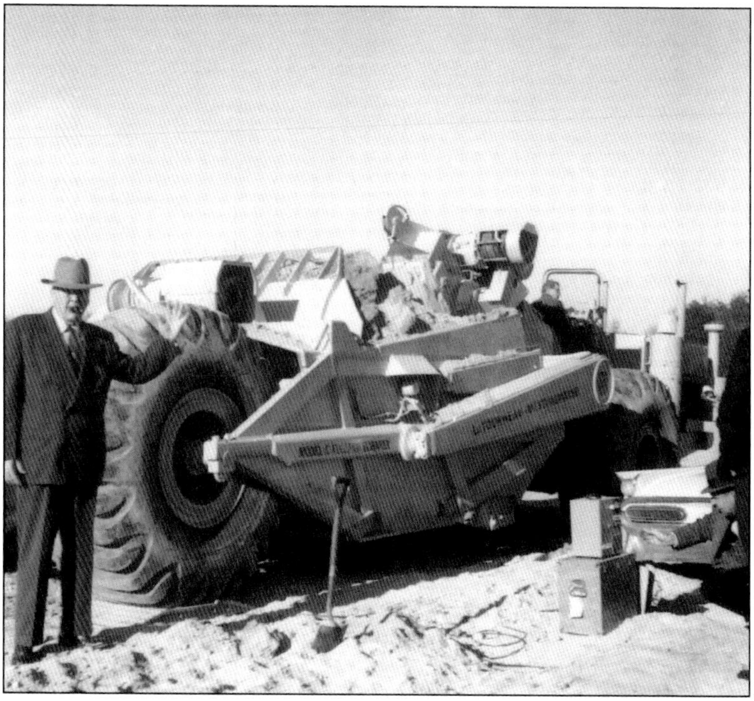

Frank Maness held a couple of positions at Carolina Tractor & Equipment Company—in sales and as branch manager for the Greensboro facility. One colleague liked to tell a story about how Maness boasted he had all the business from Guilford County, where the Greensboro facility was located, "in his hip pocket." In this photograph that dates back to around 1961, Maness is selling a scraper.

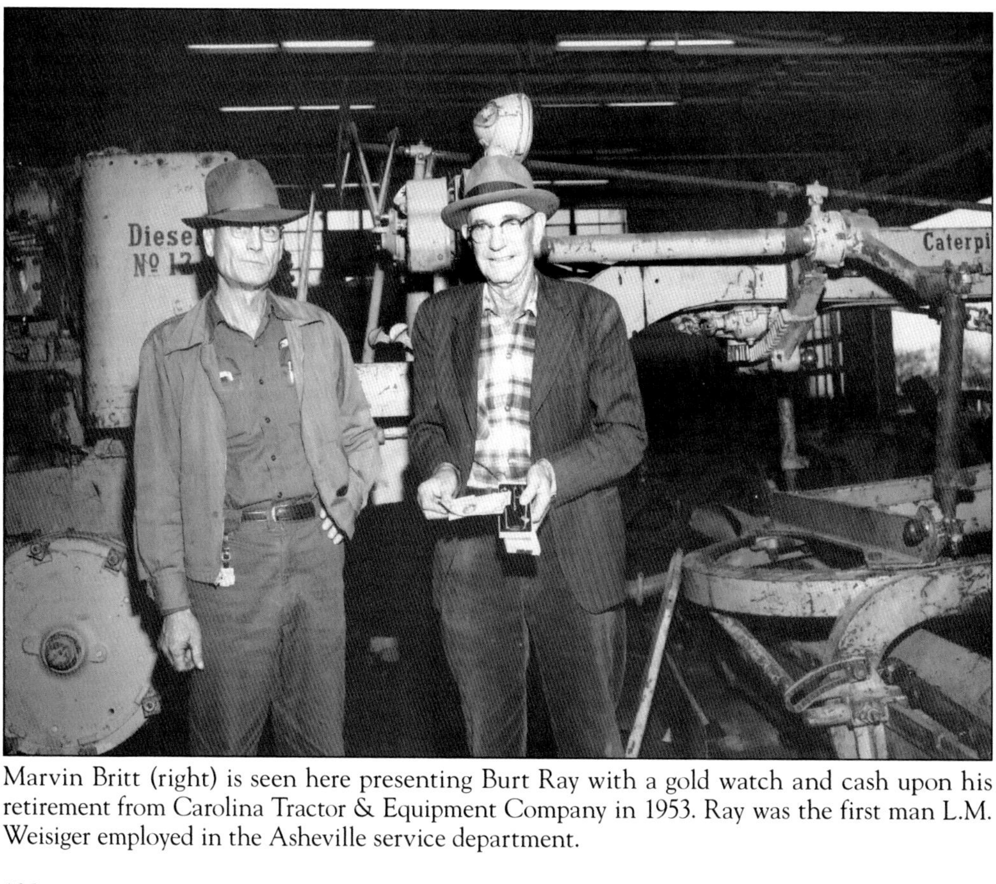

Marvin Britt (right) is seen here presenting Burt Ray with a gold watch and cash upon his retirement from Carolina Tractor & Equipment Company in 1953. Ray was the first man L.M. Weisiger employed in the Asheville service department.

Longtime Carolina Tractor & Equipment Company employee Marvin Britt was the service manager at the Salisbury facility. His responsibilities included training new employees in the job duties they would be expected to perform. Ed Sr. thanked the shop foreman for his years of dedication upon Britt's retirement in the 1970s.

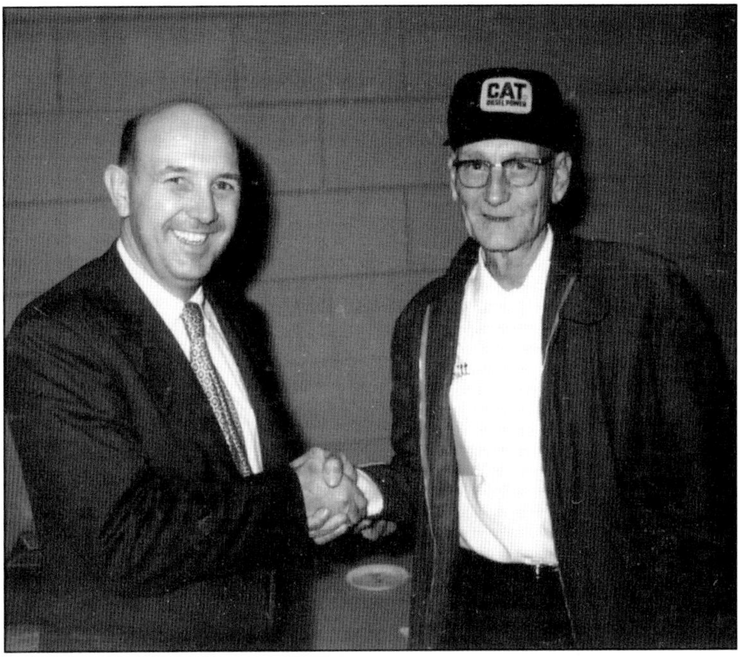

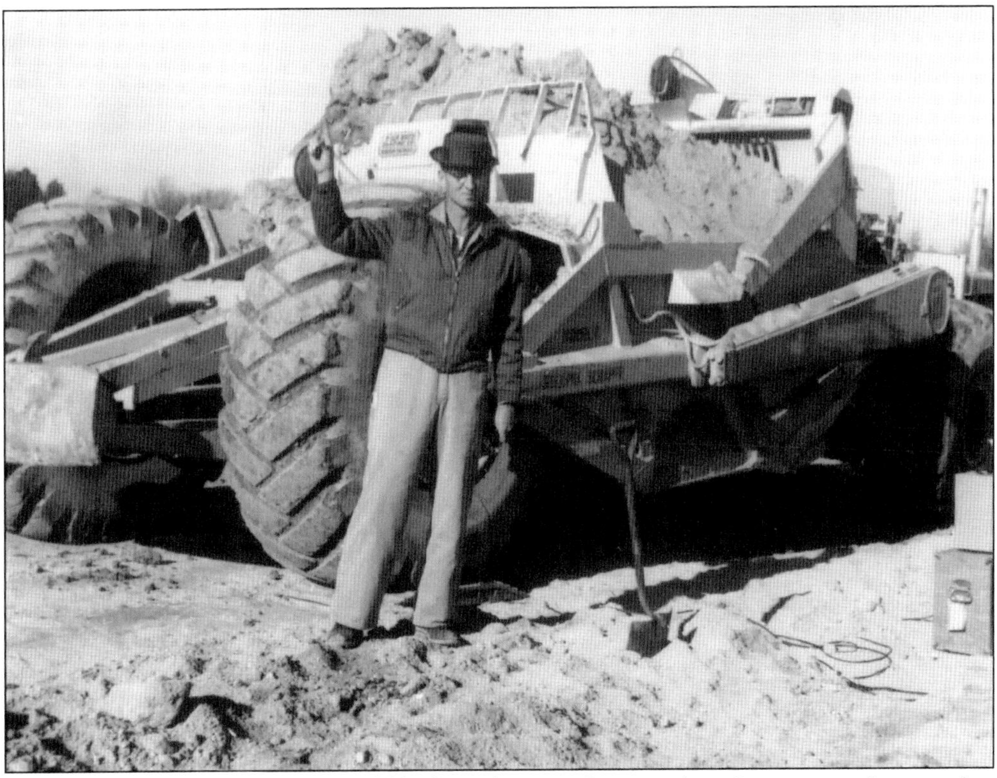

Portable scales such as this one could be brought to a job site and used to measure how much a machine was hauling. Carolina Tractor & Equipment Company employee Marvin Britt is utilizing this device on a customer's job site. The information from these readings would also help a customer determine when equipment was no longer operating efficiently and needed to be replaced.

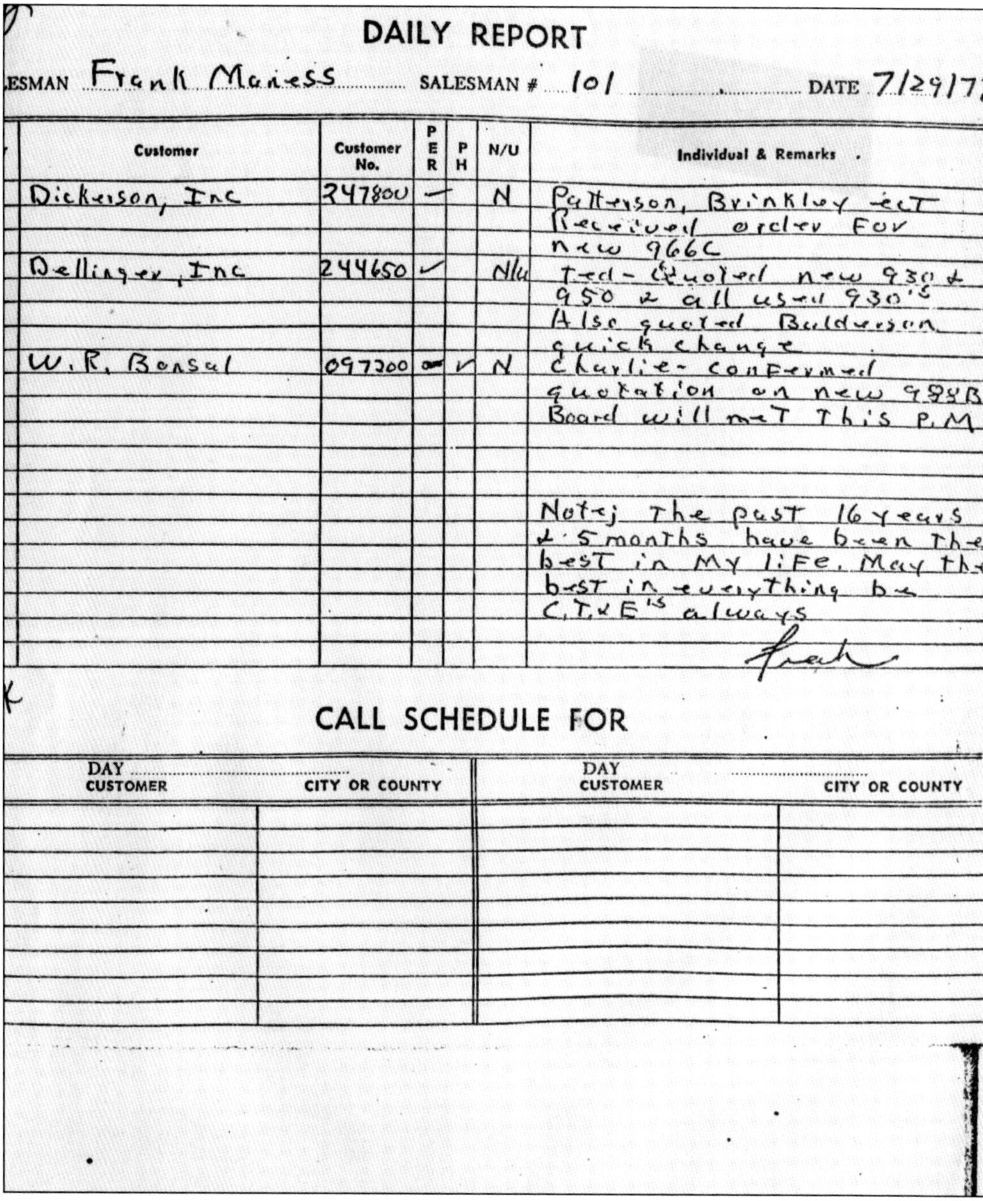

DAILY REPORT

SALESMAN Frank Maness SALESMAN # 101 DATE 7/29/77

Customer	Customer No.	PER	PH	N/U	Individual & Remarks
Dickerson, Inc	247800	—		N	Patterson, Brinkley ect Received order for new 966C
Dellinger, Inc	244650	✓		N/U	Ted - Quoted new 930 & 950 & all used 930's Also quoted Balderson quick change
W. R. Bonsal	097200	—	✓	N	Charlie - confermed quotation on new 988B Board will meet this P.M.

Note; The past 16 years & 5 months have been the best in my life. May the best in everything be C.T.&E's always

Frank

CALL SCHEDULE FOR

DAY CUSTOMER	CITY OR COUNTY	DAY CUSTOMER	CITY OR COUNTY

Frank Maness's daily report call sheet from July 1977 details the services he provided to his customers and closes with a note that reads, "The past 16 years and 5 months have been the best in my life. May the best in everything be 'C.T. & E.' always."

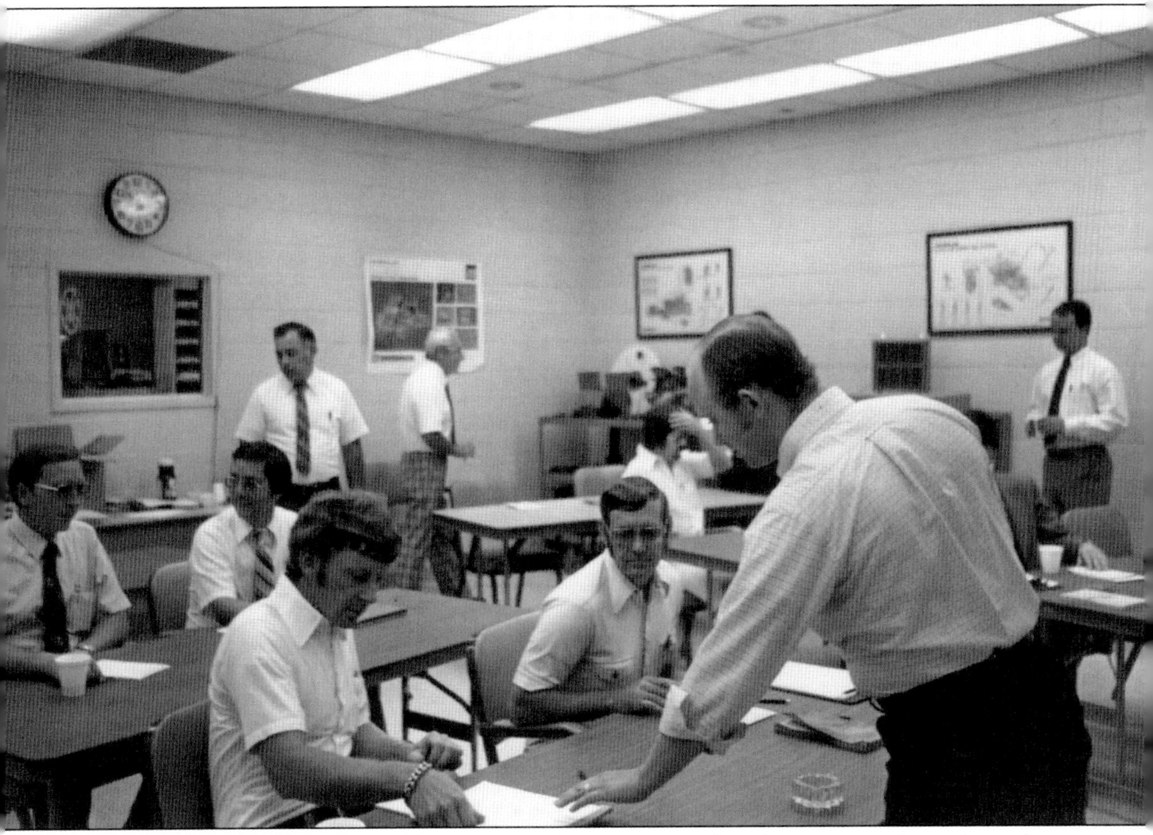

Carolina Tractor & Equipment Company employees received training not only on how the machines operated, but on the parts required to run the equipment optimally and the customer service that created customer loyalty. Managing administrative tasks for everything from sales reports to inventory could be quite laborious in the era before the digital age eliminated the need for such time-consuming, longhand recordkeeping

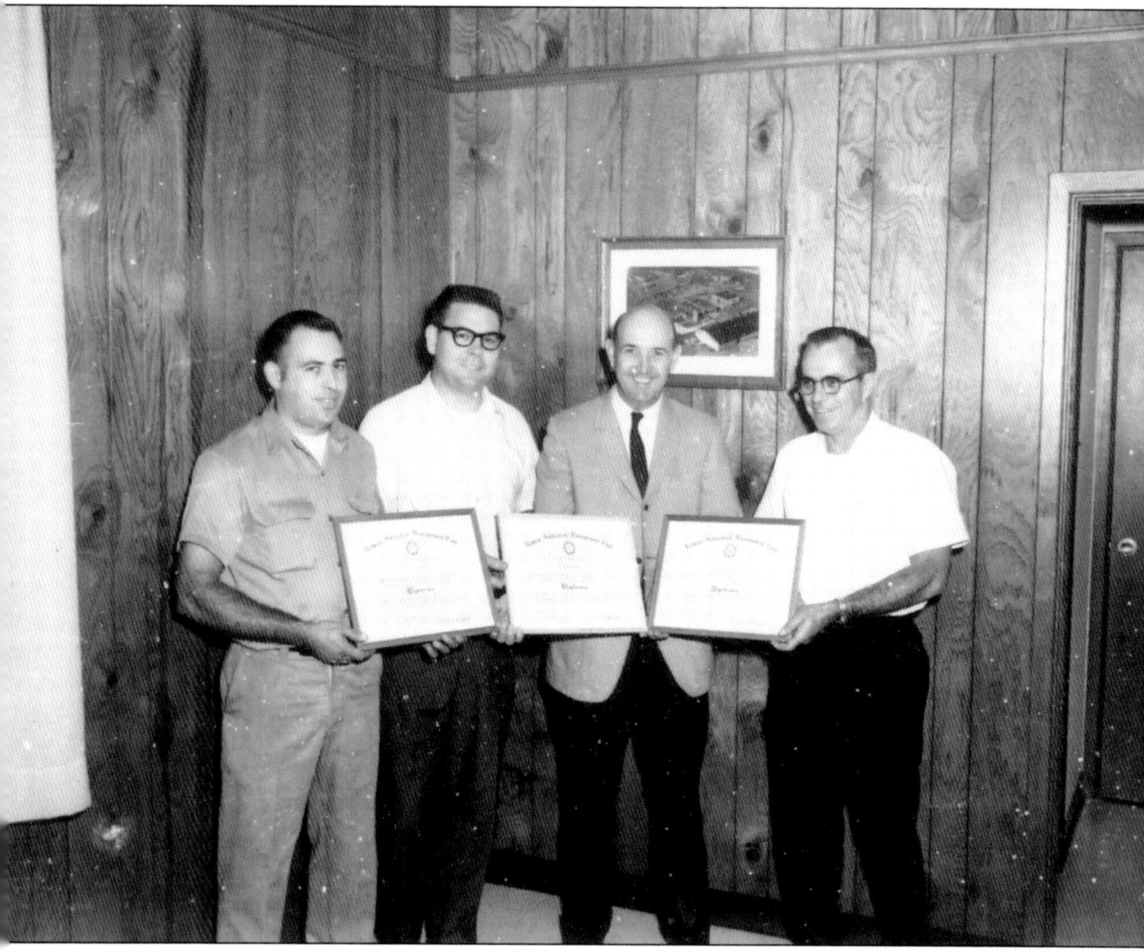

Ed Weisiger Sr. (third from left) is shown in this photograph from the 1970s presenting training certificates to employees, from left to right, Larry Watson, Rayvon Curran, and Sam Baker. The men completed the instructional sessions they traveled to attend at the Caterpillar central offices in Peoria, Illinois. Although such trips required traveling nearly 800 miles each way, Carolina Tractor saw the value of the training that not only kept the company competitive, but strengthened their workforce—a workforce that continues to remain an invaluable asset.

Five

The Weisiger Family

Weisiger family patriarch L.M "Mr. Les" Weisiger could not have envisioned when he was a soldier in World War I or an engineering student at the University of South Carolina that his tractor company would grow to international prominence in less than a century. He first worked as a highway engineer in the 1920s. Like many early entrepreneurs, his rise to success began modestly. He began building roads with a partner in the 1920s. He and his wife, Katharine, settled and raised their children, Katharine, Leslie Jr., and Edward (Sr.) in Salisbury, North Carolina. With fortitude and business acumen, Mr. Les and his company were able to weather the turbulent economic times of the Great Depression. World War II and the resulting postwar prosperity created an unexpected boom that would likely have been cause for the family to celebrate—were it not for 21-year-old Leslie Jr.'s death as a result of a car accident in 1950.

Son Ed Weisiger Sr. followed in his father's footsteps by studying engineering at North Carolina State University. He served as a lieutenant in the US Army during the Korean War, where stationed in Germany he supervised a heavy equipment maintenance unit. Upon his return from active duty in 1956, he went to work at Carolina Tractor, and in less than 10 years, he was ready to take on the role of company president when Mr. Les stepped aside in 1965 to serve as chairman of the board.

The company now operates under the leadership of a third generation Weisiger family member, Ed Jr., who was named president in 1991. Like his father, he earned an engineering degree from North Carolina State University and also received a graduate degree in business from Harvard University.

What each generation shares is a commitment to the company's illustrious history of service, cost-effectiveness, integrity, focus on customers, value of employees, accountability, and adaptability. The Weisiger family's legacy is one that continues to honor the mission and values of Carolina Tractor, both within the company and in the surrounding local and global community it serves.

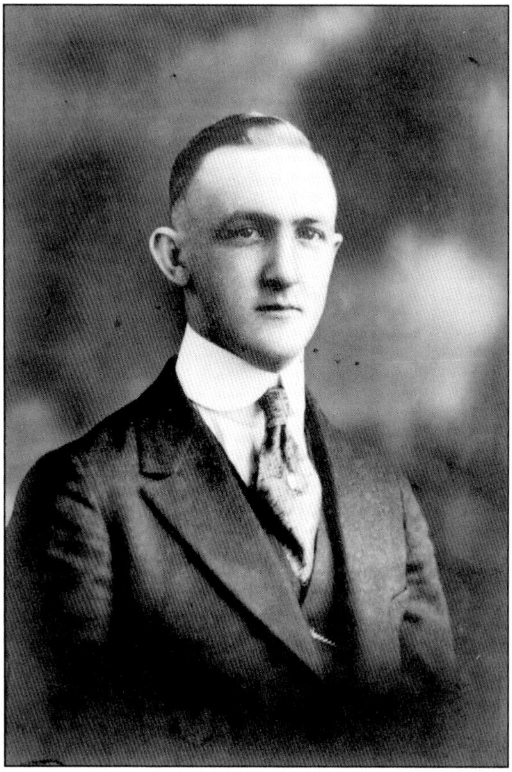

Leslie Marshall Weisiger, born in 1895 in Granite, Virginia, was the eldest of five children born to Elizabeth Marshall Innes and Peter Henry Weisiger. He attended school in Richmond but went to live in Columbia, South Carolina, with his aunt and uncle, Jenny and Donald Innes, when he was 14. He attended the University of South Carolina, where he earned a degree in civil engineering. Although he completed his military training and received a commission as a second lieutenant, World War I ended before his unit was deployed to Europe.

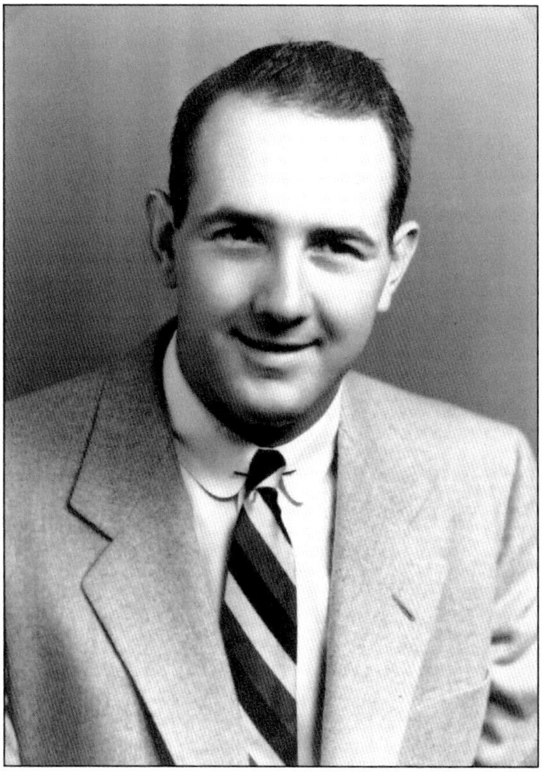

This 1951 photograph shows a dapper Ed Weisiger Sr. as a student at North Carolina State University. Born in 1931, he was the youngest of three children born to L.M. "Mr. Les" and Katharine Weisiger. After graduation, he would enter the US Army Reserves and serve abroad in Germany, where he would supervise a heavy equipment maintenance unit before being assigned to the 334th Engineering Dump Truck Company. It was good experience for the family business that he would enter upon his return stateside.

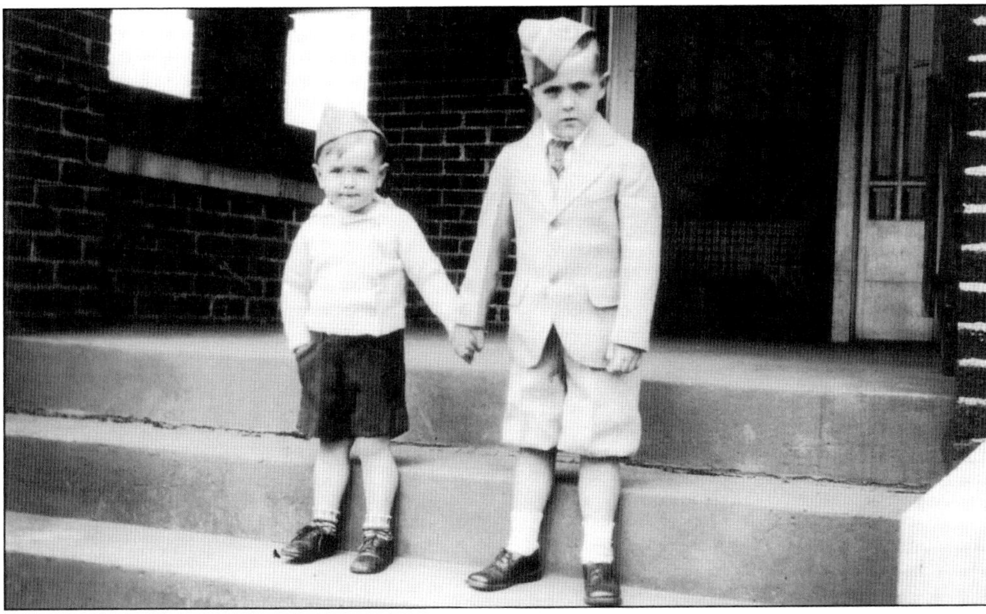

What would later come to be known as Veterans Day was originally called Armistice Day. It commemorated the end of World War I in 1918 and was a somber occasion that paid tribute to fallen soldiers. Here, brothers Ed Sr. (left) and Leslie Jr. (right) display their youthful patriotism in this mid-1930s photograph.

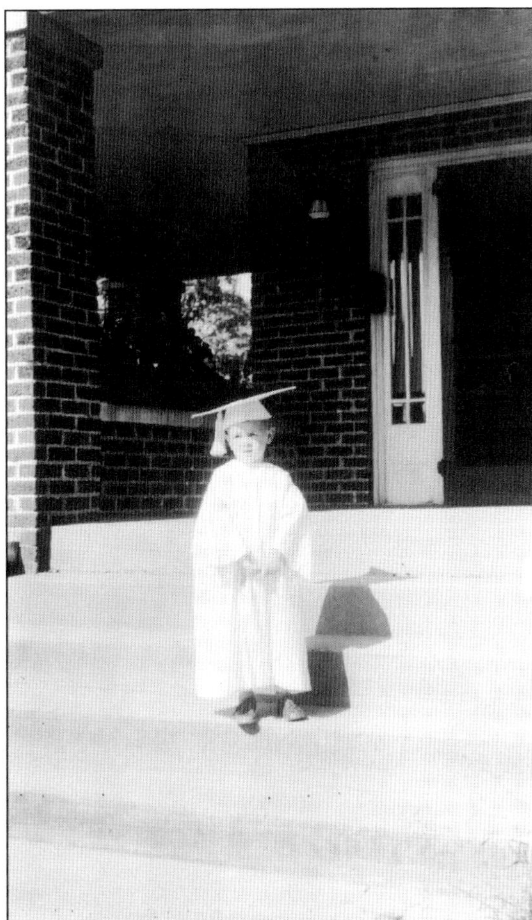

Never one to be camera shy, a young Ed Sr. poses for his first graduation photograph, from kindergarten in the 1930s.

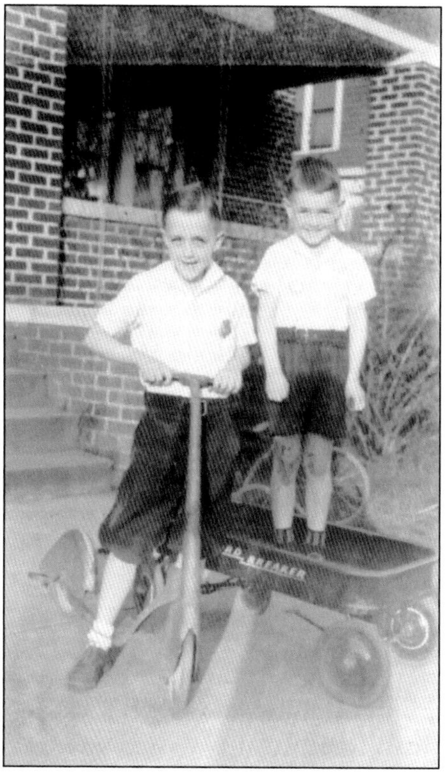

A five-year-old Ed Weisiger Sr., standing in the wagon, and his big brother, Leslie Jr., with his scooter, are at play in this 1936 photograph. Sister Katharine, the middle of the three children, most likely chose not to join in the boyish antics of her brothers.

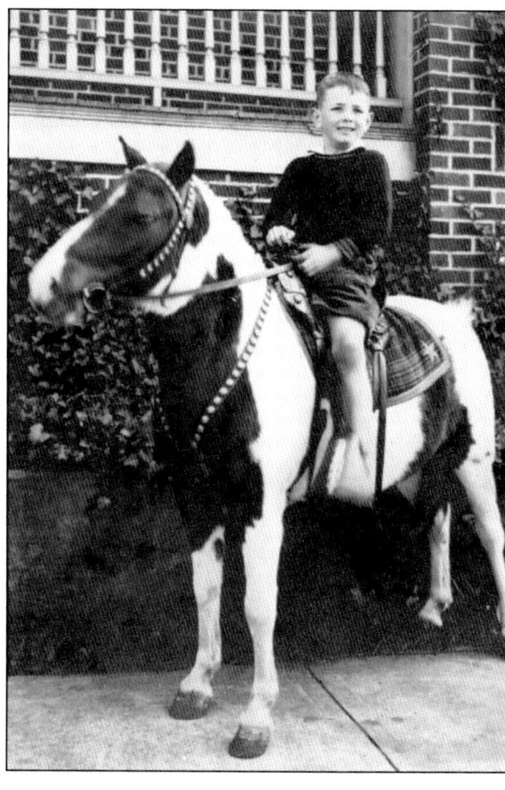

Weisiger family members in South Carolina welcomed their North Carolina relatives. At age 14, Mr. Les had gone to live with an aunt and uncle, Jenny and Donald Innes, in Columbia, where he went on to study engineering at the University of South Carolina. This photograph shows Mr. Les's son Ed Sr. as a child astride a pony during a family visit to South Carolina in the 1930s.

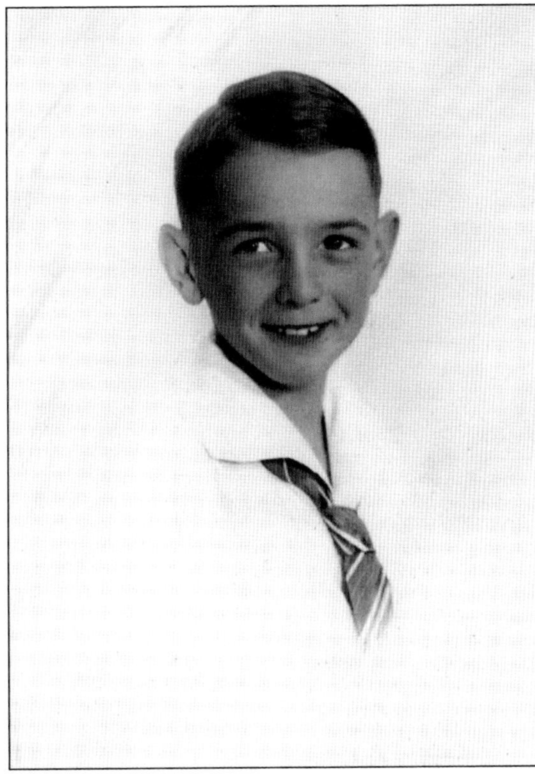

This style of portraiture was popular in the early 20th century, in the era before color photography was widely available. An artist would use paints to enhance a black-and-white photograph, and the technique produced a result that was quite realistic. These portraits from 1941 depict Leslie Weisiger Jr. (below) and his younger brother, Ed Weisiger Sr. (at right).

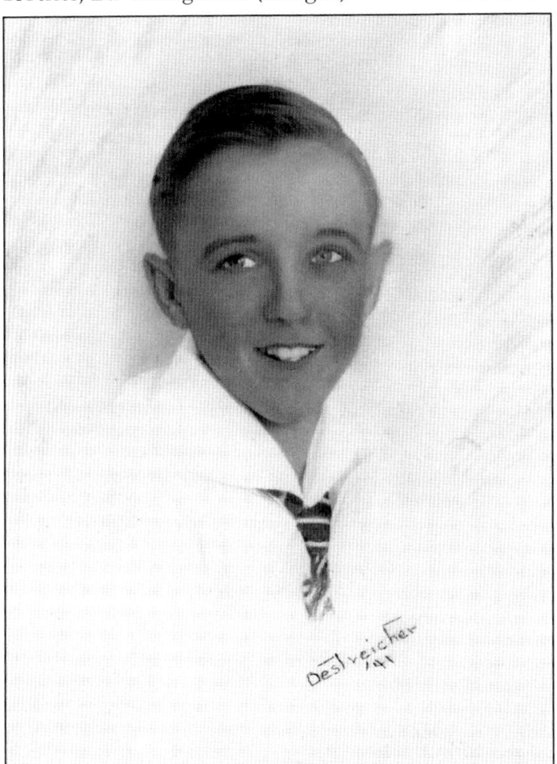

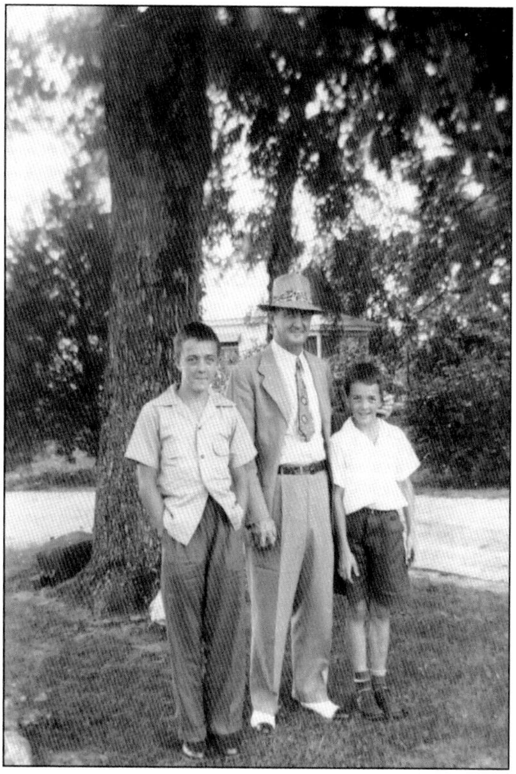

Mr. Les is flanked by his sons, Leslie Jr. (left) and Ed (right), in this photograph taken at the family home in Salisbury during the 1930s. Sadly, Leslie Jr. died in a car accident near home in 1950 when he was just 21 years old.

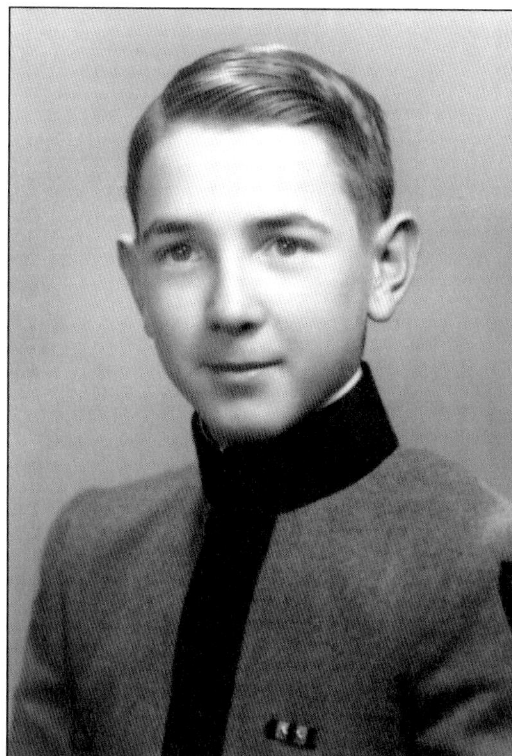

This photograph from 1946 shows Ed Sr. as a freshman at Fishburne Military School in Richmond, Virginia. Although World War II would be over by the time he graduated, the college preparatory work he completed at the school would help him pursue the engineering degree he would earn from North Carolina State University.

Teenaged cousins Don Weisiger and Ed Weisiger Sr. pose in their Fishburne Military School uniforms at their grandmother's home in Richmond, Virginia, in this photograph from 1947–1948. Although World War II had ended, other conflicts around the world meant that military service would still be critical to the country. Ed Sr. would serve abroad before coming back home to work at Carolina Tractor & Equipment Company.

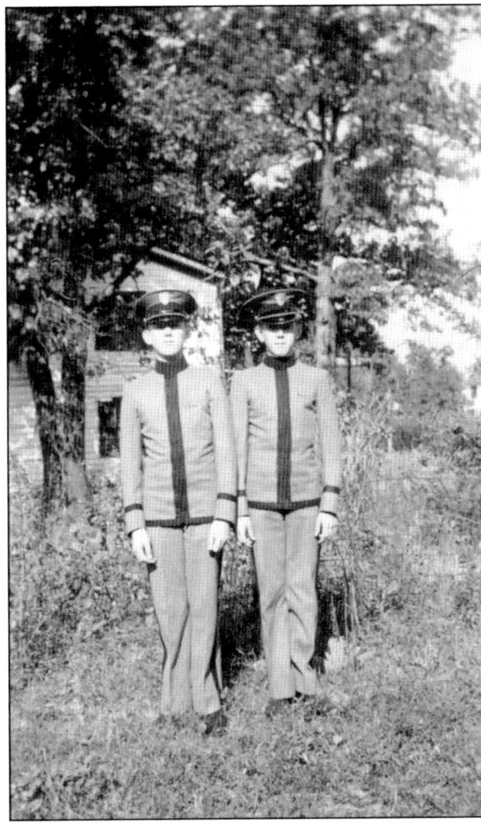

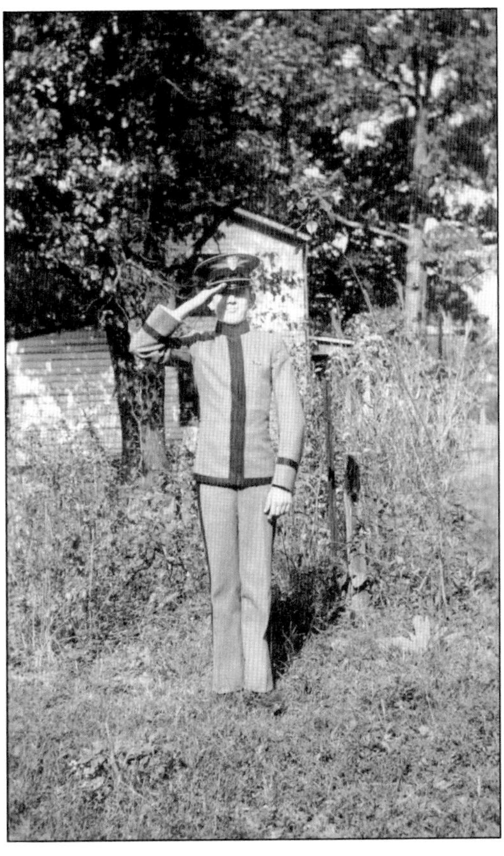

Cousin Don Weisiger attended school with Ed Sr. Both young men were students at Fishburne Military School, one of the oldest military schools in the country. Located in Waynesboro, Virginia, the school was not far from their grandmother's home in Richmond. Ed Sr. remembers that he was sent to the school not specifically to prepare him for a military career, but because the education would prepare him for college.

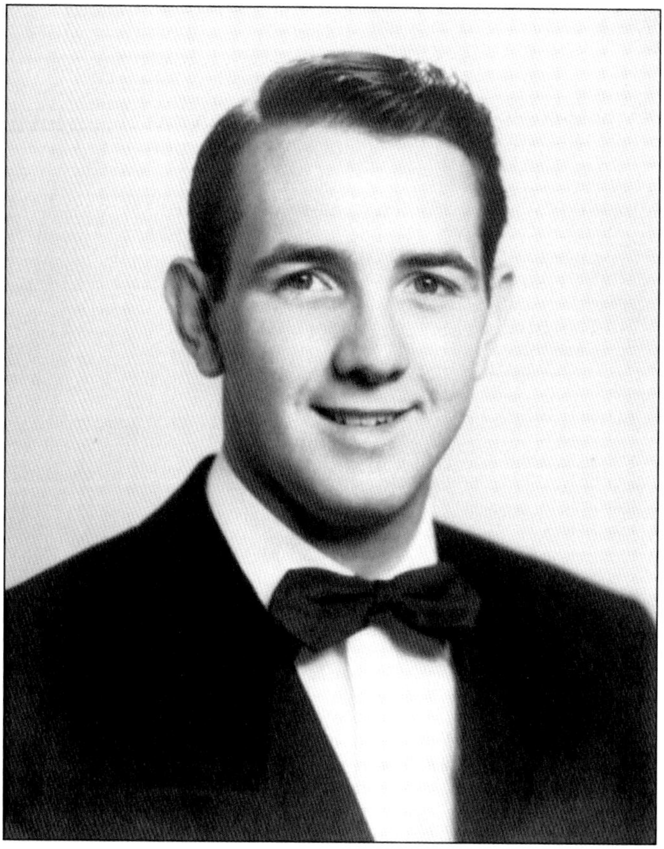

This portrait of Ed Weisiger Sr. most likely dates back to 1953, when the North Carolina State University engineering student would work during the summers at his father's business.

In this informal photograph, family and friends pose on the wraparound porch of the Weisiger family home in Salisbury. Pictured are, from left to right, Gus Wright, "Aunt" Nell, Katharine Weisiger (next to the column), and "Aunt" Jeannie. The date is unknown.

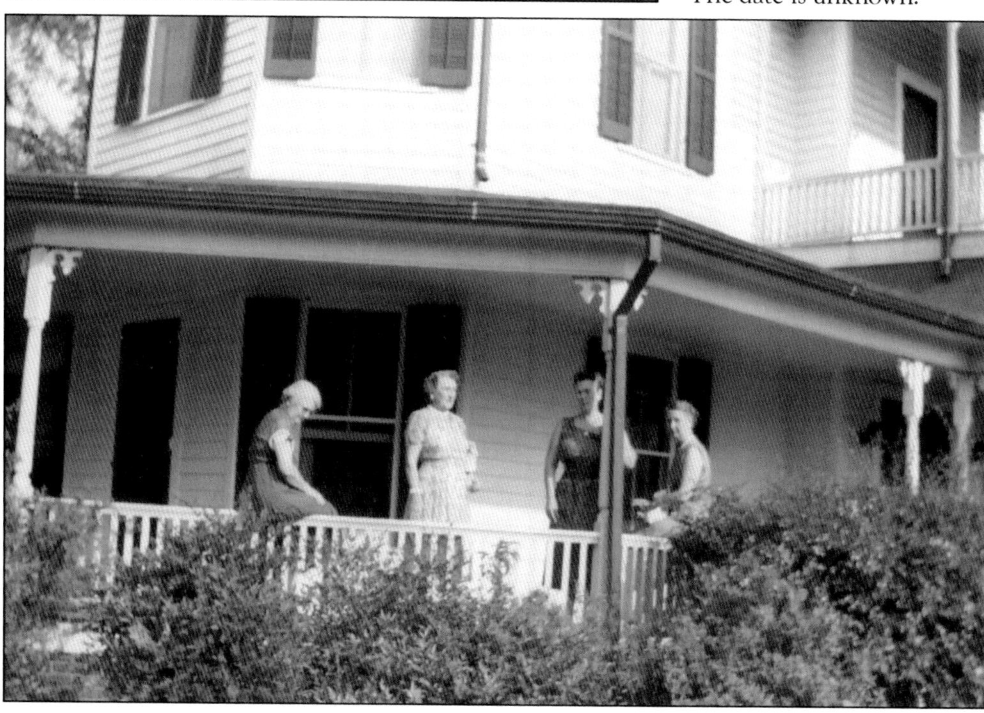

Well-to-do families often sent their sons to military schools, where the boys would receive not only academic instruction, but also preparation for service or careers in the armed forces. This formal portrait of Ed Sr. in his Fishburne Military School dress uniform dates back to 1948–1949.

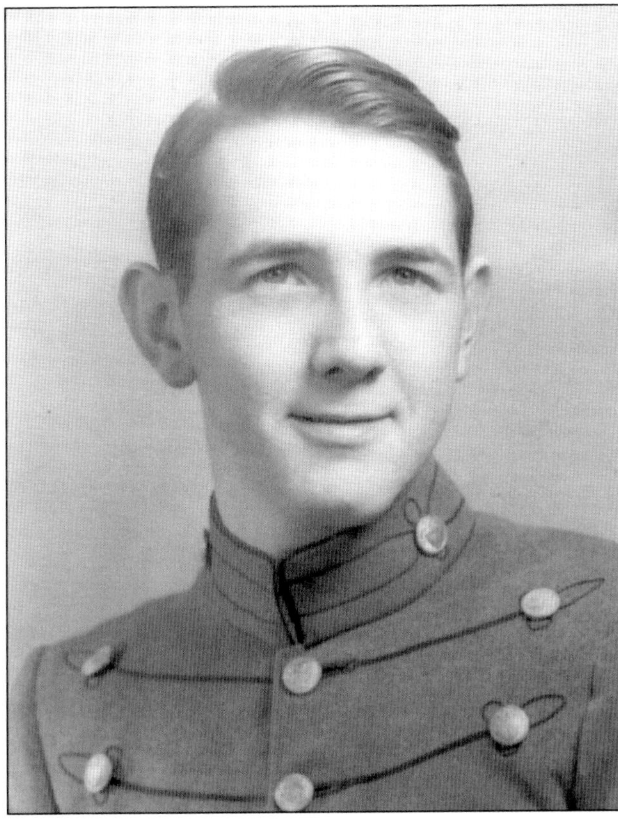

A young Ed Weisiger Sr., smiling in this school portrait from around 1953, could not have envisioned the changes and challenges his family's company would face in the years to come. The legacy his father created would continue under his leadership. Later his son Ed Jr. would become the third generation to helm Carolina Tractor & Equipment Company, as it entered the 21st century.

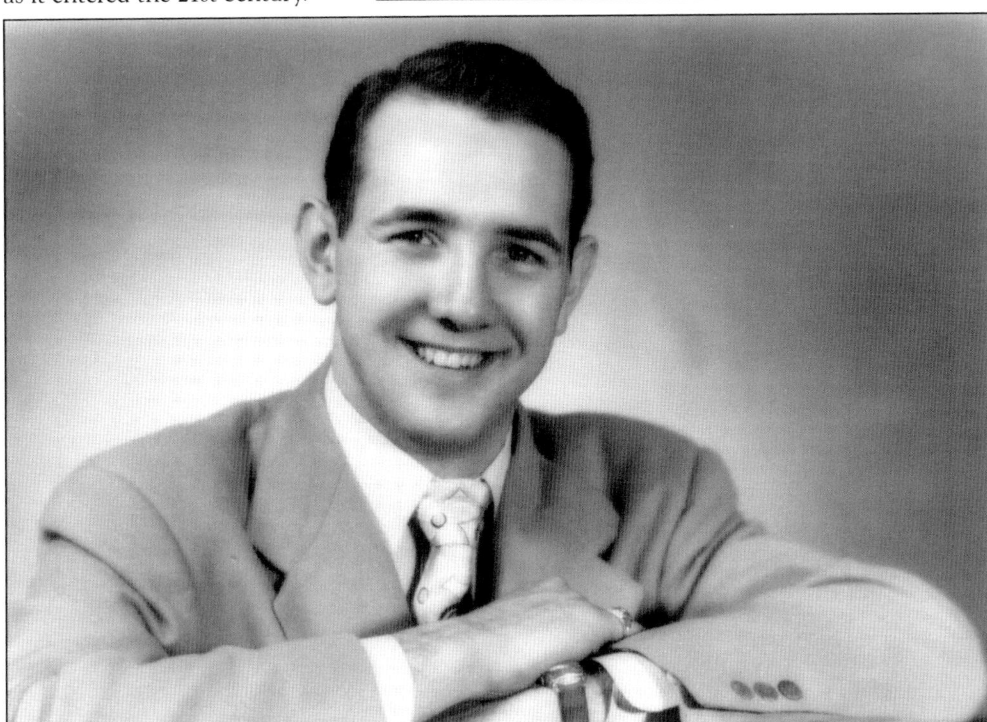

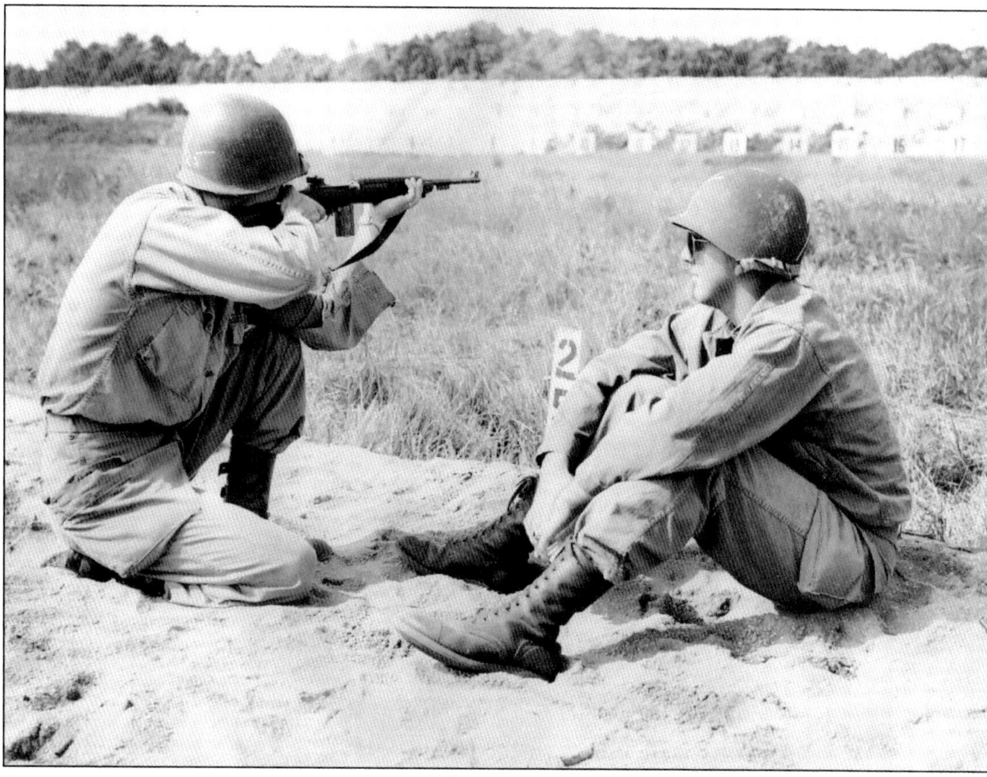

Ed Weisiger Sr., seated at right, waits his turn to practice his marksmanship during ROTC training during college at the Aberdeen Proving Ground. This photograph was taken in the 1950s.

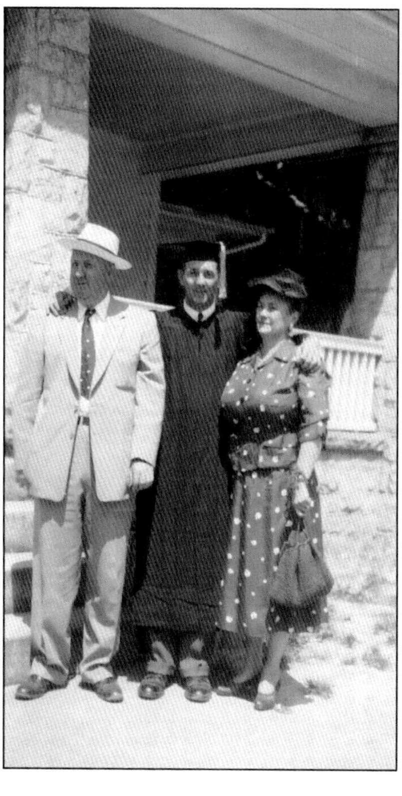

Ed Sr.'s proud parents flank the new North Carolina State University graduate in this photograph. The young man from the class of 1954 would go on to military service in Germany before he returned home to lead Carolina Tractor & Equipment Company through times of challenges, opportunities, and significant growth.

While a student at North Carolina State University, Ed Sr. was accepted as a member of the Pi Kappa Alpha fraternity, now one of the largest fraternal organizations in the world, becoming a "Pike." He earned a degree in engineering in 1954 and achieved the rank of lieutenant in the US Army Reserves.

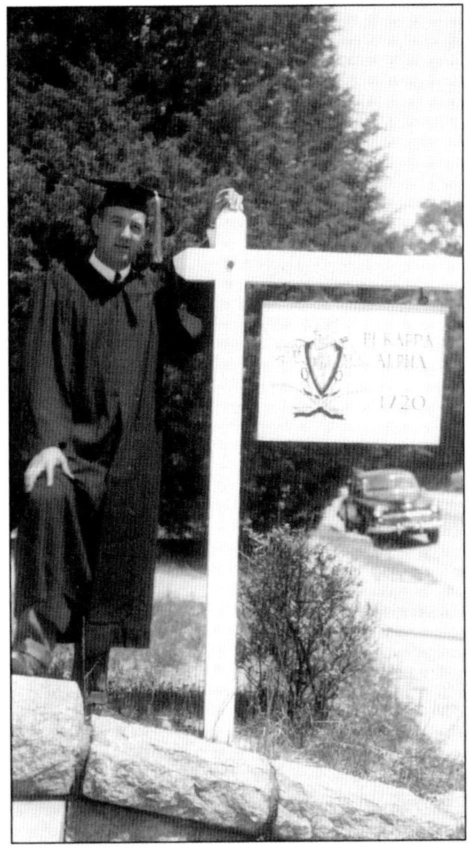

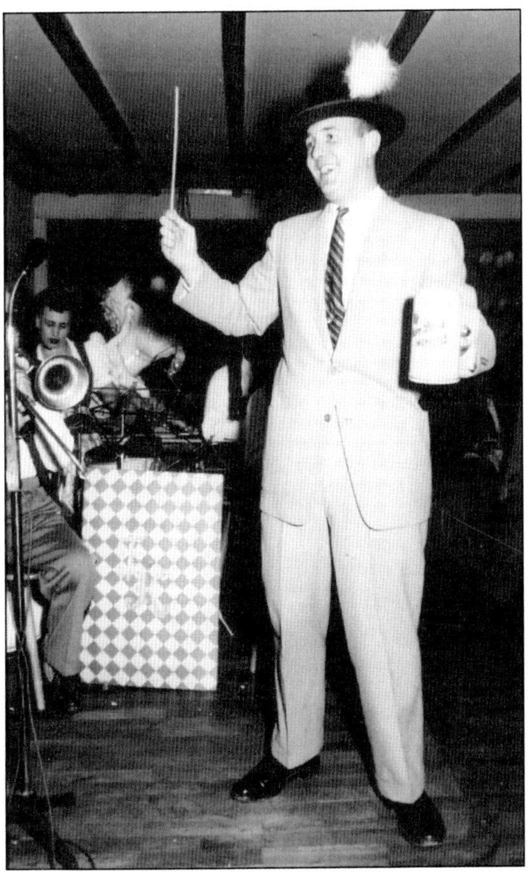

Ed Sr. was stationed overseas in Germany between 1954 and 1956 while serving in the US Army. Although most of his time was spent working as a heavy equipment maintenance officer in Mannheim in 1955, he is seen having some R & R at a local establishment that offered libations and live music.

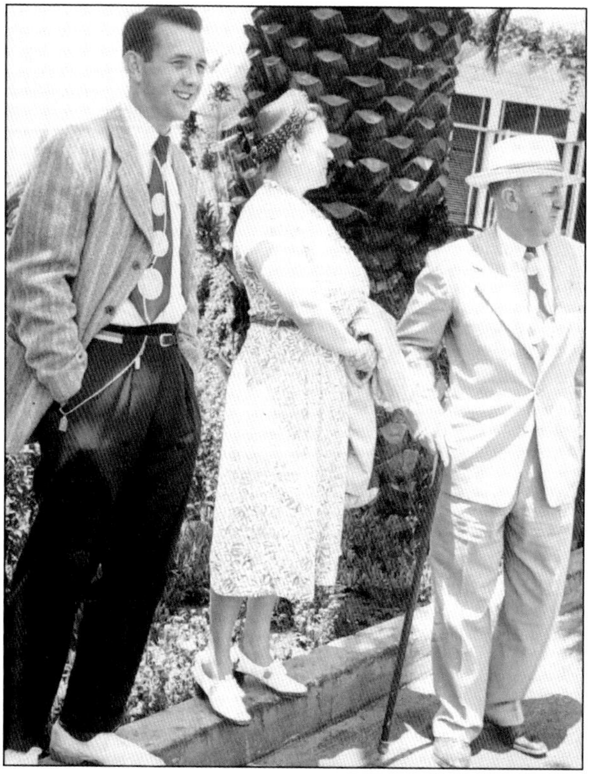

Ed Sr.; his mother, Katharine; and father, L.M. "Mr. Les," visited Florida for a Caterpillar dealers' meeting, where a photographer caught this informal moment on film. Ed's style of dress—bold necktie, watch chain, and pleated trousers—was characteristic of the 1950s.

Weisiger family members have always been committed to doing good works to support their communities. This certificate of appreciation from 1948 recognizes L.M. Weisiger for his contributions to the Franklin Presbyterian Church in Salisbury. His son Ed Sr. remembers that Mr. Les donated the organ to the church.

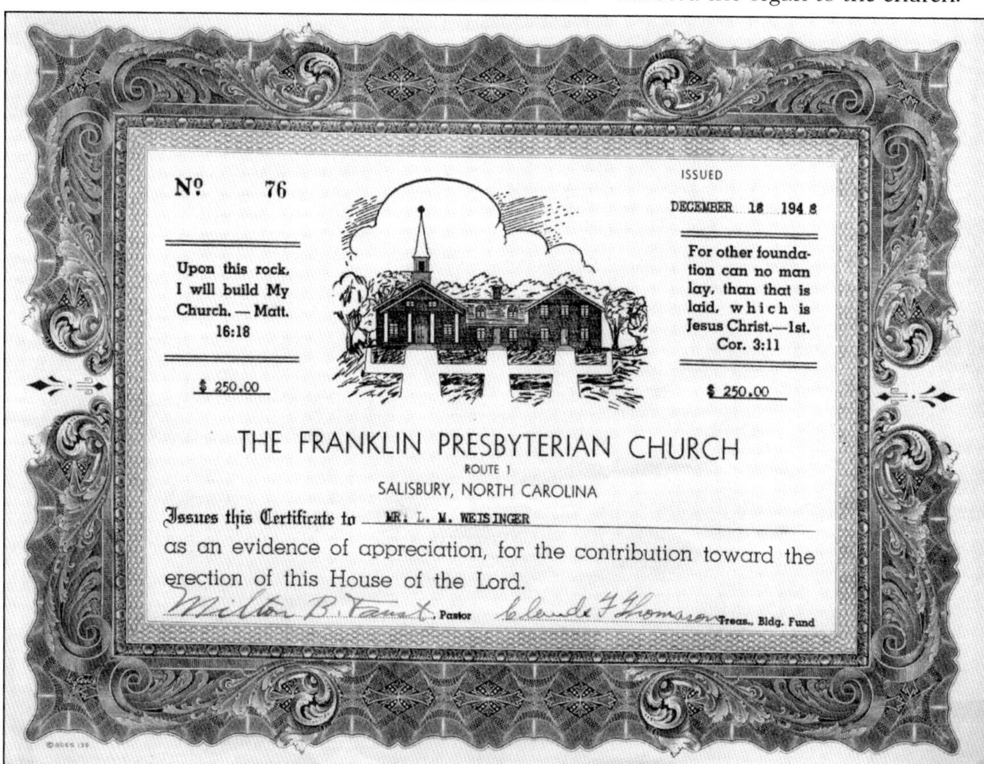

Nº 76

ISSUED

DECEMBER 18 1948

Upon this rock, I will build My Church. — Matt. 16:18

For other foundation can no man lay, than that is laid, which is Jesus Christ.—1st. Cor. 3:11

$ 250.00

$ 250.00

THE FRANKLIN PRESBYTERIAN CHURCH

ROUTE 1

SALISBURY, NORTH CAROLINA

Issues this Certificate to MR. L. M. WEISINGER

as an evidence of appreciation, for the contribution toward the erection of this House of the Lord.

Milton B. Faust, Pastor

Claude F. Thomason, Treas., Bldg. Fund

The Weisiger family's home church was Franklin Presbyterian Church in Salisbury. Franklin Presbyterian dates back to the early 1820s and continues to minister to its congregation today.

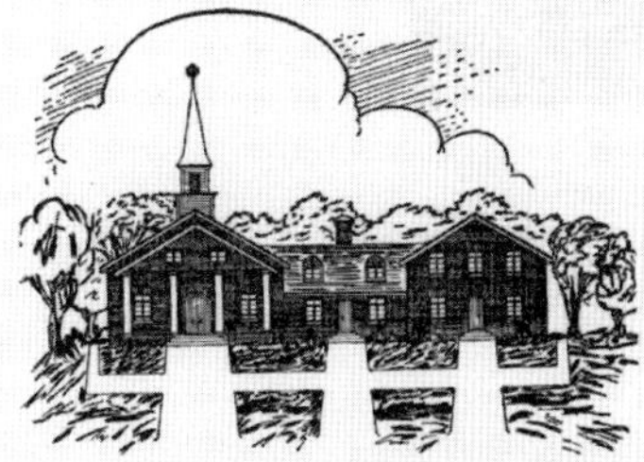

HISTORY OF FRANKLIN PRESBYTERIAN CHURCH

Mr. William Franklin Watts attended school at Chapel Hill September 5, 1821. Mr. Watts was licensed September 5, 1823, to preach the gospel in the bounds of Concord Presbytery. He was ordained Saturday, July 16, 1825, and died May 11, 1826.

The land was purchased April 28, 1828, on which Franklin Presbyterian Church was built.

Franklin Presbyterian Church was received by Concord Presbytery April 2, 1829. Pastors filled the pulpit for sixty-six years and was supplied or vacant fifty-three years. When Rev. N. E. Oplinger resigned June 10, 1945, Franklin Church was grouped with two other churches; Concord Presbytery later regrouped them. Franklin was left without a Manse and had fifty-nine active members. The Congregation has built and paid for a seven-room manse, costing $14,000.00, and has added eleven new members. May 18, 1948, we received our first full time Minister in 119 years, Rev. Milton B. Faust. Since May we have received 15 new members. The congregation has adopted plans for our Educational Unit, like the picture on this card. The new addition will cost $40,000.00. We need your prayers as well as your financial support. Any donation will be greatly appreciated. May the Lord bless you and yours.

YOURS IN THE LORD'S WORK.

Claude F. Thomason, Treas.
Box 127
Mt. Pleasant, N. C.

Mrs. Gara Weant, Sec.
R. F. D. No. 1
Salisbury, N. C.

FRANKLIN PRESBYTERIAN CHURCH
Route 1, Salisbury, N. C.

MILTON B. FAUST, Minister
Manse Route 1 — Box 378-A
Phone Salisbury — 3602-W3

CLAUDE F. THOMASON
Box 127, Mt. Pleasant
Clerk of Session

December 18, 1948

Mr. L. M. Weisinger,
Melford Hills,
Salisbury, N.C.

Dear Mr. Weisinger:

The Pastor and Congregation of Franklin Presbyterian Church want to tell you how much we appreciate your nice gift for the Building Fund.

It is the gifts of our friends like you that keep us inspired to go on with the Lord's work. We feel sure that God is with us in our building program. We will not fail if we will just put our trust in Him.

We have a full time pastor now. The first in a 119 years. We have taken in 23 new members since May 18th. That is when our pastor Rev. Milton B. Faust, moved into our new manse. We like him and his family very much. They are fine people to work with.

We would like to start our Educational Unit next year. Our new unit will cost $ 40,000.00.

I am sending you a picture of our new structure as it will be when we complete it; also under this picture will be a brief history of the Church.

I am sending you a receipt for your nice gift. It looks like a bond.

We would be very happy to have you come and worship with us at any time. We an excellent pastor now.

Again we thank you for your donation for our Building Fund. It is greatly appreciated and will help us to start our Educational Building. May the Lord bless you and yours.

Yours in the Lord's work.

FRANKLIN PRESBYTERIAN CHURCH

Claude F. Thomason

Claude F. Thomason, Clerk of Session,

This letter recognizes L.M. Weisiger for his contributions to Franklin Presbyterian Church.

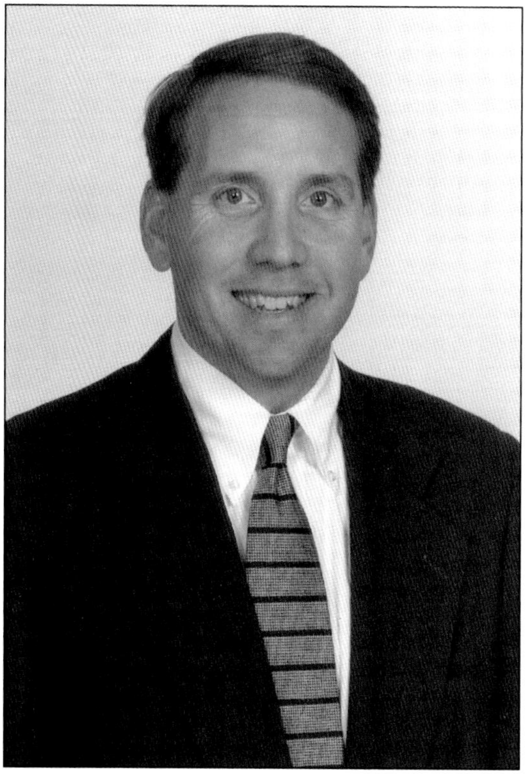

Like his father, Ed Weisiger Jr. graduated from North Carolina State University. He earned a BS degree in industrial engineering, then went on to earn an MBA from Harvard University Graduate School of Business. Ed Jr. started working at Carolina Tractor & Equipment Company in 1988, in the position of general manager of the engine division for his family's business. He was named president and CEO in 1991. Ed Jr.'s responsibilities include overseeing the company's four divisions, corporate strategy, customer service culture, and day-to-day operations.

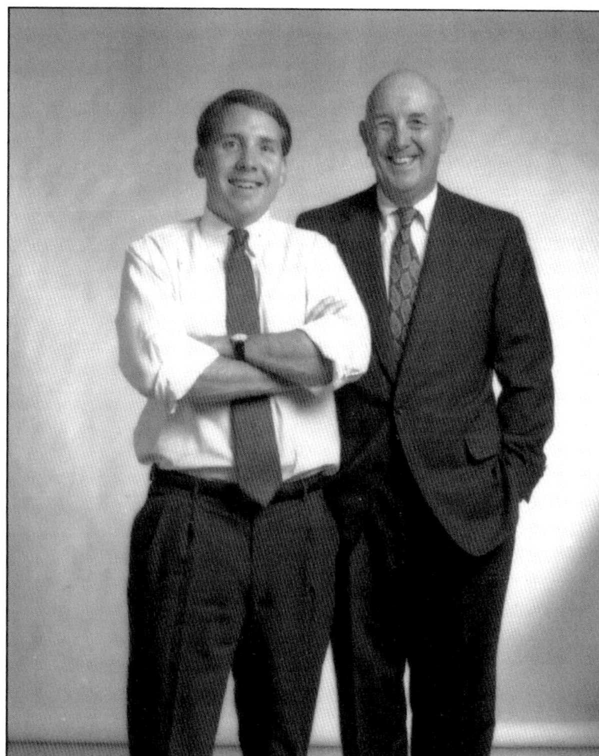

The third generation of Weisiger family leadership is represented in this modern-day, father-and-son photograph of Ed Sr. and his son Ed Jr. When the younger executive rose to become president and CEO in 1991, he succeeded his father, who took on the role of chairman of the board—just as the prior generation of Weisigers had done. And like his father and grandfather before him, Ed Jr. also serves on the boards of civic and charitable organizations. At the helm of the company founded by "Mr. Les" Weisiger nearly 90 years ago, Ed Weisiger Jr. upholds the legacy—and charts the course for continued success in the future—of Carolina Tractor & Equipment Company.

AFTERWORD

Nearly 90 years after L.M. Weisiger started out operating a small paving business, the prosperous company he founded continues to grow in the 21st century. Today, in addition to offering a full line of construction, forestry, and paving products, Carolina Tractor & Equipment Company now offers expanded lines of material handling equipment, engineered solutions, cranes, truck engines, and power generation capabilities backed by superior product support.

Carolina CAT, the construction equipment division of Carolina Tractor (the current name was established in 2000), partners with the construction, forestry, power generation, paving, and truck engine customers serving Western North Carolina. Additionally, Hydraulics Express partners with customers throughout the Carolinas to service hydraulic needs of the construction equipment, industrial production equipment, and mobile equipment, such as dump trucks, garbage trucks, rollbacks, and wreckers.

The material handling division of Carolina Tractor, LiftOne, partners with material handling and warehouse solutions customers for new and used product sales, rentals, parts, and service. In 2012, LiftOne acquired the Hyster and Yale lift truck lines from Barloworld Handling. Currently operating 17 branches, LiftOne serves the Carolinas, Alabama, Georgia, and Tennessee.

Pinnacle Cranes, the crane division of Carolina Tractor, partners with crane, boom truck and aerial platform customers in North and South Carolina for product sales, rentals, parts, and service needs.

While the equipment has changed dramatically over the years, there are some things that never change at Carolina Tractor—the personal relationships between the company, its dedicated employees, and the customers it serves so reliably. A number of customers are in their third and fourth generations doing business with the company. Blythe Construction, whose association with Carolina Tractor & Equipment Company dates back to the 1930s, and Duke Energy, whose association dates back to the 1960s, are two examples of the long-standing relationships the company will always value.

For this loyalty, and for the privilege of serving the people of North Carolina, Carolina Tractor & Equipment Company wishes to express its deepest gratitude for helping build the great state of North Carolina.

Consistent with our mission to preserve history on a local level, this book was printed in South Carolina on American-made paper and manufactured entirely in the United States. Products carrying the accredited Forest Stewardship Council (FSC) label are printed on 100 percent FSC-certified paper.

MADE IN THE USA